D1414272

LONGING

STORIES OF RACIAL HEALING

LONGING

STORIES OF RACIAL HEALING

By Phyllis A. Unterschuetz

and

Eugene F. Unterschuetz

Bahá'í
PUBLISHING

Wilmette, Illinois

Bahá'í Publishing
415 Linden Avenue, Wilmette, Illinois 60091-2844

13   12   11   10   4   3   2   1

Library of Congress Cataloging-in-Publication Data
Unterschuetz, Phyllis A.
  Longing : stories of racial healing / by Phyllis A. Unterschuetz
and Eugene F. Unterschuetz.
      p. cm.
  Includes bibliographical references.
  ISBN 978-1-931847-68-1 (alk. paper)
  1. Race relations—Religious aspects—Bahai Faith. 2.
United States—Race relations. 3. Unterschuetz, Phyllis A. 4.
Unterschuetz, Eugene F. I. Unterschuetz, Eugene F. II. Title.
  BP388.R33U58 2010
  297.9'317—dc22
                                        2009054034

Cover design by Bob Reddy
Book design by Patrick Falso

For our parents,
Jane and Louis Wilder,
Georganna and Eugene E. Unterschuetz,
with our gratitude and love

We find after years of struggle
that we do not take a trip; a trip takes us.

—John Steinbeck,
Travels With Charlie: In Search of America

CONTENTS

CONTENTS

ACKNOWLEDGMENTS

Throughout our ten years on the road we've been encouraged and supported by hundreds of people around the country. While we cannot possibly mention all of your names, we offer our deepest gratitude and affection to everyone who has played a part in bringing this book to life:

To the members of the Bahá'í communities who arranged, publicized, and attended our workshops and story-readings; you spent your time and resources finding places for us to speak and frequently drove long distances to make sure we'd have someone to speak to.

To the Regional Bahá'í Councils and their travel-teacher coordinators who worked tirelessly to contact communities and fine-tune our itineraries during the first few years of our travels; without your service we would never have been able to undertake the adventure that yielded the stories for this book.

To those special African-American Bahá'ís who, throughout our journey, opened to our eyes an entire reality of which we'd been unaware and who offered their truth with such patience and persistence.

1

To those who assisted in the development of our race unity workshop by providing training and critiques, sharing materials, and helping us hone our facilitation skills.

To everyone who listened to our stories over the past several years, gave us valuable input on their content and style, caught our mistakes, called us on our faulty assumptions, and challenged us to keep learning; and to all the people who disagreed with our viewpoints and thereby forced us to examine more thoroughly our understanding of the dynamics of race.

To those who, even though they'd never met us before, extended hospitality without a second thought; you invited us into your homes for meals, took us along to your church services, and eventually included us in your weddings and your children's birthday parties—in short, you treated us like family.

To our cherished South Carolinian friends, who embraced and loved us even though we were really ignorant and naive; your affection, along with that of many others in the Deep South, strengthened our resolve to look squarely at our racial conditioning.

To the Native Americans who welcomed us into their homes and told us their stories; the brief time we spent with you changed us profoundly.

To the white people we've met whose hearts have been moved and who have, in spite of their discomfort, courageously arisen to make changes in their personal lives; your willingness to be open about the challenges of addressing racial prejudice and your commitment to doing something concrete to bring about healing has been an inspiration and example to us.

To the black friends who made us believe that the work we were doing was crucial, that our book must be finished and our stories made available to everyone. We can never adequately express how we've been transformed by your generosity of spirit and your courage and openness. You have educated us, shared with us your lives, your pain, your trust, and your hope. We only wish it were possible to acknowledge each one of you by name, but we're comforted by the belief that you know who you are.

To the people of all ethnicities who risked speaking out in public about their concerns and expressed their emotional truth with openness and honesty.

To Dr. Richard Thomas, respected educator, author, historian, and widely-recognized expert in the field of race relations, who asked us to read our stories in his classroom; your belief in the importance of our work has sustained us, and your lifelong commitment to addressing the most vital and challenging issue of racial prejudice has been a model for people of all colors throughout the country.

To our departed and sorely missed Nat Rutstein, prolific author, educator, and dedicated race unity worker. He was one of the first white men we knew who talked openly about his racial conditioning, and in doing so he made it a little easier for the rest of us to look inside ourselves. After we read our stories for a large gathering of people in his living room one evening, he took us aside and said, "You've got a book here." And because he said it, we believed it was true.

To Caswell Ellis, who always took time from his impossibly busy schedule to look at our photos and ask about the people we'd met; he reminded us to drink enough water, buy quality tires for our trailer, and work hard to preserve the unity in our marriage. Most importantly, he warned us not to get distracted and continually reassured us we were in God's care. Though he is no longer giving us advice in this world, we feel his presence and sustained guidance from the spiritual realm and hope that he is proud of us.

To all the people who believed in us when we found it hard to believe in ourselves and never doubted our ability to write this book; to the close friends and family members who didn't laugh or lose hope in us when we assured them year after year that our book was almost finished. To those who prayed for our protection and success. And especially to the staff at Bahá'í Publishing: Tim Moore, general manager; and editors Ariana Brown, Bahhaj Taherzadeh, and Christopher Martin.

To our recently departed friend, senior editor Terry Cassiday, who guided us lovingly and patiently through the process of submitting our manuscript for publication. We miss her calm wisdom, steadfastness, and continual assurance that everything was unfolding according to divine plan. We are humbly grateful for her confidence in our ability to become real authors.

To Liz and Jerry Helt, who have provided not only moral support and decades of friendship but also a long, level driveway to park our RV and a room in their home when we needed a non-mobile place to stay for a while.

To Phyllis's sister Jean Smith and Jean's husband Steve (without whose co-signature we would have been denied the loan for our first RV); our brothers Kurt and Karl Unterschuetz, Rob and Ralph

Wilder; our sisters-in-law Caryn Unterschuetz and Dena Wilder; and to our nieces and nephews: Tara, Tyler, Andre, Sienna, and Kati.

To our two splendid sons-in-law, Gary Sandine and Bill Wood; thank you for becoming part of our family. To our beautiful, gifted, and compassionate grandchildren Bria, Ian, and Maya Sandine, who frequently begin phone conversations by asking where we are and never know which state their birthday presents will be sent from.

To the three of our parents that have departed this world; although they are not here to see what we've accomplished, we know they are watching and cheering us on from that spiritual world they now inhabit. We thank them for the qualities they taught us that allowed us to undertake this amazing journey.

To Phyllis's mom Jane Wilder, who listened to our stories and responded by setting goals of creating racial unity in her own life, and who believes in us with a fervor that only a mother could sustain.

We offer our deepest gratitude to our children Karla Sandine, Heidi Wood, and Erik Unterschuetz—two of whom thought they were leaving the nest temporarily, only to return a year later to find that the nest had sprouted wheels and taken off. Our lifestyle has presented you all with hardship from time to time, and your understanding and support of our decision to travel has been unfailing. We love you beyond words and will forever cherish your gifts of encouragement and empathy.

And finally we want to express our appreciation to all of you who appear in our stories—the ones that are included in this book as well as the ones that remain untold for now. Without you, who would we have become?

FOREWORD

For decades, the race relations publishing industry has been saturated with popular and academic books on various aspects of race in the United States. Many of these books have greatly contributed to the expansion of our understanding of the historical origins of racism, the impact of racism on racial minorities, and the social construction of white racial identity. As a history professor for over three decades, I have taught many courses on race relations but often failed to find experience-based books that focused on building genuine and loving relationships among people of racially diverse backgrounds.

Over the years, I have been particularly interested in the history of interracial and multiracial unity in the United States and the roles of the courageous black and white Americans who dedicated their lives to the struggle for racial justice and the promotion of unity and cooperation among racially diverse peoples. These souls are the precious agents of change that have contributed so much to the healing of the nation's racial wounds.

Many whites have played a crucial and vital role in this healing process. From the abolitionist and civil rights movements to the present-day struggle for racial justice and racial unity, there has always been a brave band of whites willing to forsake comfort and safety to join their sisters and brothers of color in their struggle for human dignity. By reaching out beyond their comfort zone to learn firsthand about the pain and suffering of the so-called "racial other," these white sisters and brothers have continued one of the longest and most cherished traditions in American race relations—that of standing up for equality and justice.

Longing: Stories of Racial Healing, written by husband and wife team Phyllis and Eugene Unterschuetz, is a personal account that contributes to this long tradition of caring whites who choose to make a difference by doing all they can to improve race relations in the United States. This book of stories is destined to stand out among the welter of race relations books published in the last decade. It is a collection of personal stories by a white middle-age Bahá'í couple who decided to leave their comfortable Chicago suburban home and embark on a spiritual journey of racial healing and, at times, painful self-discovery.

In their introduction to Part I, Phyllis and Gene wrote, "We were like many other whites in this country; we believed that all people were created equal, that unity was a wonderful goal that would eventually come to pass, and that we had some part to play in its realization. We had grown up with all the same conditioning and misinformation that everyone in this country receives and had both spent the majority of our lives in nearly all-white environments. We were well-intentioned—but quite ignorant—white folks." They readily admitted that, not unlike many "well-intentioned whites," while they talked about unity of all people, they chose to raise their children in a white suburb—a choice that many whites made that contributed to the perpetuation of residential racial segregation and racial isolation. Phyllis and Gene set out to correct this decision as best they could by making different choices, which they present in this book.

Their journey took them around the country, where they visited dozens of communities in which they conducted racial unity workshops that focused on healing the racial divide. They engaged in a very deliberate effort to learn more about the delicate nature of black / white relations. In the process, they shared stories of their "ignorance and mistakes" to illustrate "specific points about how [white] racial conditioning works."

This took courage. Few whites are willing to delve into their racial past and wrestle with their racial demons in front of an audience or in a book! It is far easier to engage in polite, nonthreatening racial chatter or write "objective" academic works about race while staying at a safe distance from uncomfortable racial interactions. By choosing the racial "road less traveled," the Unterschuetzes opened up new and more challenging domains of racial healing, especially between blacks and whites. They pushed the envelope of racial unity discourse by demonstrating how much more whites are capable of achieving in racial healing and unity when they make conscious choices to reach out and embrace racial minorities on their own terms. This was often tough and scary, with no readable road map to serve as a guide.

One can almost feel the pain and anguish of the authors' self-discovery as they share stories of how their racial conditioning over the years affected their interactions with African-Americans. The stories reveal how the Unterschuetzes made special efforts to connect with African-Americans and learned to listen to their heartbreaking stories about their daily life experiences in which they encountered racism.

Eugene recounts embarrassing interactions with African-Americans in which he felt "inept, clumsy, and ignorant." Phyllis learns about black mothers' fears for their black sons, who are growing up in a racist society, and she compares them to her white son's racial privilege in the same society. These efforts to reach out and connect with the so-called "racial other" is based upon the authors' spiritual beliefs and their years of involvement in the multiracial and multicultural Bahá'í community. "We are all part of one organic unit," write the authors in the introduction, "and our Creator has placed the same drive in this body as in each of its cells—the desire to thrive and be healthy in all aspects, to evolve, to become more refined, more efficient, and more closely attuned to our purpose."

One cannot walk away from this book and count it as just another interesting read on race relations. For whites, the book is a primer on how best to engage in racial self-discovery and reflection in the realm of meaningful racial change without the burden of guilt and shame. For people of color, especially those who have grown tired of the seemingly endless and often fruitless discussions on race, these stories will renew their faith in that band of brave white souls who remain dedicated to the healing of racial wounds and the promotion of the unity of humankind.

—Dr. Richard Thomas, coauthor of *Lights of the Spirit*,
author of *Understanding Interracial Unity* and
Life For Us Is What We Make It,
which was awarded the Wesley Logan Prize
in African Diaspora History

PREFACE

On February 19 of the year 2000, we stood at the front of a room in a building near downtown New Orleans. Outside, the city was busy preparing for Mardi Gras; inside, a small audience of African-Americans sat facing us, listening attentively. We recounted some of the things we'd learned in two and a half years on the road and explained how we as white Americans had been conditioned to perceive race in general, and black people in particular. They were a patient and encouraging audience, but at one point a woman in the back of the room stood up and asked, "Who exactly are you talking to here? Shouldn't you be out there telling this to white folks?"

The only response we could think of was, "Well, this is what we have to say, and you're the ones who showed up to hear it." Then we assured them that our goal was to share our understanding with white folks as frequently as possible.

The book you're holding in your hands is our attempt to do just that; it's a collection of true stories that illustrate what we have come to know about racial conditioning over the course of a ten-year journey around the United States. We invite you, whatever your ethnic background, to share this journey with us, and we're confident that people of all colors will find encouragement, hope, and inspiration within these pages.

If someone had told us in 1997 that we would coauthor a book about racial healing, we would have been highly skeptical. We were not writers—Gene was a graphic artist, and Phyllis worked for a German company. Neither of us is a researcher, journalist, or scholar; in fact, we have no academic credentials in the area of race studies. There were other, less traditional forces at work guiding us on this path. While some authors have purposefully undertaken adventures to gather information for their books, we got drawn into the adventure first, unaware of what we were researching or why. It was only after we'd been traveling for several years that it occurred to us we'd been given a mandate to publish our findings.

In the fall of 1996, we were living in a big, empty house in the Chicago suburbs. Our older daughter had moved to Washington and gotten married, our younger daughter was gone for a year of volunteer service in Israel, and our son had flown to Australia to do his own year of service. We were rattling around within our suddenly quiet walls feeling somewhat left behind, and we decided that we should travel and engage in service, too. So at the end of September, 1997, we set out on what we thought would be a six-month trip to visit Bahá'ís around the United States.

We have both been members of the Bahá'í Faith most of our lives; its teachings form the basis of our spiritual identities and the focal point of our activities. It is a young religion, and its communities are in various stages of development; traveling around the country to meet with them seemed like a great idea. We would get to know our fellow Bahá'ís from different backgrounds and at the same time have the opportunity to render a service and share our beliefs with others. It's what Bahá'ís call "travel-teaching." Then, after a half year or so, we would return and move into a smaller house. That was our plan. So we sold our home, transferred our belongings into a very small travel-trailer, and set out late one night driving east.

We began our journey in New England with very little understanding of what we were actually going to do. We had contacted communities ahead of time and offered to give presentations, for the Bahá'ís themselves or for public meetings, and had sent them a list of topics we felt comfortable speaking about. Included on this list were subjects such as the equality of women and men, the spiritual education of children, the agreement of science and religion, and the elimination of racial prejudice. We assumed different groups would have various interests and were prepared to give impromptu talks on any of these issues. By the time we left the second community on our itinerary, our focus had narrowed considerably.

In one of his stories, Gene writes about an occurrence that Phyllis named the hairdresser/taxi driver/bartender phenomenon. Apparently because we were itinerant, people seemed to feel safe talking to us, and somehow—we don't know why—our African-American Bahá'í brothers and sisters began telling us of their experiences with racism. And once we became attuned to their pain, our list of topics was reduced to one: the elimination of racial prejudice. In the third community we visited, all the Bahá'ís we met were black; they took us in like long-lost relatives, and because we were receptive, their stories poured out. By the time we had travelled down the east coast into the southern states, there was no other subject we wanted to talk about.

In two of our stories, you will read more about what happened to us in South Carolina. We had the opportunity and the honor of facilitating a series of workshops on creating racial unity, and that experience changed us so thoroughly that we felt utterly different from the two people who had left the Midwest only a few months before. Combining Gene's previous training as a race unity dialog facilitator with the new materials we'd developed, we created a workshop entitled "From the Same Dust" that we began presenting for the communities we visited.

The more workshops we facilitated, the more often we messed up. We said things that hurt people's feelings, we let slip our unconscious stereotypes; we had stepped out of our theoretical understanding of racism and into the spotlight, where our own racial conditioning was exposed for all to see. At some point there was a shift, and we realized we were no longer simply rendering a service for the benefit of others; this was our own personal issue. We were so embarrassed by our mistakes that sometimes we felt like quitting. But we had an unending source of love, support, and encouragement; our new African-American friends, whether Bahá'ís or not, never gave up on us. They told us we must keep moving, learning, and sharing what we learned with others as we travelled. And this, more than anything else, explains why nearly all the stories in this book are about the relationship between blacks and whites.

As we got braver, we began talking about our ignorance and mistakes during our workshops to illustrate specific points about how racial conditioning works. It quickly became clear that these personal anecdotes were by far the most effective part of our presentations; workshop participants responded by spontaneously revealing their own painful or embarrassing incidents, and people of all ethnic backgrounds shared anger, confusion, and frustration. More importantly, they shared honesty, courage, and hope. Eventually we stopped presenting workshops altogether and concentrated instead on storytelling followed by group discussions. It was at this point that we began writing the stories down for the sake of consistency, and soon people were encouraging us to put them into book form. And that is how *Longing: Stories of Racial Healing* came into being.

The experiences you'll read about took place all over the United States and involved individuals from a wide range of economic, occupational, and educational backgrounds. Each story is a memoir; the people are all real, although we've changed their names and avoided mentioning their locations to protect their privacy. Our interactions and conversations with them are related here as faithfully as possible. It was always our intention to portray each person authentically; we have used accurate physical descriptions—although not with so much detail that someone might be identified—and we also tried to capture speech patterns, in particular with the use of Southern dialect. This use of dialect in no way implies lack of education or sophistication; it is merely the standard way of speaking in that region. Even though we put much effort into creating truthful depictions, we relied only on our own recollections and journal entries; in some cases, the accounts were written years after the events took place, so we are not claiming perfect recall.

With a few exceptions, Gene's and Phyllis's stories alternate throughout the book, and they are presented somewhat chronologically. However, they do not form one single, cohesive narrative with a beginning, middle, and end. Everything we experienced was influenced by what we'd learned in previous communities, and in that sense the stories, taken as a whole, relate one continual journey from ignorance to deeper understanding. But each story is also complete by itself; each relates an interaction—sometimes with flashbacks or subplots—and ends with some kind of resolution. The month, year, and state are listed at the beginning of each chapter; these refer to the main event in the narrative and will hopefully help our readers make sense out of our erratic itinerary.

Several stories include brief quotations from the central figures of the Bahá'í Faith; they have been used to clarify concepts and to explain the reasons for our beliefs and decisions. These citations are from the religion's Founder, Bahá'u'lláh, His son 'Abdu'l-Bahá, and His great-grandson Shoghi Effendi. The passages were written in the late nineteenth and early twentieth centuries and contain terms—such as "the colored" and "colored people"—that were standard usage at the time.

Most of the stories are followed by commentaries in which we attempt to uncover the deeper truths underlying actual incidents and to define not only the broad concepts but also our own private thoughts and feelings. These insights have come with time and as a result of processing our thoughts together, having additional experiences, and receiving feedback from our listeners, both black and white. They were not things we realized at the time the events in the stories took place; frequently, we didn't even have the words to express the deeper meaning at that time.

In fact, everything you will read in this book is the result of an intricate and dynamic process of learning. We had interactions with people and then came home to our RV and talked together about what had happened, sometimes for weeks following particularly poignant or intense experiences. We asked each other questions: Did you hear what I heard? What did that mean? Where have we heard that before? How did you feel? What are you going to do? Then we shared our conclusions with others and incorporated their reactions into our understanding. We put all of that into our stories, read them to diverse audiences, and through comments from our listeners discovered even more layers that we'd been unaware of. When it came time to decide which stories would be included in this book, we chose the ones that shouted to be told, the ones that chronicled an epiphany or a deep sense of shift, which we frequently understood only in retrospect.

Because we have had mostly shared experiences, you'll find overlapping insights in our commentaries; we've processed these occurrences together so thoroughly that it often seems as if we're speaking with one voice. But at the same time, our insights are deeply influenced by gender and by our very different personalities. We're not proposing universally applicable solutions to the problems caused by race, nor do we mean to suggest that our decisions were always right and should be used as examples in all situations, because what we decided to do in each case was influenced by our individual temperaments, conditioning, life experiences, and level of understanding at the time. We might do something different now. Thirteen years after our decision to travel, we are still meeting new people and still learning more about ourselves. Our hope is that you will be encouraged by our stories to find answers of your own.

We understand that there are many other serious issues besides race that need to be addressed in order for this country to become a just and nurturing place, and we're well aware that many other groups have been the targets of prejudice and discrimination. This book, however, is specifically about how racism has ruptured the connection between white and black people living in the United States, and how bonds of friendship can heal that rupture and give us back the freedom to behave according to our noble design.

One of the best ways to use this book, we believe, is as a starting point for group discussion. You may want to read a story first, then allow people to share their own experiences, thoughts, and feelings before reading the commentary. This approach gives group members the freedom to express themselves without being influenced by our interpretations of the events. It is our hope that the book will also be used for personal reference and inspiration, for in our stories you will meet the people who inspired and uplifted us, who instructed and challenged and loved us. We found them everywhere we went in this richly blessed country.

We have a photo that clearly depicts the beginning of our travels. In this picture Gene is hammering a "For Sale By Owner" sign into the ground in front of our split-level suburban home. In the driveway behind him sits our newly purchased Nomad travel-trailer, all shiny and ready to go, and the big blue van that will haul it along the highways of the United States and into the heart of our as yet unimagined journey. The trailer is quite modest by RV standards— just 22' long and 8' wide—nothing fancy. In fact, it was beginning to seem awfully small that day as we made trip after trip from the house, carrying sheets, towels, pots and pans, art books, and small appliances, all of which we crammed into our little box on wheels.

Nothing about our life seemed all that extraordinary. We lived in a tree-lined residential area of a suburban community and considered ourselves fairly average, with our nice house, big yard, two cars, and cat and dog. We had a sizeable mortgage, and both of us worked full-time to support our lifestyle; like everyone around us, we were settled securely in the middle of the middle class. And like most of those neighbors, we are both of northern European heritage—second- and third-generation Americans profiting from the efforts of our German and Danish immigrant grandparents and great-grandparents. To us, our lives were just normal. We never thought of ourselves as privileged.

So as we moved into our new home, we didn't foresee the real adventure that awaited us. We thought we were setting out to discover something about the country we lived in; we ended up discovering more about the country within—the mountains of our own conditioning, the oceans of our ignorance, the valleys of our private psyches. Through our friendships with the people we met along the way, we came to understand something about our true selves.

We'd be honored to have you accompany us on our journey.

INTRODUCTION

We'd like to begin our journey with a word of welcome to our readers. If you've picked up this book, then you are apparently interested in the topic of race. Maybe you're curious about the idea of racial healing or hopeful of discovering some new approach to the problems associated with race. Some of you might already be deeply engaged in the work of creating unity and committed to building relationships. Perhaps you've read other books about the causes of racism or ways to overcome prejudice. Whatever your level of involvement in the issue of race, and whatever your reasons for joining us, we're pleased that you've chosen to read our stories. We hope you'll find something new in these pages—some insight or confirmation that will leave you optimistic about your ability to make a difference.

It will be helpful to understand some basic concepts that form the framework of this book, so before beginning with our stories, we'll present a few of the principles from which we've drawn our focus and inspiration.

We believe that there is only one race of humanity, so when we talk about racial healing, we are not referring to the coming together of different races because, in reality, there is no such thing as "different races." While we use the terms *black* or *African-American* and *white* or *European-American*, we feel these are social constructs that have nothing to do with our true reality, which is spiritual.

Racial healing is a process, ordained and directed by God, which is unfolding on several levels. As individuals, we all need to heal from the toxic effects of our own racial conditioning. Each ethnicity or group of the human family must be healed from the cumulative effects of its particular experience of racism, and the body of humanity must seek healing from the diseases caused by separation and disunity.

Each one of us human beings is created in the image of God and is therefore born noble, with the potential to develop divine attributes. In the same way that the physical body is designed to heal itself, the soul is designed to seek spiritual health, and anything that causes us to behave in a less than noble fashion impedes that goal. Individual racial healing is not so much about ceasing conscious oppression or violence; it's more about uncovering and eliminating any attitudes we may be carrying around unconsciously that result in mistrust, fear, avoidance—and consequently separation.

Each part of the human family—whether identified by skin color, ethnicity, or culture—has something unique and essential to bring to the process of unity-building. But in order to do that, we need to heal the injuries that each particular group has suffered. It's not our place as white authors to address the problems facing the black community; our stories focus on how whites have been impacted by racial conditioning and how that dynamic has resulted in unhealthy patterns of behavior that thwart our collective well-being.

The same healing process is taking place in the organism of humankind. Imagine a physical body that is striving to be healthy and has at its disposal everything necessary to attain that state. Imagine that you can zoom in and see each individual cell attempting to function in an optimal, healthy way, to take in nourishment, rid itself of toxins, and combine with other cells in the formation of new tissue to repair wounds. This is the process in which we're engaged as a human body. If the organism is to function optimally, then each of us must constantly take in nourishment—emotionally in the form of love, intellectually in the form of new knowledge, and spiritually in the form of our connection with the divine. We need also to rid ourselves of toxins—attitudes and feelings we've absorbed that aren't good for us. And we must always be looking for new ways to connect with others to heal the wounds in our society. We are all part of one organic unit, and our Creator has placed the same drive in this body as in each of its cells—the desire to thrive and be healthy in all aspects, to evolve, to become more refined, more efficient, and more closely attuned to our purpose.

Our desire to be connected with one another is innate; we have been designed to seek association with other members of our human family. But things have happened to us throughout our common history that have thwarted our design and resulted in separation, and the repercussions of that separation are the social and spiritual ills that plague us. The cure for the disease of separation is the recognition of our oneness; it is this recognition at a soul level that is the source of the longing.

What exactly do we mean by *longing*? We see it as a form of energy—a force of attraction that exists within every one of us, inherent even when it lies dormant. And it is spiritual rather than physical in nature. If our souls live eternally, and if they are associated with bodies that live at most about a hundred years, then our reality is far more spiritual than material. We're not trying to ignore the fact that we are all material beings with physical drives, but the attraction we are talking about in these stories has nothing to do with our physical selves. It is spiritual love, an extension of the love between God and humankind. We are drawn to each other as cells in the body or planets in a solar system, responding to a kind of human gravitational pull, one soul to another. To regard this attraction as biological or physical is a sullying of the gift.

The longing is an innate aspect of our human nature, and its emergence is a natural development, similar to the stage of puberty in an adolescent. In the same way that an adolescent's hormones—which were built into his design and lay dormant since his birth—force his body to begin the process of maturation, this longing was built into us by design and has lain dormant until we collectively reached this point in our development. It has now been activated and is forcing the body of humanity to enter a new phase in the process of maturation. Just as hormones draw us to one another physically to ensure the propagation of our species, this urge to connect is the spiritual counterpart, drawing us to one another to ensure the continuation of our collective development.

We believe that the coming together of our human family is God's plan; it is the inevitable next stage in our social evolution and is as crucial to our normal development as a baby's learning how to crawl before it walks. It is a spiritual truth that exists even when we can't see it. And though the accomplishment of this unity is a God-driven process and exists already in the spiritual realm, it is we individual humans who are the means for bringing it about on the material plane.

This is what our stories attempt to describe—the process of manifesting a divine reality in the physical world. You will read about our efforts to define the nature of the work. You will watch us struggling to make appropriate choices. You will share in our experiences of transformation and faith, as well as our challenges, setbacks and disappointments. Each story presents some aspect of our learning—insights and questions, defeats and triumphs. We fully expect that you will see things we've missed and ask questions we haven't thought of. We assume that your own unique life experiences will allow you to discover truths that remained hidden to us.

The process of building racial unity needs everyone's input. We're profoundly grateful for your decision to participate and we hope your engagement in this process will bring you blessings and confirmations beyond your expectations.

PART 1

Before 1997

In this first section, we have included a few stories about incidents that occurred in our lives before we moved into our trailer and hit the road. They were specifically chosen for two reasons: to explain how we became attracted to the work of building unity and to illustrate our state of awareness about racial issues when we made the decision to travel. We want our readers to understand that neither of us was out of the ordinary in our ability to form interracial friendships. We were like many other whites in this country; we believed that all people were created equal, that unity was a wonderful goal that would eventually come to pass, and that we had some part to play in its realization. We had grown up with all the same conditioning and misinformation that everyone in this country receives and had both spent the majority of our lives in nearly all-white environments. We were well-intentioned—but quite ignorant—white folks.

This is a point we hope to communicate clearly. Because if we did in fact have extraordinary abilities to connect with people from different backgrounds, then this book would be merely a collection of stories about our own adventures—interesting perhaps, but not applicable to others' lives. The truth, though, is that we had absorbed countless stereotypes, prejudices, and irrational fears, and these were things that constantly tripped us up and frustrated our efforts to create relationships. While many of our readers are certainly less ignorant than we were at the beginning of this journey, we believe they may still see in our stories a reflection of themselves and may recognize some of their own experiences and attitudes about race.

1

FIRST GRADE

Gene, September 1951
Illinois

I felt a little breeze as she walked by me. She made her way between the rows of desks with a bounce in her stride. I paid attention whenever our teacher asked her to write a new spelling word on the blackboard at the front of the classroom, and now I leaned into the aisle to get a better look as she placed one hand on her hip and picked up the eraser with the other hand. Her whole body was involved in the task of cleaning the blackboard. As her erasing arm waved back and forth, wiping off another classmate's word, her hips swayed from side to side, mirroring her arm's motions. I was enchanted by the grace of that movement.

While she wrote, I looked at her arms and hands, the back of her neck, her ankles—dark brown. Her jet-black hair was tied up in several small braids on top of her head, not in two long pigtails like the other girls wore. A couple of weeks after the beginning of school, she had suddenly become one of our classmates. This new girl fascinated me.

When she walked back to her desk, she was smiling; her spelling was correct, and the teacher said she had neat printing. I looked at her bright eyes as she neared my desk, hoping for a sign of friendship. She smiled at me as she passed on the way to her seat.

In another three weeks, she was gone as suddenly as she had appeared. I don't remember if our teacher explained where she went, but I missed her.

Over fifty years have passed, and I wonder where she is. What has happened to her since first grade? If she had stayed in our school, would she have had to deal with cruel remarks and behaviors from our peers? Would I have joined in with them, or would I have stood up for her? After all these years, I still remember her. I hope she is well.

2

CONFRONTATIONS

Phyllis, June 1993
Illinois

Close your eyes and imagine a five-year-old in the checkout lane at any grocery store. Take your time. Picture her clearly. She is sweet-tempered and adorable; she stands about three feet high, her eyes perfectly level with the shelf that holds brightly-colored packages of chocolate, sugar-coated goodies. She looks from the candy to you and, when you respond with a firm shake of your head, is suddenly overwhelmed with such dire *need* that all sweetness evaporates. In a voice that can be heard way back by the meat counter she whines, "PLEEEEEEASE, OH PLEASE, PLEASE PLEASE PLEASE PLEASE, PUH-LEASE, PLEE-EEE-EEEASE."

Horrible, yes. Embarrassing, infuriating—nevertheless, it is a situation I can handle. I have raised three children, and I am im-mune. But take that same word, spoken in the same way by the voice of a grown man, and I am shaken, hyper-alert and ready to fight. It was that word, floating up from dormant memories of a twenty-

31

three-year-old man named Emilio, that helped me understand how racial prejudice works.

In July of 1967, I was freshly graduated from high school and working a summer job at a factory—and as naive as a girl my age could be. It's not that I'd had no experience at all, but my forays into the world of passion had been quite innocent by anyone's standards. When my coworker Emilio asked me out, I was surprised and flattered that he was interested in me, but also curious and somewhat cautious because he was Mexican—in fact, the only Mexican I'd ever met. Predictably, flattery won out over caution; I set aside my concerns and agreed to go with him to—of all places—a drive-in movie. This somehow made sense to me in spite of the fact that he spoke almost no English. Perhaps he wasn't worried about understanding the dialog; perhaps he just enjoyed the music, or the hot dogs, or the stimulating environment. . . .

I spent two hours deftly evading his amorous moves, and all the while Emilio begged, implored, pleaded in a manner most unbecoming an adult, "PLEEEEEASE, OOOOH PLEASE, PHYLLIS, PLEE-EEE-EEEASE!"

Fortunately he was just obnoxious, not aggressive; when I continued to resist, he finally got the message, and I survived the encounter unscathed. Or so I thought. I had no warning of the real danger, of the damage that had been done—not by Emilio, but by my own treacherous mind.

A quarter century later, as I lay awake one night thinking about my racial conditioning, Emilio stepped out of my memory and into my restless mind, bringing with him another invitation. This time he didn't want to go to the drive-in; he wanted to take me instead to a place of deeper awareness.

Have I lost credibility here? Do you think it unlikely that anyone actually lies awake thinking about such things? Well, the truth is, it was on my mind a lot that summer. I had recently resumed my college education and was writing a paper about prejudice; in this essay I examined Mexican culture to see if I could find a reason—any reason—for the stereotypes and intolerance that became increasingly prevalent among my neighbors as more and more immigrants moved from Mexico into our previously un-diverse community. These attitudes enraged me, and I poured my anger into my composition. I considered myself, if not completely prejudice-free, then at least as enlightened as a white person could be. I believed passionately in the oneness of humanity; when I was younger, I had been unofficially engaged to a black man, for heaven's sake—surely there was not a bigoted bone in my body. At my office, I was taking Spanish lessons and talking on the phone almost daily with Mexican clients, suppliers, and customs agents. And there were a number of Mexican-Americans at my place of employment; not only did I work closely with these men, I counted many of them as friends. So when I heard anti-Mexican rhetoric, I was filled with indignation, for I was above such preposterous ideas. And yet . . . and yet . . . whenever I passed a group of young Mexican men standing outside on a street corner, I avoided them, crossed the street, averted my eyes.

My behavior plagued me. It seemed utterly illogical. I searched my psyche for some insight, but the explanation for this hypocrisy eluded me. And it kept me awake. On that particular night—the night of Emilio's unexpected reappearance—I was, as I mentioned before, lying in bed, unable to fall asleep. Duplicity is a troublesome thing and can prevent one from enjoying the restful sleep of the righteous. As I wrestled my demons, stirring up the muddy waters of my unconscious, a fuzzy memory began to float up, becoming more vivid as it rose until it burst onto the surface of my consciousness in the form of a single word: PLEEEEEEASE.

Only this time I was willing to cooperate. I sat straight up in bed, grabbed my journal and, so as not to awaken Gene, went into the bathroom to write. There was a crowd gathering in my head—Emilio, the guys at work, the guys on the corner—all of them bunched together and looking at me with clear irritation. "Look back," they said, "if you dare. If you really want to know, look back. Please."

I did want to know. And with the clarity of hindsight, suddenly I could see the conclusions I had come to, based on that one experience at the drive-in movie theater. Conclusion #1: Well, at least now I know how they are, and #2: that's what I get for being friendly; I sure won't do that again. Then those conclusions, which were strongly linked to my memory of feeling discomfort, settled so deep in my subconscious that they were unchanged by all my later positive experiences with Mexican men. My avoidant behavior—which for some odd reason applied just to groups of young men standing on street corners—had served only to reinforce my conclusions, which continued to affect me twenty-five years later.

But the realization was not enough for me; I knew I had to do some intentional reprogramming, so I designed an experiment. I would go the next day to the corner by the post office, where there was nearly always a group of young Mexican men hanging out. I would walk straight up to them, look them in their collective eye, say "hola" and see what happened.

And this I did, on the following day. I drove to a spot near the post office, emerged from my car bold and brave, and set off down the sidewalk, super-charged. But as I got closer my resolve began to falter, and soon I found myself stopped ten feet from a few young Mexican men standing on the corner. They were talking and laughing, and probably wondering what the heck was up with this woman who looked at them so strangely. What kind of a look was it, you might ask. Fear. It was the look of fear. There was just something about the group of them standing bunched together like that . . .

Time for a reality check. Did I really think they were going to jump on me in the middle of the day in front of the post office? Was I really *so* alluring that they would be unable to control themselves, drawn like hypnotized mariners to an overweight, forty-four-year-old siren breathing shallowly through her open mouth? I closed my mouth, shook off my stupor, and got a grip.

Once I had my overactive imagination under control, I was able to proceed with my Great Experiment. I walked right up to them, looked each man in the eye and smiled, said my "hola," then continued casually on my way. The response was . . . what one would expect. They stopped their conversation, smiled and returned my greeting. No violence, no frothing at the mouth. Just some folks acknowledging each other on a pleasant day in front of the post office.

What to do now? Of course I had to either go into the building or continue walking down the street, getting farther away from my car with each step. So I went in and bought some stamps I didn't need, then retraced my route back down the stairs and past the corner, where the men and I nodded to each other again in a reaffirmation of goodwill and mutual recognition.

I did a quick self-assessment as I walked toward my car. I felt slightly foolish, having created such a spectacular sense of drama around such a commonplace event. But I was also exhilarated, and though I didn't know it then, I would experience that feeling every time I intentionally challenged my own conditioning. And I felt something else, or thought I did. There was the slightest weight on my shoulders. It was not a heaviness or burden, but rather a gentle pressure, as if someone had put an arm around me. I turned and looked behind me; no one was there. Then I heard that voice again from my memories, now sweet and shy.

"Thank you," it said.

No, Emilio, it is I who thanks you.

COMMENTARY

When I had the awareness that led to my great experiment in front of the post office, it was the summer of 1993, and I was taking a college course in which we used the Kolb Cycle of Learning to help us evaluate our learning styles. This model, developed by educational theorist David Kolb, suggests that people have concrete experiences and feelings, which we then reflect on. The reflections, in turn, become generalized to form a theory, and we go out and test that theory by having new experiences.

Just before encountering Kolb's model I attended a race unity workshop and saw a flowchart diagram called the Cycle of Racial Conditioning.[1] The overlap of these two pieces of new information had a profound effect on me and formed the groundwork for my understanding of how this conditioning functions—both in me and in our society.

According to the diagram, racial conditioning begins with misinformation. From childhood, we receive messages—not by our own volition—about who we are and who others are, and this training leads to a belief in the superiority of one group over another. The conditioning is sometimes deliberate, sometimes unintentional. It comes from our families, friends, institutions, entertainment, media, and classrooms.

The flowchart shows that misinformation results in fear, mistrust, and then in separation, which is sometimes voluntary—we just don't want to be around folks who are "like that." Other times the separation is institutionally enforced; now that segregation is no longer legal, our society is still adept at finding ways to keep us apart. When we're separated, we have no way to disprove the misinformation. I was eighteen before I met someone who was Mexican, and because of that separation, due in my case mostly to where I lived, I'd had no other interactions with Mexican men to draw on.

In the next phase of the cycle, we learn that separation is a breeding ground for the development of stereotypes, which are nothing more than generalizations applied to a particular group of people. Unlike a cultural norm, a stereotype resists change in the face of new information; it's an emotional attachment to an untruth. I had one experience with Emilio, and I generalized from that single incident that all young Mexican men were sexually aggressive. And I clung to this idea at an unconscious level even though later in my life I had many interactions that ought to have disproven my conclusion, which is something I find particularly odd.

The diagram goes on to explain racial prejudice, discrimination, and denial. When stereotypes take on negative feelings—especially fear—they become prejudice. If the targeted group has a different ethnicity or skin color, the stereotypes turn into racial prejudice. The negative feeling I experienced with Emilio was discomfort verging on fear, and the emotion became inextricably interwoven with the thought that all men like Emilio were dangerous.

Racial prejudice that is expressed in some kind of action or behavior becomes discrimination. Whether on an individual or institutional level, discrimination is usually accompanied by denial—an unwillingness to look at our unconscious thoughts and a belief that we are, in fact, free of prejudice. Nat Rutstein, author and dedicated race unity worker, described denial as "a carefully conceived mental maneuver that springs from shame."[2] In my case the discrimination manifested itself as avoidance of a very specific situation, and so the cycle became self-perpetuating. But all the while, I continued to perceive myself as untouched by racial prejudice.

The final—and to me the most disturbing—phase in the cycle of racial conditioning is identified as "internalized oppression." This is when some members of the targeted group come to accept the stereotypes of themselves and act out the labels that have been put on them. The devastating result of this is that it effectively serves to reinforce the prejudice—those who have believed the misinformation all along can say, "See, we were right to mistrust them; they're exactly the way we expected them to be." And they feel justified in continuing to keep their distance and to practice injustice, bringing the cycle full circle.

So the chain of separation, mistrust, and oppression perpetuates itself, leaving us doomed to dig ourselves deeper and deeper into the hole of disunity. Unless, that is, we can discover a way to break the cycle.

While the Cycle of Racial Conditioning made perfect, undeniable sense, it did not give me hope; I left the workshop feeling overwhelmed and depressed. I had completely missed the most important part of the presentation—that the cycle can be effectively broken at the stage of separation.

It was when I studied the Kolb Cycle of Learning just a couple weeks later that I had my moment of clear insight. I could see that I'd had the concrete experience with Emilio, reflected on that experience with its accompanying negative feelings, and then formed a theory that I never disproved because I never tested it. So in the middle of the night, realizing exactly what I'd done, I decided to reevaluate based on different, more positive experiences. I had a number of safe, trusting relationships with Mexican men at my workplace; when I reflected on those relationships, the inconsistencies in my attitudes became very apparent. Perhaps my original conclusions had somehow incorporated scenes from movies or media images of gang members hanging out on street corners. Or maybe because the men I worked with were professionals, or because I interacted with them in an office setting, I had come to see them as exceptions. In any case, once I acknowledged the irrational nature of my prejudice, it was easy to come to a different conclusion—that young Mexican men are no different than other young men. Some of them are violent, pushy, or obnoxious, but the vast majority of them are not. Having a neighborly exchange with a group of them standing on a street corner in broad daylight, I concluded, was not a dangerous thing to do. Then, of course, came the assessment—testing my theory to see if it held up in real life. The result of that was, I admit, fairly amusing; but it also set a precedent for my future efforts to unlearn my own conditioning.

My bold experiment was really only a baby step, and that's what I would recommend to anyone who wants to confront her racial conditioning. Baby steps yield only a little progress, but that's better than no progress at all. Because each step leads to another step, and before you know it, you're taking daring risks in exchange for the reward of new relationships. And relationships are the cure for separation; they are the simplest, most logical, most joyful way to break the cycle.

3

CRACK IN THE WALL

Gene, October 1993
Illinois

"I need fifty of each of these—black and white. This has to be enlarged 300% and printed in color. I'm going to need a hundred of these with envelopes, and these have to be collated and put into binders."

Typical shop talk at the local copy center. The person giving the instructions was a young African-American woman. I had entered the store preoccupied with my own project, but when I saw the woman at the service counter, I positioned myself behind a kiosk of supplies to observe her interaction with the white employee assisting her. I had never seen a black person in this shop, and I wasn't even sure if any African-Americans lived in our town. I wondered how the guy serving her would handle this unusual situation.

The woman took one item after another off a large pile of documents, organized them on the counter, and gave the man explicit directions. As I watched her I thought, *Look at that young black woman. Man, she is really competent. Look how confident she is; she really knows what she's doing. And she's well dressed. Nice pants suit. I'll bet she works for some law firm around here. She's really doing a great job.* I looked around at the other white customers to detect if they too were appreciating the young woman as much as I was, but they seemed to take no notice, and I was miffed. *What's wrong with these people; why can't they see what I see? Would it hurt them to give her a little acknowledgement?* And the white guy assisting her? Not a trace of anything out of the ordinary. He just listened and took notes.

While I stood smiling at the young woman, basking in the warmth of my own charity, a distressing thought—like an ogre trudging out of a murky swamp—threatened to blot out the serenity radiating from my altruism. I felt defenseless as the grim image of it came into focus: *I'm being patronizing!*

The night before, I had attended the third session of a race unity workshop series offered in a neighboring town. During three weekly classes, I had listened to lectures about racism in America, watched videos, and processed insights with other participants; now I felt I knew something about racism that other white folks were unaware of. The message of the workshop so far was that we white people feel we're superior to black people, and this sense of superiority is a result of conditioning. We aren't born racists; we learn racism—and, therefore, we can unlearn it. So here I was in the copy center, applying my new understanding, appreciating the young woman as an equal.

Of course she's competent, I chastised myself. *Did you think she would be inept just because she's black? That's ignorant. Remember in the workshop, when they asked those participants who thought they were racists to raise their hands, and you raised your hand because you knew it was the cool thing to do, and you got good feedback for that from the facilitators? Well, guess what? This patronizing stuff is racist, whether you raised your hand or not.*

Three weeks earlier, if I had noticed the young woman at the copy center, I would not have obsessed about patronizing and wrestled with my conscience. Now I was asking myself, *Do I feel superior to African-Americans and other people of color?* For the first time in my life I was consciously confronting my racial conditioning.

Shortly before I heard about the workshop, I read Toni Morrison's *Beloved.* I'm not sure why I decided to read *Beloved,* but I remember feeling totally confused and lost as I forced myself to make my way through the book. The manner in which the author narrated the story—and depicted characters who seemed like aliens to me—left me feeling stupid. After all, Ms. Morrison was awarded a Pulitzer Prize for *Beloved.* But I didn't get it. The protagonist in the novel, Sethe, seemed so dysfunctional. I concluded early on that the book was simply a tale about a crazy woman. Or maybe a ghost story? Then I finally understood that Sethe had been assaulted by the school teacher's nephews. It was so horrific. I felt her helplessness. The beastly injustice of it all. SNAP! It hit me. *That's what her whole life has been like! How does she continue to function at all?*

Beloved awakened in me a feeling for the injustice of racism, but I was very ignorant about the causes. Just a few days after I finished reading the book, a friend called and invited me to attend the race unity workshop. I wanted to decline—or at least put it off—because I sensed my life would change, and I wasn't sure I was ready. What kind of commitments would I have to make? In spite of my anxiety, however, I was attracted to the possibility of getting some clarity about the dynamics of racism.

In the workshop, I got more specific information about institutional racism—how the racial prejudice of individuals gets woven into the fabric of the institutions to which they belong. The presentations provided convincing evidence that white Americans have not only accepted racial stereotypes as truth, but have also wielded power in key areas of public life. We were given a definition: racial prejudice plus power equals racism. The logic was compelling but disconcerting because it led to the following deduction: to be white in America is to be racist. My reaction was: *But I don't feel superior. I don't have any power. I'm just a cog in the corporate machine.*

The lectures, videos, and testimonies of black participants described the inequalities in our society. It is easier for whites to get loans and more difficult for blacks. Whites have few limits on our mobility; blacks are barred from—or at least not welcomed in—many suburbs, social clubs, and positions of authority in corporations. The law treats black citizens differently. Black students often struggle to learn with inadequate resources. Medical care is frequently inferior for black citizens. We examined how African-Americans are disadvantaged in every institution and are, in general, regarded with suspicion, punished unfairly, and excluded. I had been ignorant of all this.

I grew up fifty miles from Chicago during the '50s and '60s and was old enough to have been conscious of race riots and protests. In the workshop classes, I saw images of African-Americans, adults and children, being blasted with water from fire hoses and attacked by snarling dogs. But these media images, decades old, seemed unfamiliar. It's not that I had blurry memories of the civil rights events that occurred in my youth—it's that I had no memories of them at all, and therefore, could not recall having been moved to talk with others and process my feelings about what was happening. Now middle-aged, I was compelled to ask myself, *What kind of person can live so close to human distress of such proportion, yet be unaware, ask no questions, have no feeling of relationship, no compulsion to do something? Is that person intelligent, compassionate, just?* I was embarrassed.

Here's an example of one way to deal with embarrassment—the magician's device of misdirection:

At recess a first-grader shouts to a classmate, "Hey! Your fly is open. I can see your underpants." Every youngster within earshot turns to see the exposed briefs.

The kid with the open fly points to the street and yells, "Hey, look! The ice cream truck just pulled up." While everyone looks toward the street, Open Fly quickly zips up and sticks his hands in his pockets.

The others realize they've been tricked, turn back, and shout in unison, "Your fly was open! Your fly was open!"

Open Fly smiles and says, "No it wasn't. Can't prove it."

Sometimes, when I'm embarrassed, I wonder whether something I've said or done will diminish my value in the eyes of others. Had I, in the past, used misdirection to squirm out of situations in which I exposed my ignorance and insensitivity with regard to racism? What unconscious mechanisms had I developed to avoid embarrassment?

These are some concerns that haunted me as a workshop participant: *Can I deal with the private embarrassment of having lived in*

45

ignorance most of my life? Should I cling to the comfort of anonymity? If I get involved in this workshop, will I be spotted as a racist?

I've discovered that fear of exposure can lead to denial. What is denial? It is something that is difficult to define but that is characterized by certain signs. For example, if we are presented with the unconscionable, and we do not acknowledge it or give it a name, and we dispute that it has any relevance to our own happiness and well-being, we are in denial. If we feel our hearts moved by another human being's need and choose not to respond, we are in denial. If we believe our non-involvement has no impact on others, we are in denial.

Denial is injustice at the subconscious level. It's not harmless. It's lethal. Not only does denial affect people whose human rights are being violated, it is symptomatic of a disorder that has grave spiritual consequence for the individual in denial.

Denial gives rise to the inability to see reality from another person's point of view. A person could point at some hideous creature standing right in front of me, could describe it in detail, could tell me what it smells like, and if I were in the grip of denial, I would say, "Nope, can't see it. You must be imagining it. Don't be so obsessive. Let's get on with normal life."

Racism is like that hideous creature. I was learning that African-Americans had been pointing at it for centuries, and yet the majority of white citizens are still unable to see it. Learning about racism in the workshop was like looking at a deadly virus under a microscope. *Oh, no! It's real, just like they said it was. And I've got it!* The prescribed treatment for removing racial prejudice from the mind, heart, and

46

will appeared to be a process beset with remissions, flare-ups, frustration, and hopelessness. Was it worth the effort?

I worked in a community closer to Chicago where the demographic was much more diverse than in my home town. I had never paid much attention to people of color during my commute, lunch break, or shopping trips after work, but now it seemed I saw them everywhere, and I could not look at them, speak to them, or think in their presence without questioning whether I was revealing my inherent racial prejudice.

For example, driving up to the pay window at a fast food place, I was conscious of a slight anxiety if the cashier was black—or the relief I felt if the cashier was white. Talking to African-Americans was a nightmare; I constantly wondered if the words I chose were racist and insulting, and if people could perceive a racism that was only gradually coming into focus for me. Watching TV became a private internal battle; when I saw black news anchors and weathermen I was conscious of questioning if they were qualified to do their jobs. In public places, I felt I had to interact with people of color differently than I had previously. *Should I look into their eyes? Smile? Say something? What should I say? Should I just act nonchalant about their presence? But that's not really doing anything.* Interacting with people of color required new social skills, and I felt uncoordinated, as if I had just read a book about the history of the piano and was now sitting at a baby grand attempting to play a Chopin concerto.

I had discovered a crack in the wall that separated my white world—an imaginary fortress of order and standards—from a much larger world outside the wall. It was as if light were filtering in

47

through the crack, energizing me and quickening a yearning for more knowledge and competence. I was eager for the whole truth, yet fearful that I might get burned by the intensity of a reality from which I had been sheltered my whole life. What lay beyond the wall? I shared with other white folks the idea that there might be a larger reality we had been overlooking. In response, some people waved their hands as if to ward off evil, and exclaimed, "There's nothing to talk about!"

It seemed the discussion of race was taboo, and my thwarted efforts to gain clarity resulted in frustration. I was just becoming aware, questioning things I had accepted as "normal," and struggling for answers. Most white acquaintances gave me no support and said things like, "Why don't they just get over it? It's not my fault. That's just the way things are. I've got my own problems." They did nothing to help me learn how I could contribute to eliminating racial prejudice.

What I did learn from other whites was that we don't have many constructive insights about racism in the United States. Not only was I overwhelmed by the resistance I encountered, but more devastatingly, I was humiliated by my ignorance. Discussions about racial issues with other white folks led to arguments I invariably lost. Some had formed opinions about African-Americans based on unpleasant personal experiences. Most kept up to speed with current events; they had data to support their stereotypes. I was going on a hunch, still processing information acquired in a classroom setting. I needed evidence from real life to convince myself first, before I could persuade others that we were missing something. But it still wasn't clear to me where I could get that evidence.

After years of participation in race unity workshops, first as a student and then as a facilitator, I felt I knew something about the dynamics of racial prejudice. In fact I was pretty impressed with my understanding. What I didn't know was that my opportunities to truly understand racism lay outside the classroom and beyond my community—outside of my comfort zone. Had I been able to foresee how many embarrassing moments I would have to experience to develop just a bit of humility—vital to learning about things of the soul—I might have declined the invitation to that first workshop.

COMMENTARY

During our travels we met hundreds of African-Americans who generously shared stories about their experiences with race that changed our hearts. We heard about life in the community and how black children were still receiving inferior education and hand-me-down books. We heard how folks driving home from church or family gatherings were frequently stopped by the police and questioned about why they were in a particular neighborhood.

Everywhere we traveled, the majority of black people we talked to, whether rich or poor, college educated or illiterate, related the same or similar stories of racial stress. Seeing the truth was for us a simple matter of connecting the dots, and gradually a bigger picture took shape. Eventually we could speak as credible witnesses with white folks about the racial challenges African-Americans and other people of color face.

At some point in our travels, I took part in a discussion of a book by a well-known black author. After we had been sharing our ideas for a while, the white man leading the discussion asked the participants, "What do you think about this 'intelligence thing'?"

Someone asked, "What do you mean?"

"Well, you know. Do you think black people are as intelligent as other people?"

I squirmed and waited for him to go on. He cited some research that classified groups of humanity in a hierarchy based on intelligence.

"Asians are at the top—and I don't feel bad about that," he stated. "Caucasians come next. Then Hispanics and then native peoples—and then last on the list, at the very bottom, are blacks." After he finished, he looked around to see how others were reacting, but there was no response. "Well, I just thought that research was interesting," he said. "Let's move on."

When we finished and the room cleared out, I told him about an African-American friend we had met in the South, a licensed carpenter who was struggling financially because none of the local banks, which were all owned by whites, would lend him enough money to take on a project that would yield a substantial profit. He and his wife have several children. Two daughters had graduated from high school and were attending college; one had been accepted at a prestigious law school, and the other was studying medicine.

"I'm really surprised to hear that," the discussion leader said. It was information he didn't have. We considered the possibility that we'd been bamboozled about the notion of intelligence. I left with the hope that this new information had revealed to him a crack in the wall. How would he choose to respond?

POSTSCRIPT

After we had been traveling a few years, I read Toni Morrison's book a second time, and it made a lot more sense to me. A few years later, I read *Beloved* again and wondered how I'd missed so much the first two times. Now in my fourth reading, I am puzzled how I failed to catch the foreshadowing references in the very first pages to the assault on Sethe later on in the story. I'm nervous about continuing, because I remember the appalling scenes of cruelty. After ten years of travel, having heard hundreds of stories about racial injustice, I'm responding to the plight of Sethe and the other characters in *Beloved* at a level I couldn't reach with the first reading.

4

WINDOW OF OPPORTUNITY

Gene, April 1994
Illinois

Spring in northern Illinois is intoxicating. On an April morning in 1994, I was driving to the grocery store with the windows open, inhaling the promise of regeneration that permeates the air this time of year. There is a brief moment in spring during which one can actually witness the birth of new leaves on trees; this birthing is a process that varies in duration from days to weeks, depending on temperature and the amount of rain that has fallen. If one's mind is preoccupied with other things, one might drive by and miss this awe-inspiring event of the North. But no matter how long it takes, whether acknowledged or not, a renewal is assured. The trees, skeleton-like but alive, having stood month after month covered with snow through the cold winter, seem confident that everything will unfold as in the past. And sure enough, one day a million tiny green buds burst forth. Rebirth! Today one can see through the branches to houses and fields that lie beyond, but soon those branches will be filled with mature foliage that blocks the view. Throughout the summer, the trees will sway and dance in the breeze until they lose their leaves in autumn and stand naked through another winter. I love spring!

There is something very comforting about the familiar. One can rely on the familiar; it provides stability, a sense of order. It's a base from which one can venture out to explore the unknown and then return safe and sound to the consistency of that which feels true. I have always found comfort in the predictability of the four distinct seasons of the North.

My community also provided me with the security of consistency. I was comfortable with my fellow citizens; most of them were a lot like me—white collar, middle class, and European-American. But local folks were nervous about the accelerating influx of people from the big city. One by one, the localities east of ours were changing as a result of recent demographic shifts. Now, when shopping at the malls and eating at restaurants in some of those suburbs, we saw more African-Americans and Hispanics among the white shoppers and diners. Sometimes I heard people in my town talking about their concerns:

"Why can't they just stay in the city where they belong?"

"They'll just bring all their problems out here."

"We like our town the way it is."

"We don't want any changes."

Many white residents believed negative stereotypes that intensified their concerns about people of color. They anticipated gang violence, drugs, prostitution, and poverty as a result of a shift in demographics. Longstanding separation from people of different ethnic groups made it hard for some to accept the inevitable—that sooner or later, those folks would be our neighbors.

People told me I was idealistic because I believe in the unity of humanity. "There have always been wars, there will always be wars, and racism will always exist," they said, and I couldn't prove them wrong. Although I could relate to their concerns, I felt optimistic that at some point in the future, we would eliminate racism and live in peace. But a mixture of idealism and ignorance can lead to a disconnect from reality. As an ignorant idealist, I could endorse the concept of the inherent nobility of my fellow humans—while remaining comforted that some of them lived far away.

But as I entered the grocery store that April morning, I had only one concern about reality—will there be a fresh supply of bratwursts in the meat cooler when I get there? We were having friends over for our first cookout of the year, an annual ritual that heralds summer.

Shopping on a Saturday morning is like driving in rush hour traffic during the week; if you're not aggressive, you don't get very far. I had been in the store for about twenty minutes and had done well. I counted my items to make sure there were no more than fifteen so I could use the express checkout lane. I had, among other things, a package of bratwurst, hot dog buns, a bottle of soda, and a container of potato salad. Altogether I had eleven items. Then I remembered that my friend likes potato chips, and I headed back to the snack food area. I grabbed a bag of chips and a carton of dip, made a U-turn, and squeezed past two shoppers who were conversing across the aisle, skillfully guiding my cart between theirs. When I reached the end of the aisle, I saw an unusual scene unfolding at the front of the store.

I stopped to get a better look and was rear-ended by another customer. "Sorry," said the woman, but her face revealed annoyance as she deftly maneuvered around me and continued on her shopping mission. I was so distracted that I was only dimly aware of the pain in the back of my legs.

Now I wanted to get a closer look. I pointed my cart toward the express lane, which had several customers with fifteen items or less. At the back of the line stood a man whose very presence marked the end of our comfort with the familiar. "Our community will never be the same," I said to no one in particular.

A shopper zipping by with a cart-full of groceries heard me, stopped long enough to roll his eyes in the direction of the man at the front of the store, and grumbled, "That's for damned sure!" then moved on.

The other customers seemed determined to maintain a cautious distance from the man in the express lane, swerving abruptly when they saw him and steering their shopping carts in a wide curve around him. While they bumped and scraped each other, he stood isolated in his own private space. But I wanted to get closer.

I watched the flow of traffic and waited for an opportunity to slip in. Finally out of desperation I pushed my cart forward, heedless of potential collision. "Excuse me. Sorry! Excuse me!" The line was moving quickly, and the man advanced toward the cashier. *I'm going to miss my opportunity,* I thought. The shopping cart was slowing me down. I stopped where I was, grabbed my food items—balancing the wet package of bratwursts on top of the bag of chips—abandoned the empty cart, and hurried over to where the man was standing; he was still the last person in line.

What the hell am I doing? I thought. *What am I going to do when I get over to him? What am I going to say?* I watched him as I moved closer. He seemed to be lost in his thoughts, looking straight ahead, unaware of the customers who stared at him as they passed by. *What's the big deal? He's African-American. So what? We're all the same— members of one human family. We're all 50th cousins. Originally we all come from Africa. An African woman is our common mother. So his skin is darker. Big deal! Just more melanin. There's a reason for that. To protect the skin in sunny climates. But he's sooo dark!*

Now I stood directly behind the man, clutching my fifteen items or less. He looked to be in his early forties, about 5 feet 10 inches, casually dressed. My gaze was drawn to the back of his neck; the deep brown color of his skin glowed warmly even in the store's cold fluorescent lighting. Little white curls bordered his hairline.

I've touched hair like that, I thought. *I know what it feels like; it's actually soft. But what's he doing here? He's shopping, stupid! But where does he live? Does he live in our community? I've never seen him before. Maybe he and his family recently moved in. I should say something to him—make him feel welcomed, like, "Welcome to our community!" But if he lives here, it's his community too. Man! Now that would be patronizing! Actually, if I say anything, he's going to know that I'm talking to him just because he's black. I'm sunk. But it would be great just to sit down and have coffee together. We could get a cup over there, sit at one of those tables and just get to know each other. I wonder if he's from the city. I'll bet he can take care of himself. He's pretty muscular. And when you grow up in the city, you learn to fight. I grew up in the country. I'm not a fighter. He could probably take me. You idiot! What's wrong with you? He didn't come here to fight. He's just shopping. Look at his groceries. He's got bratwursts! He's probably going to have a cookout with some friends too. Wouldn't it be great if we had some coffee together, and then he invited me over to his cookout? But his whole family would be there, and their friends, and everyone would be grooving to soul music and dancing.*

Images of black people suddenly flooded my mind. I remembered cartoons from my childhood in the '50s: African natives with exaggerated features and bones stuck through their nostrils, scantily clad and dancing around a cauldron of boiling water in which a hapless white man stood terrified.

But I can't dance. I would look so stupid just standing on the sidelines. And that handshake, I can't do that either. How could I possibly relate to everyone at his place? They'd probably laugh at me. I don't think I'd be welcome. Maybe he and his wife would come over to our home. I could handle that. I could play some of my jazz albums; we could bond over music. After we became friends, I could learn how to dance; maybe he'll teach me how to do that handshake too. But I think I'm too short for basketball.

The man placed all his items on the checkout counter. The cashier looked down at the groceries as she scanned them, glancing up every once in a while to sneak a peek at his face. When his items were taken from the belt, there was space for me to set my groceries down. I moved nearer. As he wrote his check his left arm was bent, elbow pointing at me. I was so close to him that if I had moved forward three inches I would have touched his elbow.

This is my last chance to say something. Just say, "How do you like our town?" No, that's no good. If he lives here it's his town too, remember? How about "Nice weather"? "Nice day"? "Good morning"? or . . .

The man finished writing his check, glanced at me nervously, and took two quick sideward steps away from me. He picked up his bagged groceries and walked to the exit. I stood immobilized as I watched him cross the parking lot to his car.

"Sir? Sir? Check or cash, sir?"

How long had I been staring out the window? My groceries had been scanned and bagged, and the cashier was asking how I wanted to pay. "Check or cash"—what did those words mean? Slowly, as if I were waking from a dream, the world of the familiar came back into focus.

"Uh, check."

Driving home, the air seemed cooler; I closed the windows and turned on the heater, dimly aware of the gray-green blur of blooming trees lining the street. My mind was preoccupied with other things. *A man. A black man. African-American man.* What had prevented me from acting on my impulse to somehow reach out to him? Reviewing the details of the entire scene, I wondered if I had been motivated by mere curiosity or had been moved by some deeper need. A window of opportunity had closed and clicked shut, and the frustration of my powerlessness to even say "hello" to the man tormented me. I slumped in the driver's seat, weighed down by ineptitude.

In my driveway, I sat quietly, listening to the engine crackle as it cooled. A robin landed on a branch full of baby leaves, and I thought about the sensation of something stirring within me, struggling to be expressed as I was drawn to the man in the checkout lane. What was that? What had prevented it from blooming and coming to life? What could I have done differently? Something in me was pressing to be born, and in spite of my clumsiness I knew there would be opportunities ahead for me to participate more fully in the birthing process.

COMMENTARY

Unlike my other stories that relate a single event, this story is a combination of experiences that happened at the local grocery store during a period of my dawning awareness about race.

My feeling of failure as I sat in my driveway might seem a bit melodramatic, yet in the supermarket, standing next to the man, I sensed at a subconscious level that something vital to my well-being was at stake. The remedy was only inches away, within my grasp, and I could not move to reach out and avail myself of its healing. I didn't understand at the time that racism is a spiritual illness and that my inability to act was a symptom.

What I understand now is that we are spiritual in essence and hunger for spiritual sustenance. Like cells in the human body, we are held together by a cohesive force that enables the flow of spiritual nutrients from person to person. When we connect, we form a relationship not only to another individual but also to the body of mankind. If we have been isolated from one another and conditioned to believe we are unrelated, we may regard association with others who appear different as a liability to our well-being. But prolonged separation makes us weak and susceptible to the disease of disunity.

The Bahá'í writings eloquently confirm the necessity to respond to the law of attraction:

> Consider: Unity is necessary to existence. Love is the very cause of life; on the other hand, separation brings death. In the world of material creation, for instance, all things owe their actual life to unity. The elements which compose wood, mineral, or stone, are held together by the law of attraction. If this law should cease for one moment to operate these elements would not hold together, they would fall apart, and the object would in that particular form cease to exist. The law of attraction has brought together certain elements in the form of this beautiful flower, but when that attraction is withdrawn from this centre the flower will decompose, and, as a flower, cease to exist.
>
> So it is with the great body of humanity. The wonderful Law of Attraction, Harmony and Unity, holds together this marvelous Creation.[1]

The outcome of responding to the law of attraction and making connections is unity. When people of diverse backgrounds are attracted and held together by the force of cohesion, the result may be called unity in diversity. Over time, both individuals and communities develop and become transformed into mature versions of themselves with new features and refined conduct.

An oak tree is an example of transformation. It begins as an acorn. After a period of germination, it sends out a shoot that grows upward, reaching for the sun. Eventually, it takes on a new identity, a sapling with roots, branches and leaves—related to both the earth and the sky. On its journey to becoming a mature oak tree, it connects with other elements of the material world. Its survival depends on those connections. The tree does not decide what connections it will make; it does not fret about windows of opportunity. Nature makes the choices.

Humans have the capacity to make conscious choices about the connections we form. Like the oak, each of us is a unique work in progress. Just as the acorn sacrifices its identity to become a sapling and eventually a full-grown tree, we leave behind the characteristics of childhood and adolescence as we mature. As adults we can make decisions that factor in the importance of healthy relationships with other people.

When I was unable to make the choice to speak to the man in the grocery store, I knew I had missed an opportunity to find some new potential in myself. I have since learned that growth is a process of leaving the familiar behind and attuning myself to the unknown until it becomes the new familiar. The challenge is to be attracted to the unknown, secure in the knowledge that there I will discover my real self.

5

SEPARATED AT BIRTH

Phyllis, November 1994
Illinois

It was the day after Thanksgiving, 1994, and for the first time in fifteen years I was not sitting at a dining room table with my family, eating my mother's famous Day After Turkey Bone soup. Instead I sat with Gene, our three grown children, and our one-year-old granddaughter in a hotel conference center in Chicago, surrounded by hundreds of Bahá'ís of African descent. The six of us represented about half the number of whites attending the Vanguard of the Dawning, a conference organized for the specific purpose of addressing the station and role of African-American Bahá'ís and inspired by a quotation from the Bahá'í writings: "Bahá'u'lláh once compared the colored people to the black pupil of the eye surrounded by the white. In this black pupil is seen the reflection of that which is before it, and through it the light of the Spirit shineth forth."[1]

The conference was open to everyone, and people of color from all ethnic backgrounds had been encouraged to attend. Gene and I had come to support and to learn, but when we first arrived, I wondered briefly if we'd made a mistake, if our presence would disrupt the safety and privacy of the consultations. I assumed people might not feel free to be honest around us, just as whites won't usually reveal deeply personal feelings about race if someone in the room is black. However, no one seemed inhibited, possibly because the spiritual intention of the conference created the safe atmosphere necessary for openness.

Just before lunch on the first full day, our chairperson thanked the gospel choir and the morning's speakers, then announced the afternoon breakout sessions. There was one for Asians, one for Native Americans, a session for Hispanics, and several different workshops for African-Americans. I waited, but the entire list had been read. There was nothing for "others." Though I hadn't really expected a session specifically for European-Americans, I wasn't sure where to go. I finally chose to attend a panel discussion led by several women who had recently been to Africa; it had the word "Sisters" in its description, and I figured at least I could relate by gender. It was a popular workshop attended mainly by black women, although a few men squeezed into the crowded room. I sat in the back, perfectly content—I thought—to remain an inconspicuous observer. But when the panelists' presentations were done and the group was engaged in passionate dialogue, I began to notice a twitchiness in my body, as though it wanted to stretch itself taller. My neck lengthened in a turtle-like movement, and the slightest feeling of impatience hovered in the air around my inconspicuous chair. Had I given these feelings a voice, they would have shouted, "HEY! Call on me! Back here in the corner. You can't miss me; I'm the only white person in here! Aren't you interested in what I have to say?" I told myself to be patient, that surely before the session's end, someone from the panel would notice me sitting back there all by myself. I imagined her standing, clearly concerned at the oversight.

"Hold on just a minute, everybody," she would say. "Let's hear what our white sister has to offer!"

But it never happened. The workshop ended, and the women filed out of the room in little animated groups, ignoring me completely. I was kind of stunned, to be totally honest. I had never in my whole life felt so . . . invisible.

As soon as that particular word formed in my mind, the realization was there too. For one stinging moment, I had experienced what I'd been hearing people of color talk about ever since I'd learned how to listen to them. Actually *realization* is the wrong word. This was physical—a sort of queasy feeling that came over me in waves as I looked squarely at my sense of entitlement, my confidence in the inherent value of my opinion, my natural assumption that people would want to hear what I had to say. It was a very tangible thing, this awareness, and was accompanied by a sense of shame that settled in my stomach.

Later, when I thought back on what happened that day, it seemed obvious that the lesson in humility had to come first. For there was something even bigger I would learn at that conference. It had already germinated and taken root, but the ground was covered with the debris of my ego, which had to be cleared away to give that knowledge a chance to push through into the air.

At dinner I processed my feelings with Gene, and by the time we reconvened for the evening program, I was ready to let go of the shame that I knew would become self-indulgent if I hung onto it. Local folks had come for the concert, increasing the number of people in the conference center to several hundred. The spirit that filled the room as the gospel choir sang transformed us all into a single, jubilant body—jumping out of our chairs, singing and swaying, giving praise and receiving blessings.

At one point between songs, we were asked to leave our seats and stand next to a person we didn't know. I walked forward a few rows, looking left and right for someone who might take me into her heart, and was drawn to a woman with silver hair and gentle eyes sitting near the front. She reached for me as I approached her, taking my hand in one of hers, putting her other arm around me and drawing me close. We stood for a while with the rest of the crowd, swaying to the music, then sat down for the last song and closing comments. The woman never let go of me, and if my memory is correct, I laid my head on her shoulder and closed my eyes. A series of images that had been moving in and out of my consciousness began to solidify, then coalesced into a vivid memory.

It was a scene from a movie I'd watched as a teenager. A woman in her mid-twenties lay across her bed, crying inconsolably. Somehow she had discovered that she'd been adopted as an infant and her parents had never told her. They'd also hidden the fact that she had several biological brothers and sisters, each of whom had been adopted by a different family. The young woman had been separated at birth from her siblings. She said repeatedly, "I have brothers and sisters out there somewhere, and until I find them, I'll never know who I am," or at least that's how I remembered it. She spent the rest of the movie searching for them.

This is what I took from the Vanguard of the Dawning Conference that lives within me at all times: it is the longing to find my sisters and my brothers. It is the knowledge that we were all separated at birth—in fact, born into separation—and that until we reconnect, none of us will ever know who we really are. It is the understanding that our best selves can develop only in relationship with the family we've been missing. I know this is true, because I saw it all in the faces of the people I met that weekend, reflected clearly in the pupil of the eye.

COMMENTARY

People are always asking us why, with all the teachings of the Bahá'í Faith, we decided to focus our presentations on racial unity. We could just as easily have chosen to talk about the equality of women and men, for example; or as parents, we might have concentrated on the education of children. So why this particular principle?

My only answer is that it chose us, not the other way around. Within a few weeks of beginning our travels in 1997, we knew there was no other conversation that was more important. The people we met and the experiences we had simply kept steering us in that direction. And the more we addressed it, the deeper became our sense of personal loss at the separation between us and our brothers and sisters of color. I'd like to say that we had no choice, but that's not really true. We always have a choice. But the longing to heal that separation took precedence over everything else.

I said in my story that my understanding of our relatedness as a human family had already germinated and taken root by the time I attended the Vanguard of the Dawning Conference in '94. It seems appropriate at this point to talk about how that happened and at the same time give you a little personal background. Because in learning something about me, you'll have the answer to the second most frequently asked question: Why are your stories focused only on your connections with African-Americans when there are so many other groups affected by racial prejudice? This is my own very personal response.

I've read that our first exposure to a new experience continues throughout our lives to influence how we feel in similar situations. My first real exposure to African-Americans didn't happen until I was eighteen, and it involved falling in love. I grew up in a suburb of Chicago that was statistically over 99% white. I know there were some black families living there; two of them had sons in my class at high school. But I never had a single face-to-face conversation with either of those students. All I remember about them is that one was on the basketball team and the other played drums at our talent show. I was surprised that he could play so well, which gives you an idea of the stereotypes I'd already absorbed. During the summer of 1967, just after my graduation from high school, I was so unconcerned about race that I have no memory of the riots in Detroit and Newark, even though I must have seen coverage on the evening news.

By the spring of 1968, I was at college and had fallen head-over-heels for a black student who worked with me in the cafeteria, where we washed dishes and sorted silverware to help pay our tuition. Like me he was a singer, but unlike me he was utterly uninhibited about sharing his songs with our fellow dish room workers; his rich voice drifted through the steam that billowed from the dishwasher. The sound of it drew me irresistibly, though the attraction alone wasn't strong enough to overcome my fear of speaking to him. It was insatiable curiosity that finally pulled me out of my paralysis at the silverware-sorting station and up to the base of the platform where he stood to put racks of dirty dishes onto the conveyor belt. Since the beginning of the school year I'd been watching him walk around the quad, fascinated by his unique ability to attract interracial groups of students. It seemed to me that wherever he went, he created a little pocket of diversity on a campus that was for the most part self-segregated. I didn't see anyone else doing that. He still laughs at me when I tell this story, amused as always by my flair for the dramatic, but I clearly remember looking up at him through the steam and saying, "OK, so what is it that makes you different?"

And I clearly remember him smiling and saying—through the steam, of course—"I've been watching you watch me, and I've been waiting for you to ask."

Omygosh I was so embarrassed. He knew. I was exposed. He ignored my reddening cheeks, focusing instead on my question.

"If I'm different, it's because I'm a Bahá'í."

When he said that word, my attraction expanded to include whatever it was that had made him so unusual. That spring I joined the Bahá'í Faith and began my own spiritual journey toward becoming my true self, guided by Bahá'u'lláh's proclamation of the oneness of humanity. And so it seems likely that this first experience of love—both human and divine—was the source of my longing.

My education about the Civil Rights Movement happened the following year when an African-American freshman from Chicago became my roommate. She and her friends would gather in our dorm room and talk about black power, and I had the privilege of hearing many things for the first time from their point of view; occasionally the words "whitey" or "honky" were spoken, but never to me. Once, when the conversation was becoming quite heated, I asked if they would all be more comfortable if I left the room (not that they seemed to be holding back for my sake). One of the girls said, "No, of course not. You stay right where you are. We don't think of you as white anyway."

I wasn't sure exactly what she meant by that, but it made me feel good—included and safe. So now an understanding of justice and a sense of inclusion merged with the experience of love, and my longing became more clearly defined.

I quit college after two years to study in France and met Gene shortly after I returned in 1971; by the fall of that year, we were married. For the next two decades, I focused most of my energy on parenting, taking advantage of the option I had as a white person to choose not to think much about race for a while.

Then about a year before the Vanguard Conference, I attended for the first time a workshop that directly addressed the dynamics of racism. There I saw a documentary that explained how stereotypical images of African-Americans had been intentionally created by the media. To illustrate their explanation, the filmmakers used excerpts of cartoons from the 1950s—the same ones I had watched after school and Saturday mornings throughout my childhood. I knew exactly what would happen next in each animated scene; my memory of the images was so vivid that I heard myself saying out loud what was coming, describing to the others in the room what each character was going to do seconds before we saw it played out on the screen. It was as if I'd just found out I had a mind-control chip implanted in my brain—only this was my real life, not some science fiction horror movie. In an instant everything changed from theoretical to personal. I realized that those images had been dished up with my milk and cookies and fed directly into my hypnotized brain as I sat on the floor in front of our TV. My mind had been poisoned without my consent, and the pictures were still in there, manipulating me subconsciously, robbing me of the freedom to choose my own thoughts. I was shaking with rage by the end of the workshop. A year later, when I went to the Vanguard of the Dawning, I was still trying to figure out what to do with that information and anger. Since then I have learned how to use the information. The anger is still with me.

Not long after the Vanguard Conference, Gene and I attended a meeting to plan a fundraiser for a group of black women who were going to Africa. Before our opening prayers, we called on the souls of people who had passed from this world, asking them to support our work of creating racial unity with their guidance and energy. I was moved during the meeting to share my experience at the conference and the longing I felt to find my family. One of the women—who has since joined that heavenly concourse and is hopefully watching over me—was standing behind the couch where I sat. There was silence after my sharing, and I was thinking about the implications of what I'd just revealed, when she placed her hands abruptly on my shoulders and said loudly, "You've been called!"

She startled me badly, and I jumped a little on the couch. I didn't know much about callings, and I had no intention of questioning her authority, but I must have looked confused because she repeated, "Yes. Yes! You've been called."

Did she come to that conclusion based on the story I told about myself, or was she seeing something else? And what would be my response to that call? And if the Caller were God, which seemed very likely, then it would be wise for me to pay attention.

Within three years of that night we were on the road, and you can read about what happened there in the stories that follow.

So now that you know some of the personal reasons I work for racial healing and unity, there's something else I want to say. We've all been called. The longing to be connected as a human family is built-in, a part of our design. I believe that it was placed within each of us by our Creator and that we all go about fulfilling that design in our own unique way. But even though it's inherent, sometimes we can't see it, and then something happens to bring it to our attention. We need only stay alert.

PART 2

1997–2002

The stories in Part 2 recount events that happened during our most intensive period of travel. As we mentioned in the Preface, our goal initially was to meet fellow Bahá'ís from different parts of the country and to offer ourselves as speakers for their gatherings. Working with a committee of Bahá'ís in New England, we began creating an itinerary and contacting communities. By mid-September of 1997, we'd bought and road-tested a small travel-trailer, put most of our belongings in storage, and put our house on the market. Then, after loading our new home-on-wheels with all the vital necessities and hitching it up to our van, we set out from Crystal Lake, Illinois on September 25, headed for our first stop in Buffalo, New York.

It was that fall, during meetings with folks in the Northeast, that our goal became more clearly defined. As a result of what we learned from new African-American friends—how their daily lives were impacted both by institutional racism and by the often subtle attitudes of white people—we began emphasizing the topic of racial unity, focusing in particular on the dynamics between blacks and whites. Several of these black friends urged us to share our insights

73

with other white people we met in our travels. "They'll believe you," our friends insisted, "because you're white, too; you are credible witnesses." It was those relationships that set us firmly on our course.

In the beginning of our travels, we would sometimes park our little RV in people's driveways, hitching our hose to their garden faucet, plugging an electrical cable into an outlet in their garage, and running a 100-foot phone cord through one of their windows to a phone jack so that we could download e-mail. After blowing a few fuses (and discovering that people have different ideas of what constitutes a "level driveway"), we decided to stay in campgrounds or RV parks. This provided the proper hookups for our trailer as well as the privacy that we quickly discovered was necessary if we hoped to stay focused.

By November it became clear that because of freezing temperatures and treacherous road conditions we would have to head south. We arranged to leave our trailer parked in North Carolina while we went back to be with family for the holidays. It was during that trip that we came up with the plan to offer our services in South Carolina. In the first two stories of this section, *Leap of Faith* and *Looking for Simon*, you'll read about some of the experiences we had there and about how we both reached a kind of internal tipping point that changed us permanently.

After spending February and March of 1998 in South Carolina and six weeks in Tennessee, we headed north again and in August crossed the Mississippi River, beginning a leg of our journey that would take us eventually to the West Coast.

The committees that helped us plan our visits had by this point matured into well-organized Regional Bahá'í Councils with travel-teacher coordinators, and these individuals worked closely with us by phone and e-mail to design our itinerary and contact the communities we'd be visiting. Then community members in each location would organize gatherings—usually in their homes or local Bahá'í centers, sometimes at universities, churches, or in their neighborhoods—where we would give talks or facilitate workshops.

With the assistance of many dedicated people, we went to twenty-eight communities in one five-week period, and we often wonder, looking back on that time, how we accomplished it. We traveled west through Minnesota and North Dakota, east through South Dakota, then west again through Nebraska. Sometimes we would go a hundred miles, unhitch our trailer at a campground, drive to the evening's event, go home to bed, then the next day, hitch up the trailer and drive another hundred miles to our next location. In the Dakotas we visited Lakota Bahá'ís on the Turtle Mountain, Pine Ridge, and Rosebud Reservations. In Nebraska we stopped for dinner at the home of the travel-teacher coordinator who had arranged our itinerary; she showed us a large map of her three-state area, covered with little pins that indicated our destinations. It looked like a map showing the route of disoriented explorers who couldn't make up their minds which way to go.

The rest of that year was spent traveling in the Northwest, then in December we drove down the coast to San Diego, which would become our winter home.

In 1999 we visited communities in Texas, Louisiana, Mississippi, and Tennessee, then returned to the city in South Carolina where so much of our early transformation had occurred. We spent nearly a month there, renewing old friendships and forming new ones, and conducting a series of trainings for local folks who wanted to continue holding race unity workshops. In April we made our first of many trips to Atlanta, after which we traveled throughout the southern states. During the summer we toured the Midwest, visited Navajo Bahá'ís at the Native American Bahá'í Institute in Hauck, Arizona, and then went back to San Diego.

We began the year 2000 with a trip to Mississippi, where we traded in our twenty-two-foot long trailer for a slightly larger model with a slide-out. In March we returned to Atlanta and facilitated one of our most exciting workshops for staff at the Carter Presidential Center. Then we spent the rest of the year circling through the Deep South before heading back to Southern California for the winter.

Until this point in our journey, we had been almost constantly engaged in interactions with communities along our route. Our schedule of workshops, public talks, and personal visits had continued with only a few periods of rest, and we realized we needed to stay in one place for a while. So we spent the first half of 2001 in California and the second half in Illinois, with a brief trip to New England in the fall. During this time we were also attempting to market our race unity workshop professionally, both in San Diego and the Chicago area. In December of that year, we drove our trailer south to Tennessee, where the last story in this section takes place.

Out of the thousands of encounters we had during the period between September 1997 and January 2002, only thirteen became stories that appear in this section of the book. Phyllis's last narrative, "Hands," is a collection of five more short anecdotes relating events that happened in five different states and over a span of eight years.

Now that we've described our itinerary, you can see why one story takes place on the East Coast and the next one happens clear across the country. The locations are not important in relationship to one another but serve rather as indications of the kinds of experiences we had in different areas. And because we wanted to alternate between Gene's and Phyllis's stories, they are slightly out of order chronologically.

So our narratives jump around in time and space, creating a collage of images that in turn form a single truth: no matter where we went in this vast country, we found individuals who wanted to heal the separation caused by racial stereotypes and fear. People of every ethnicity were willing to step out of their comfortable assumptions, to reach out a hand to someone who might normally make them suspicious, and to make great sacrifices in their quest for unity.

We hope you enjoy reading about these courageous people in the stories that follow.

6

A LEAP OF FAITH

Phyllis, February 1998
South Carolina

This is the story of an everyday miracle. If you already believe in signs and omens, my tale will confirm their importance; if not, perhaps you'll be convinced. It's the account of a few minutes of my life that I now realize formed a bridge between what I was and what I became. But above all, it is a love story, set against a backdrop of centuries of oppression, hatred, and injustice.

The story takes place in a small city in the Deep South, but before I relate it, I'll give you some background. We had begun traveling with our little trailer only a few months earlier. After visiting Bahá'í communities in several New England states, we had worked our way southward along the coast; then we'd taken a break from our scheduled engagements to spend Thanksgiving with my sister and her family in the mountains of North Carolina. Afterward we planned to head back north for a month-long visit with family in Illinois and Wisconsin.

By this time, we had already encountered sleet and freezing temperatures as we'd driven south through the Appalachians, and we realized that the 22-foot-long RV we now called home had not been designed for winter use. So we wisely decided to leave it parked at the bottom of a long, steep, curving driveway in my sister's backyard and take just the van on our trip north.

One evening, a couple of weeks after Christmas, I sat in my parents' cozy house in the far north woods of Wisconsin, looking at my atlas for inspiration about where we should go when we left North Carolina. Remembering the chilly mountain nights and inspired by the thirty inches of fresh snowfall blanketing the trees outside the window, I did what any reasonable person in my situation would do—I looked at the route to Florida.

As you read this, you may be wondering how we determined our itinerary. Although later our schedule of visits became much more organized, at this early point in our travels, everything was still pretty loose. Basically we decided where we wanted to go and then called someone in that area to help make arrangements with the communities along our route.

Fortunately for all of us, I am a lover of maps; I was made that way by a mother who studies maps for fun, even if she has nowhere to go. Maybe my passion started with plotting hikes for my Girl Scout troop and was reinforced by my short career as a logistics specialist. However it began, it has served me well in our journeys, and I was happy as I traced my finger along the highways that would take us out of the Blue Ridge Mountains to the land of perpetual warmth.

The next morning, I telephoned a member of the Regional Bahá'í Council of the Southern States[1] and explained our idea of visiting communities in her area; she assured me that there was indeed much service we could render in Florida and that we would be most welcome there.

"You know, I was just looking at the map before I called you," I told her, "and I see that with only a small detour, we could go right by the Louis Gregory Bahá'í Institute in Hemingway, South Carolina. We've heard so much about the school, but we've never been there; it would be great if we could stop for a short visit on our way south."

She liked my idea, gave me the phone number of a woman who lived near the Institute, and said she looked forward to hearing from me again when we were on our way to Florida. And that's how it happened that in the second week in January of 1998, I phoned someone I'd never met and initiated a series of events that would permanently change our lives.

"Hi, is this Gina?" I asked the woman who answered. "You don't know me; my name is Phyllis, and my husband Gene and I are travel-teaching in our trailer." I remember thinking that the phrase "travel-teaching in our trailer" sounded vaguely like some kind of circus act. "We'll be on our way from North Carolina to Florida in a couple weeks and thought we might stop for a few days in your area. We'd like to be of service to your community; we have experience facilitating discussions on race unity, and my husband is a graphic artist."

I'd hoped this brief summary of our circumstances would be enough to get the conversation started, but Gina was silent for so long that I wondered if I'd caught her at a bad time or maybe even called the wrong number. Then quite abruptly she began a passionate prayer, loudly enough that I nearly dropped the phone.

"Oh God! Dear God! Thank you, thank you. I can't believe it! Yes! Yes! I *can* believe it! Oh thank You, God, thank You!" and on she went in this fashion for some time.

Later, as we got to know Gina better, we learned that she saw miracles everywhere; to her eyes the Hand of God was at work even in happenings that others might find insignificant. But at this point she was still a stranger, and all I could think was, *What's up with this woman?*

I waited patiently as she expressed gratitude, astonishment, disbelief that turned to belief and then back again; finally she calmed down long enough to relate an amazing series of events.

She told me how some of the Bahá'ís in the area had been talking with the mayor of a neighboring community that was experiencing racial tension. The city was located in that part of the South where huge plantations had once supplied the nation with tobacco and cotton, picked by the hands of slaves. In 1998, the city was still populated by descendants of those slaves, most of whom lived—literally—across the tracks from descendants of the slave-owners. As was common in this part of the country, positions of power—whether political, social, or economic—had been held by whites since the end of Reconstruction, even though the majority of citizens were black.

Over the course of our visit, we would hear different accounts of the changes that had taken place. People told us that a few years before, local political activists had registered many citizens to vote and in some cases accompanied them to the polls, resulting in the election of a black mayor and city council. In fact, people of African descent now held most of the positions of political power in this city, which found itself turned upside down. White families still controlled nearly all the economic assets, and some of the white residents, apparently still a little shell-shocked at this unexpected turn of events, were wondering how in the world they would ever have fair representation and how they could restore things to their previous—and "proper"—order. We heard stories of white flight to areas outside the city limits and concerns about a white county government that was trying to gain control of city resources. So while the African-American residents seemed to feel a cautious hopefulness, there was at the same time an acknowledgement that many difficult issues still needed to be addressed.

In the midst of this unsettled atmosphere, the mayor had met with a few Bahá'ís from neighboring counties to plan a nine-week series of workshops on creating racial unity. In the spirit of the moment, and in an impulsive act of complete faith, the Bahá'ís had offered to provide facilitators for those workshops. One of the local community members would lead the first session, but they'd not yet found anyone for the remaining eight weeks. Although they had initiated an intense e-mail and telephone campaign to find a person to conduct the remaining sessions, their efforts had yielded no fruits. The night before my call, the planning committee had gathered for prayers and apparently spent hours beseeching God to send them some travel-teachers who could facilitate race unity workshops. And in addition they had asked Him, if it wouldn't be too much trouble, to also send someone who could do the graphics for their advertising.

A journalist who was writing a newspaper article about our travels once asked me if I had a motto. At first, all that came to mind was an image of our son's Boy Scout troop jumping out of their seats shouting "Be Prepared!" This seemed appropriate but was probably protected by trademark laws. So I had pondered for a moment, and my own motto came to me in a flash of inspiration: "Plan as though everything depends on you, and then proceed knowing that nothing does." After listening to Gina's account of recent events, I knew the idea to stop in South Carolina had come from somewhere besides my map.

What happened between that phone conversation and the moment my real story begins will not be recounted here. The details of our drive from Wisconsin to North Carolina in the bitter cold of January, of the unexpected snowstorm that trapped our trailer for days in my sister's driveway and caused us to miss our briefing by the planning committee, of the town meeting that kicked off the workshop series and brought together black and white community leaders, the tales of the people we met and the things we experienced—and of how we didn't make it to Florida for several more years—all these are for telling another time.

As I said before, this is a love story. It takes place in front of a Catholic church in a small city in South Carolina. It was mid-February, a couple of weeks after my forty-ninth birthday. For nearly half a century, I had lived in the bubble created by white suburbia. Now here I was: a northerner in the Deep South, a suburbanite in the country, a pale-skinned cork, floating and bobbing along optimistically in an ocean of people of darker complexion—people who buoyed me up at the same time that they watched me and waited to see what I would do.

Gene and I had agreed to spend at least a week—maybe two—assisting the Bahá'ís with their service. Gene had gone through extensive training to conduct race unity dialogues and had facilitated two 12-week workshop series in Illinois, so he was the one with experience. I was his co-facilitator by virtue of being his wife. He also put his graphics skills to work designing invitational flyers to be posted around town, and we spent many days carrying those flyers from store to store. In addition, I wrote articles for the newspaper and called potential locations for the workshops. Fortunately we had a committee of people helping us with organization.

On the evening the events of my story transpire, we had just parked along the street in front of the Catholic church, which was at the time the only racially integrated church in the city. Gene had already gone inside and was setting up the room for our meeting. We were expecting a good turnout, as the previous week's session—the first one in the series—had been well-attended. It would be my first time co-facilitating a workshop. I am not at all a shy person; normally I feel at ease in new situations and comfortable speaking in public. But on this day, I was jittery and unfocused—a poor condition for someone who's supposed to stand in front of an interracial group and guide a discussion about racial healing.

As I got out of the car and started toward the church, I was assaulted by doubts about my abilities and motives and plagued by feelings of unworthiness and ineptitude. Who did I think I was, walking into a situation like this? What could I possibly have to offer about the workings and the effects of racism, coming as I did from a life of privilege and ignorance? The sidewalk leading to the entrance seemed to lengthen under my feet, and the church door looked farther away with every step I took. I suddenly knew how astronauts preparing for their trip to the moon must have felt as they moved slowly in their cumbersome spacesuits, step by step along the gantry toward the rocket that would propel them into an unknown universe.

The door of the church opened, interrupting my disquiet, and an African-American woman stepped out with her two children. She was carrying a little boy in her arms and holding the hand of her daughter, who looked to be about five years old. As the woman smiled and started walking, the little girl's face lit up in an expression of surprised delight, and she suddenly broke free of her mother's hand and came running toward me at full speed down the sidewalk. I was truly confused as I watched her run, and then astonished as she launched herself into the air. She jumped high, flung herself off the ground and was airborne, sailing toward me in what thankfully seemed like slow motion, which gave my brain time to shout out instructions to my body: *"Catch her! Put your arms out like this! Catch her or she'll fall down on the sidewalk!"* And like a stunned toddler watching, wide-eyed, the approach of a tossed ball, I stretched out my arms and caught her in mid-flight.

Having landed safely in my grasp, this child of light, daughter of Africa, wrapped her little arms tightly around my neck, kissed me repeatedly on both cheeks, and proclaimed for all the world to hear that she loved me. I had no context for this declaration; my mind darted about in search of some explanation for her delightful but highly unexpected behavior, and I finally settled on the only one that made any sense to me: *Maybe she thinks I'm someone else; probably there's another white woman who attends her church and looks like me.*

Such were my thoughts when the woman arrived at the spot where I stood clasping the affectionate girl to my heart. I assumed the mother would be embarrassed that her daughter had mistaken my identity, but I wasn't sure exactly what to say to put her at ease. Holding tightly to this child who continued to hug me enthusiastically, I asked, "Does she think I'm someone else?"

The woman didn't answer right away. She seemed to be sizing me up, as though I had said something really dumb and she was deciding just how much nonsense she was willing to put up with. The expression on her face distinctly said, "What's wrong with you, woman? You think my daughter is some kind of fool?" But as she watched me her features softened, and when she actually spoke, her words were extraordinarily gentle.

"No, she doesn't think you're someone else. She just loves you."

As though this behavior were commonplace. As though there were nothing at all unusual about her young daughter launching herself into the arms of a stranger. As though this were not a miracle.

But for me, everything changed in those few minutes. No wand-wielding wizard could have effected a more thorough and immediate transformation. It was as though the Hand of God Himself, moving through a child, had taken hold of me, galvanized me, electrified me. I was filled up with the courage and heavenly power that is born of love, and all my nervousness was channeled into focused energy and confidence. If this child could leap into the arms of the unknown with total trust and express her love with complete freedom and spontaneity, then so could I.

"I'm Miriam," said the woman. "This is my son Terrence, and you've already met my daughter Shandra. Are you one of our workshop facilitators?"

I nodded and managed to squeeze my name out through Shandra's hugs as we walked together to the entrance of the church. Miriam held the door open, and I stepped over the threshold into the next phase of my journey.

COMMENTARY

I've never been so thoroughly unprepared for any occasion as I was for my stay in the city where this story takes place. At the same time, I was perfectly prepared. Events in my life had conspired to bring me to that exact spot at precisely that time; I knew this the moment I made the call to Gina, and it would have been unthinkable to hesitate. Yet I had not a clue what I was doing, and I was sure everyone could see that.

First of all, I had never been in the Deep South. I hadn't seen swamps or the extreme rural poverty that is common in that part of the country. I had traveled to Israel, lived in France and Germany, but there was no other place I'd been in my life that felt so *unlike* what I knew. Twice before I had been completely surrounded by black folks—at a conference for Bahá'ís of African descent and at Black Expo (a trade-fair showcasing African-American owned businesses) in Chicago. But this experience was different in so many ways. To be the only white person in a restaurant, a store, a church—this is something many of my fellow Caucasians never experience.

Once, when we drove over the state line into South Carolina, Gene had asked me, "Did you feel that?" just as I was shivering slightly and wondering if we'd passed through some kind of electrical field generated by a hidden power plant. A friend later told us that what we felt was the spirits of all the runaway slaves who perished in the swamps. The history of slavery is the identifying characteristic of the Deep South, the element that distinguishes it from neighboring states. To me, a person who had spent half a century in the North, it felt disorienting, inscrutable, and intimidating. The disorientation lasted several weeks; the intimidation vanished as soon as we started meeting people.

Another reason I felt insecure was because, while I'd attended many race unity workshops, I had never before served as a facilitator. And every workshop I'd been to had attracted primarily white participants. It was common, where I came from, for only a few African-Americans to show up, and frequently there were none at all. But at our first workshop in South Carolina, the only whites who came were Bahá'ís from surrounding communities, some quite far away. Gina, the woman I'd called from my parents' house, drove with her husband sixty miles to be there. I laughed every time I heard people asking each other, "Don't you know any white folks?"

"No, I don't know any."

"Well we ought to have some white folks here, don't you think?"

"Yeah, sure we should. They're the ones that need to hear this stuff. But I certainly don't know any who'd come."

"Me neither."

"Let's ask Pete—I think he knows some white folks."

I laughed not so much because it was funny—it really was more sad than funny—but because it was so uncannily *different* from what I knew as reality.

We ended up staying much longer than two weeks in this lovely city in the Deep South, as you may have already guessed. We conducted the remaining eight workshop sessions, and eventually white folks started showing up on their own. The first was a young man with fire-orange hair who always looked sunburned; he had been unofficially adopted as a young teen by a black family. Then a white high school student came after seeing a flyer and brought a couple of friends the following week. The white editor of the local paper, though he never attended a workshop, became one of our strongest supporters. The night we held a session at the fire house, a group of both black and white firemen hung around afterward for a couple hours, talking about the effects of racism on the city.

We had our final gathering at the Elks Club south of the tracks, on the black side of town. When we mentioned the location to a white acquaintance, she was quite distressed.

"Why on earth would you want to have it down there?" she asked us, frowning her disapproval. "No one will come."

What she'd meant, of course, was that no white people would come, but she was wrong. That week we had the highest attendance of all the workshops—maybe thirty or more folks showed up—and the colors were evenly balanced. When the workshop series was completed, we helped to plan and carry out a unity festival in a park that had in the past been off-limits to African-Americans, and attended the first meeting of a steering committee organized by some of the participants to keep the workshops going.

I wish it were possible to fully describe here the effects these sessions had, both on the participants and on us. Unfortunately, I can't relate all the stories about the things that happened and the people we met, not just that year, but also the many other times we visited. What I will tell you, though, are some of the things I learned. I don't know how to combine them into one cohesive narrative, so if you don't mind, I will simply list them, in no particular order.

People told us they had never before sat down black with white, knee-to-knee, eye-to-eye, to discuss issues of race. I learned that even in places with a history of severe racial oppression, there is a movement toward reconciling and creating unity.

The coming together of humankind is God's plan. If you have the desire to work for it, He will put you where you need to be.

Respond to attraction; take risks. Mistakes are OK.

The power needed for action can be found in small moments, touching moments, courageous moments. Human connection generates massive amounts of power.

Love is stronger than fear.

If you intentionally put yourself in situations that are a little bit intimidating, you will receive help from unexpected sources.

If you want to make a difference and wonder what you can draw on for direction and motivation, I suggest drawing on love. If you look for it and expect it, it will find you.

The very act of making a decision and taking a step will attract confirmations.

Check yourself, and then step out. If your motives are pure, you will witness transformation; if your motives are not pure but you step out anyway, they will be purified by the process and you will experience transformation in yourself.

You don't have to wait until you have courage before you act; often the courage comes as a result of taking action.

I don't mean to be overly dramatic—although I do realize that's my tendency—but the truth is that my life changed when a little girl jumped into my arms. She didn't know me, but for some reason she had faith that I would catch her. With her leap, she taught me that I could leap too. And from the moment I walked through the door of the church, nothing was ever the same again.

A few years later when we were visiting Miriam and her family, I asked ten-year-old Shandra if she remembered how we met. At first she didn't, so I told the story, holding out my arms to recreate the scene in vivid detail. Terrence, who'd been just a toddler at the time, was delighted with this story, especially the part about his sister flying through the air and my fear of dropping her. Each time I finished, he would jump up out of his chair and beg, "Tell it again, Miss Phyllis, tell it again!" And I would oblige.

After several repetitions, when Terrence was finally satisfied and ran off to play, I looked over at Shandra. She was introspective, apparently pondering the mysterious nature of her behavior on that day. Then her face brightened, and she looked back at me with an enigmatic smile, shaking her head in bemusement.

"I must've known somethin'!" she proclaimed.

Clearly, she did.

7

LOOKING FOR SIMON

Gene
Prologue

"Did you feel that?" I asked Phyllis. I scanned the road and surrounding area for evidence that would explain the sudden wave of energy that passed through my body.

"Yeah," she said.

"What was that?"

"I don't know."

We had just left North Carolina, and as we crossed into South Carolina, I shuddered as if we had just driven through a force field. The feeling was deep, molecular. I glanced at Phyllis. "You really felt that? It wasn't just my imagination?"

She nodded.

Silently we rolled along a narrow strip of asphalt that cut through an immense swamp. The surface beneath us provided tenuous security, for a moment's neglect to the task of steering could easily cause the van to veer to the right, slip off the thin dirt shoulder and slide down an embankment into a quagmire that seemed hungry, waiting for a mishap. What forms of life had nature brought into being that found in that primordial bog a nurturing environment? The swamp seemed indeed to be a living communal entity that survived by breaking down higher, more sophisticated forms of life into simpler primitive elements—all the easier to assimilate. The sun, filtered through moss-laden branches, produced a yellowish light that brightened slimy patches of green punctured by decayed tree trunks poking through—vestiges of defeated life forms.

Moss hanging from trees, tobacco fields, rickety shacks. Whatever I knew about the South I had gleaned from movies and conversations with folks up North. Although I didn't remember anything specific from history classes, my brain was nevertheless sorting through pictures, words and phrases. Swamps. Snakes. Nooses. Disappearing. Lynching. We had entered a different reality, and I was both fascinated and wary. What would happen to us? Could we handle the situations we would encounter? We had definitely left the familiar behind. I had thought North Carolina was the South, and geographically, it was. But in South Carolina I *felt* the South—and its history. Families split by slavery. Sons and fathers sold. Reconstruction foiled. Jim Crow. Separate but equal. Civil rights. The atmosphere was charged with a strange energy; the spirits of folks who had lived that history seemed to hover over the surface of the swamp we were passing, and I wasn't sure if they were friendly or vindictive. In the warm embrace of the descendants of those souls, I would find my answer.

We were at the beginning of a ten-year journey that took us not only into the Deep South but also into other regions of the country, where we learned about the effects of racism from people we met along the way. The real odyssey for me took place internally, in my mind and heart, as I found myself drawn into situations that required me to think and respond in new ways. In the mire of my psyche, I discovered a tangle of notions, impressions, and conclusions about African-Americans that had impacted my ability to pull myself to a moral high ground.

In the South, grasping the meaning of race depended on feeling and intuition—capacities of the heart. Could I trust my heart to recognize the truth, and would I allow that truth to guide my decisions and actions? Could I trust African-Americans and initiate interactions with them? Would I be trustworthy? If I relied on my heart as a built-in compass, might I slip into a morass of my own racial conditioning? Or might I, while immersing myself in a strange and mysterious social context, discover unimagined inherent capacities that would enable me to gradually progress toward my true potential as a spiritual being? The drama of this story arises from the uncertainty of navigating an uncharted reality and trying to get my bearings with logic and cultural norms that proved impractical.

June 1998
South Carolina

I glanced over at Marcus sitting in the passenger seat of the van. I was driving, and our wives, Gina and Phyllis, were in the back seat. We were looking for Simon. Phyllis and I had met Simon a couple of weeks earlier at a workshop. When he found out I was an artist, he told me about the small-scale battleships he had constructed out of found objects, and he invited me to drop by sometime and see his work. Marcus and Gina had driven out to the town where we had parked our trailer, and I'd suggested we visit Simon and check out his battleships. They'd known Simon for a while but were unaware he had this creative outlet, so my idea was well received. Simon had no phone, none of us knew his address, and we weren't even sure if he would be home. We were just excited about hanging out together, and it really didn't matter what we did. Gina knew he lived in the next town over and was convinced she also knew what street his house was on. So now we were cruising around the town where Simon lived, up one street and down the other, with Gina confidently maintaining that as soon as she saw "that fence that's right across from his place," we'd find him.

"Whaddaya think?" I asked Marcus. I had met Marcus only a few weeks earlier, and I was still somewhat incredulous that he seemed to enjoy my company. But then, I hadn't been the same person since we crossed the border into South Carolina. I was having a lot of those "out of body" experiences during which I stood on the sidelines watching myself do things I'd never done before, wondering, *Who is this strange guy in my body?* Maybe Marcus was relating to that guy. It was all a bit unsettling because I didn't seem to have much control over this impersonator, who looked like me but who was far more impulsive and daring and who took me into situations I would normally run away from.

Marcus grew up in Harlem, and when I thought about what his childhood must have been like, the images that surfaced were those of an urban war zone with people running for cover, screaming for help over gunfire. Where did that imagery come from? When I thought about my childhood, I saw cows grazing contentedly in the neighbor's pasture and heard the gurgling creek that separated their property from ours. It was hard to imagine that Marcus and I had grown up in the same country. I'm sure that for most of my life, I regarded Marcus and other black men as people from a different world, possessing little regard for human life. The warnings I had heard growing up about the dangers of driving through black neighborhoods had led me to the conclusion that those areas were life-threatening for whites who might accidentally make a wrong turn and end up in the "ghetto"—easy prey for any black man who had nothing better to do than shoot a lost white guy. And thinking about being lost in the ghetto reminded me of those movies I used to watch as a kid about white hunters trekking through the jungle, obviously out of their element. Suddenly one of them would fall down dead after having been shot with a poison dart from a blowgun. The message for me was clear: "Stay out of the jungle!"

Everything I had learned as a child, teenager, and young adult about African-American men can be distilled into one axiom: *black men are dangerous wherever they are, in the ghetto or out, on the bus, in a museum, in the grocery store, at the office; therefore, avoid them at all costs and keep them away from us.* This is what I think of as the "white peoples' code of survival." It's not written down. We don't talk about it (well, maybe discreetly, with other white folks), but many live by it, cling to it. It becomes written in our cells. By the time I had become an adult with my own family, my conclusions about black men had solidified into rigid thinking and patterned behavior. Although I talked idealistically about the unity of all people, I chose to raise my children in a white suburb. My association with black men was limited to brief, "safe" encounters where whites were in the majority. In the years just prior to beginning our trip, I was finally becoming aware of my ignorance. But in South Carolina, my understanding of reality was turned upside down. What I thought was truth didn't correlate with the experiences I was having.

Marcus leaned over, cast a furtive glance toward the back seat, then looked at me with a mischievous smile and said, "Well, man, I don't know. Maybe they moved that fence." We chuckled—a bit too carelessly.

"What are you guys laughing at?" Gina wanted to know. Gina was direct and assertive. The intensity of her personality was heightened by her appearance. I peeked in the rear view mirror and saw an Italian-American beauty with fiery dark eyes and thick, jet-black hair that seemed unwilling to lay flat and reached out in all directions as if challenging any brush or comb to just try and break its spirit.

"Nothing, honey. Nothing," Marcus assured her.

Marcus put his hand over his mouth to stifle his laughter while his body convulsed with suppressed mirth; it looked like he was about to explode. I watched him out of the corner of my eye as I continued driving. He and Gina made a striking pair. He was tall, with the broad shoulders and tapered waist of a bodybuilder, his dark complexion intensifying the superhero proportions of his physique. In any gathering, his mere presence drew attention. And where others might have used their stature to intimidate and keep people at a distance, Marcus invited connection. He could break me like a twig if he wanted, but I felt no threat. No need for fight or flight. I was attracted to his gentle spirit.

Men generally estimate one another's worth by some contrived standard of power that we attempt to quantify: How much can he lift? Did he set a new record? What's his IQ? What's his net worth?

My relationship with Marcus was supported by a different value system. I appreciated his humanity, and there was no way I could measure that and assign a number to it. What I saw in his face was compassion and acceptance. He liked me. And although at first I didn't feel deserving, I believed that what he saw in me was real, because I trusted his capacity to know character. Through his eyes, I became aware of some virtue in myself that I had neither identified nor embraced.

We finally gave up the search for Simon's home and decided to visit Miss Eva; she was another new friend we had met at the workshop, and she lived in the same town as Simon. We were sure she would know how to find his place. After a few attempts to locate Miss Eva's house, it was clear that we didn't have a clue where she lived, either. "I think we're going to have to visit Simon another time," I conceded.

"Look! There's a gas station," Marcus said. "Let's ask those fellows if they know where Miss Eva lives." It was around 5:00 p.m., the end of a workday for a group of six African-American men who were relaxing by a vending machine that sat just outside the gas station garage. I pulled in and parked away from the pumps near the street. As soon as the van came to a stop, Marcus said, "I'll go over and ask the guys about Miss Eva," and hopped out. He looked happy to be leaving the confines of the van and joining the men over by the garage. I was a bit apprehensive about interacting with the group, so I stayed in the van with Phyllis and Gina.

The men watched Marcus approach. When he reached the little area where they stood in the shade in front of the garage, they greeted him warmly, and every one of them shook his hand. Leaning against the garage door, the vending machine and a rack of tires, they formed a semicircle around Marcus, who positioned himself in front of them with his back to the van. I studied the scene. Marcus rocked side to side as he interacted with the others, each of whom was animated in his own way, slapping hands, laughing. It looked like a party, and suddenly I wanted to be part of it.

"What's taking him so long?" Gina asked.

"I'll find out." I said, and jumped out of the van and headed toward the gathering at the garage.

As I made my way across the concrete lot, I thought, *Uh oh! The other me—the impersonator—has taken control! What's going to happen when I get over there?*

The intensity of the animated interaction I had observed from inside the van decreased the closer I got to the garage, and now the group was quiet, watching my approach with curiosity. When I reached the men, I stood next to Marcus, who put his arm around my shoulder and announced, "This is my brother."

I looked around to see how the men would react to his statement. There were a couple of guys in their twenties, some in their forties, and one older man with a weathered face, wearing a baseball cap pushed back on his head. He took a drag on his cigarette and eyed me intently. The men were silent. I watched the old guy exhale, and when the last bit of smoke was out of his mouth, floating away in the breeze, he took another breath and stated authoritatively, "He sure don't look like you."

I panicked. Was he judging me? Had I been rejected? Then suddenly everyone was laughing, and I joined in, sharing the joke—included. The men introduced themselves and shook my hand, and I was welcomed into the gathering. Where was I from? they wanted to know. How had Marcus and I met? The lively exchange resumed, and now I was part of it.

We heard a horn, and turned around to see hands waving at us from behind the windshield of the van. "Well, guess we'd better get going," Marcus said. After parting farewells of "Y'all take care," and another round of handshakes, Marcus and I made our way back to the van.

The men did know Miss Eva and told us where she lived, but when we got to her house, she wasn't home, so we decided to go back to the town where our trailer was parked and get some dinner. We didn't find Simon, and I never did see his collection of ships. But that day I found something else—a part of myself I hadn't known existed. I discovered it in the eyes of Marcus and the men at the gas station.

COMMENTARY

When I first wrote this account, I was simply recalling the incident to the best of my ability. As I reread the story and thought about writing the commentary, I remembered the same quotation from the Bahá'í writings that's found in chapter 5 of this book: "Bahá'u'lláh . . . once compared the colored people to the black pupil of the eye surrounded by the white. In this black pupil is seen the reflection of that which is before it, and through it the light of the spirit shineth forth."[1]

I realized that Bahá'u'lláh's comparison of black people to the pupil of the eye applied to my experience with Marcus. I saw trust in his eyes and recognized it as the reflection of a quality he saw in me. That reflection of trust helped me discover new potential in myself. In spite of all the violent imagery that surfaced when I thought about his childhood in Harlem, I trusted him.

Moreover, I was moved to jump out of the van and walk over to a group of black men who were complete strangers. Earlier in my life I might have thought the men were watching me and working out a plot to come over, grab me, and mess me up—like when you hear people speaking a foreign language and laughing, and you're sure they're laughing at you. For some reason I didn't care about safety; I just wanted to be with the guys and share in the fun.

And then the old guy studied me and made a joke aimed to include me. Why did he do that? He could have said, "Well, time to go home," and left. What did he see in me? I think he noticed how comfortable I was around Marcus and the other men and had determined that he could trust me to respond to the joke. The work continues as I am able to recognize and take advantage of opportunities to develop trustworthiness and other spiritual qualities that strengthen relationships.

8

BE CAREFUL WHAT
YOU WISH FOR

Phyllis, February 1998
A city in New England

When will you learn? I scolded myself harshly.

The young man waited, not very patiently it seemed, apparently unaware of my distress. He sat across from me at the kitchen table, looking at me with his intense eyes.

This is what you wanted, now isn't it? You know you brought it on yourself.

I carried on my private reprimand, mentally wagging an I-told-you-so finger in my own face.

And, once again, you're in over your head. So now what, Miss Smarty-pants?

I hadn't called myself that in a long time. Then again, it had been a while since I'd gotten myself into such an uncomfortable situation. The person responsible for my anxiety was quiet, and now I addressed my paralyzed brain once again,

Say something! He wants an answer. You can't keep sitting here with your mouth hanging open. He's waiting! Speak!

But no answer was forthcoming, and he shifted in his seat without releasing me from his gaze. How long had it been since he asked me that question—the question for which there was no possible satisfactory response? And how had I gotten myself into this spot, anyway?

I'd met Jason for the first time several months before at a weekend conference. His magnetism had affected everyone in the auditorium; whenever he'd stopped moving—which wasn't often—he'd been quickly encircled by men and women of all ages and complexions. There was something about this young man that made all sorts of folks feel good in his presence, something that had continued to pique my curiosity long after the conference was over. My encounters with him that weekend had been superficial, and I'd headed home with a strangely compelling sense of missed opportunity, an unexpected regret at not getting to know him better. At the time I didn't think I'd have another chance.

And then a friend in New England invited Gene and me to a workshop on healing racism. She told us the facilitator was excellent and that many respected people from the community would be attending; she even offered to put us up at her house. So we gratefully accepted, even though it was a seventeen-hour drive from where we were staying in South Carolina. We arrived so late that we thought our hostess and her other guests would already be in bed. But the living room was filled with laughter, and everyone was wide awake, even though the workshop sessions were beginning early the next morning. When our friend introduced us all around, I had a pleasant surprise.

"You remember Jason, right?" she asked. "I think you guys met at that conference back in October."

"Sure, I remember you!" I said, hoping I appeared laid-back, trying to conceal my sudden feeling of expectation. If I had known what was actually coming, I would have fled on the spot. But I didn't; I was just glad to see him again, to have another opportunity to get acquainted. And I was really looking forward to experiencing the next day's sessions together.

However, this workshop was unlike any other I'd attended. The already stressful subject of racism was presented in such a direct and honest way that it created extreme discomfort for the members of this racially diverse group. We started out the Saturday morning session citing overt acts of discrimination and violence perpetrated against people of color. We all know that racism exists, but it's difficult to talk about how bad it really is. It is so difficult, in fact, that those of us who are white usually end up feeling guilty. We have an urge to confess to something we don't really feel responsible for, to convince some random African-American that we are sorry. We wish to weep, to experience forgiveness, relief, catharsis. Or better yet, we wish to not speak of it at all. I know that many of us in the workshop hoped the next topic would be easier.

And it was easier, or at least it seemed to be at first. We talked in the afternoon about covert prejudice—the stereotypes and subtle attitudes that have such a profound effect on the way we perceive each other. We looked at the most insidious of these attitudes: the subconscious sense of superiority that whites seem inherently to possess. Our discussion was guided by a quotation from the Bahá'í writings that describes how whites should relate to their black compatriots: "Let the white make a supreme effort in their resolve to contribute their share to the solution of this problem, to abandon once for all their usually inherent and at times subconscious sense of superiority, . . . to persuade them through their intimate, spontaneous and informal association with them of the genuineness of their friendship and the sincerity of their intentions . . ."[1]

I've thought about this a lot in the recent past, and I think I understand how it happens, how white people grow up with this idea floating just below the surface of conscious awareness. It is a whispered reassurance that we are somehow the norm, the "typical" Americans, the ones who rightfully call the shots. We know instinctively that ours is the color of validity, that whoever is unlike us needs a label, while we require none. Very few people acknowledge these thoughts, and yet there they are, coloring everything we think and do. I've heard it said that this feeling of superiority is in the air that we breathe and that we take it in with our mothers' milk. It seems patently unfair and overwhelming, impossible to deal with. How exactly does one go about addressing something that's not conscious? I realized during the workshop that I had been wrong. Discussing the topic of covert racism was even harder than talking about obvious discrimination and violence.

But it was in Sunday's workshop that my greatest shift in perception occurred. The group was engaged in an intense dialogue when something happened that shook me abruptly out of the realm of the abstract where my mind had sought escape from painful feelings. Later I recorded the incident in my journal with an odd detachment:

During this morning's session, we were talking again about the appalling injustices perpetrated against African-Americans. Suddenly one of the black participants stood up and said that he was tired of bleeding for the purpose of educating white people—that all these workshops did was reopen wounds without providing any means for healing, so that white participants could experience an epiphany, express their guilt and regret, and then feel better. This is a whole new point of view for me to consider.

It was Jason who stood and spoke, and my journal account does not even hint at the anguish in his voice or the grief in my heart. For reasons unknown to me, I heard him as if he were my own son, suffering some indignity at the hands of an unrepentant tormenter. And then images came unbidden to my mind, gruesome photographs I had seen in books about slavery, jumbled together with pictures of racial violence from newspaper articles. All of them showed black people bleeding. In a brief instant of clarity, I realized that what Jason and the other African-American participants had experienced in the workshop session was no different than the hundreds of other injustices cited that day; they had been wounded so that the needs of white participants could be served—the very thing we were trying to figure out how to avoid. How deeply entrenched and cleverly hidden these attitudes must be, that we could unwittingly perpetuate an injustice we'd identified only minutes before. And how baffling that they appear so subtle to some and so blatant to others!

That's when I had an impulse that resulted in my present troublesome situation. I made a wish. I wished that I might have the chance to talk with Jason one-on-one, to find out who he was and how he had come to possess such a powerful energy, to understand more clearly the feelings he had just expressed. But mostly I wanted to learn why, when I was around him, I had this sense of impending recognition and urgency.

The workshop had ended before dinner, but the impassioned conversations had continued all evening. It was now very late, and those who had not gone to bed were still talking in the living room. I don't know exactly how it happened—maybe it was an act of divine humor—but suddenly I found myself in the kitchen sitting across the table from Jason, realizing with a little start that my wish had been granted. My heart was all pumped up into a state of fervent anticipation. We were one-on-one. I sat on that chair trying to appear casual, knowing he would speak first, wondering what he would say, all anxious and excited. . . . *like it's my birthday and the doorbell rings and people are coming in carrying beautiful presents and I don't know what's in them but I'm hoping it's something really great, and. . . .*

"You're white," he said.

His deceptively simple statement fell onto the table between us with a soft thud. It didn't sound like a question or the first line of a riddle but more like the opening premise in a debate. I had no idea what was coming. I did notice, though, that some of the intensity from that morning was starting to build up around him; the air in the kitchen felt charged and slightly ominous.

"Well, yes. I am." Why did this sound to my ears like an admission of guilt?

"There's something I need to know, something I've been wanting to ask a white person."

"Oh." A small flutter of unease tickled my stomach. Where was this heading?

"I've come to trust you over these past couple days," he continued, "and I'm willing to believe that what you tell me is the truth."

Now I felt full-on panic. This I had not foreseen. I was here to learn about him. Why was he asking *me* a question? What if I couldn't answer it? What if I answered it wrong, or worse, said something stupid? "Go on," I said.

"I want to know"—and now the intensity escalated—"how this sense of superiority that you whites have can possibly be unconscious. I mean, you have eyes, don't you? You can look around and see what you're doing, right? So how can it be unconscious?"

And here he leaned forward, reached across the table with that forceful energy of his, and held me in place as surely as if he'd gripped me by the shoulders. "Please," he said. "I'd just like to know."

And then he sat back in the static charge that buzzed around us and waited for my answer, while I sat in my own private fog and waited for inspiration. I looked around for support, forgetting for a moment that my husband was the only other white person in the house, and he was very busy hanging out with his friends in the living room. But no one else could have helped me anyway; this was *my* wish come true, mine alone to redeem.

If only I could think! OK, yes, like he said, we have eyes. We can look around and see . . . what? What do we see? What does he want me to say? No eloquence here—not one coherent thought. I know that I know this stuff; weren't we just talking about it earlier today? Didn't I have the gist of it just a few hours ago?

I tried to regain my earlier clarity, to remember my insights during our workshop. Unconscious sense of superiority. I looked down at the table as though I were thinking hard, pondering an essay question on a college entrance exam. Then I chanced a quick peek at him, hoping he wouldn't see the movement of my eyes. He was still watching, still waiting.

I take back my wish; I don't want to do this. This is too hard.

I just wanted him to *like* me, wanted desperately for him to perceive me as good white folk, to consider the possibility that here he had found one white person who was completely, utterly free of every trace of racism. I wanted this so badly that the imagined taste of it glued my words to the roof of my mouth like peanut butter straight from the jar. I knew with certainty that whatever sounds I uttered would betray me and reveal my fatal flaw—my inherent, unavoidable, undeniable, *unconscious* racial prejudice. Then that would be the end. And I really didn't want it to end.

Too much time had passed since the asking of the question, and it was clear that saying nothing would be worse than saying something dumb. So I took a deep breath, stepped out onto the ledge of my own ignorance, and began to speak—slowly at first, then faster and faster—calling on all my verbal and logic skills, analyzing furiously, citing this and that theory, explanation, excuse—anything to convince this young man with the earnest eyes that it was not really our fault, that we can't in all fairness be held accountable for some sneaky idea that hides below the conscious level of our collective white mind.

What did he ask again? How can it be unconscious?

As I rattled on and on, I began, miraculously, to get some clarity. It was as if the words tumbling out of my mouth had generated enough energy to disperse the fog in my head. I told him about the insidious programming of young minds, about caricatures of black people in our after-school TV shows and Saturday morning cartoons. I described denial as a mental illness that prevents our seeing what's in front of us.

What else can I say? I wish he could see through my eyes.

And with that thought, suddenly I had my answer. So simple! How had it taken me so long to figure it out?

"Surely you've heard women accuse men of being condescending or chauvinistic?"

There was a thick silence while Jason considered his response. Then finally, "I don't know. Maybe. Sure," he sort of admitted.

I went on, feeling bolder. "Do you think it's possible that most men have been conditioned to have a superior attitude toward women, and that this attitude just might be"—here I paused dramatically—*"unconscious?"*

He gave the slightest nod before speaking. "OK, I think I get your point."

And that was all he said. Not, "Oh Phyllis, thank you so much for illuminating the darkness!" Not, "I can't believe it's that simple, and I'm so grateful for your insight!" No, not those or any of the other things I wish he'd said. His almost-concession hung in the air between us, making us suddenly aware of how tired we were. We acknowledged the lateness of the hour, said good-night, and slowly got up from the table. I felt like a little girl who just wanted to be his friend and saw him for a brief moment as a very young boy who just wanted people to stop hurting him. Then that moment passed. He joined the lively group in the living room, and I headed up the stairs, the heaviness of my steps due more to emotional than to physical fatigue. I didn't want the day to end; I was afraid the next morning I would see aloofness in the eyes that had engaged me so directly. I fell asleep vowing to keep tighter control over my impulsive wishing.

COMMENTARY

I was greatly relieved the next morning when there was no trace of remoteness in Jason's demeanor, and I realized I'd been worried more about rejection than anything else. I read this story to one of my mentors for her feedback, and she asked me, "Why all the drama? What's the big tragedy here?" Clearly the drama was all in my head, and it was about the fact that I really liked this guy and hoped we could become friends. I was sure that somehow in the course of our discussion I had unconsciously said something racist and that he would write me off. So maybe I didn't mess up, or if I did, he had far more generosity of spirit than I was giving him credit for.

This same mentor, an African-American professor of literature, warned me against characterizing Jason as a boy at the end of my story. I believe she said, "Don't you dare do that to him!" And because she is my friend as well as my mentor, I paid special attention to what she was saying. Certainly everyone in this country is aware that whites have called black men "boy" since the beginning of slavery, with the intent to demean, humiliate, and emasculate them. She also pointed out that portraying him as a child could be interpreted as an effort on my part to downplay or deny the attraction I felt, which apparently came through quite clearly when I read her my story.

In the end, and after much soul-searching, I made a few revisions but left the image intact. I intend to speak the truth about my private thoughts and feelings, and in truth I felt at that moment as if we were both little kids trying to figure out how to relate. I'll leave the rest to my readers, and hope that you judge my intentions fairly.

I've had many conversations with Jason in the years since my story took place, none of them quite as intense, but all of them rewarding. Even though I don't see him often, I consider him my friend. I don't know if he remembers our late-night conversation, and he surely has no idea how many times I've recalled his trust and felt grateful. But I've learned something important since that night. Usually when people of different ethnicities have a conversation about race, the content is less important than the level of honesty. What really scares many of us white folks is that if we talk about it, we'll expose ourselves as unintentional racists. We fear we'll slip and reveal attitudes we don't even know we have. Then we will be judged and found inadequate. It's tremendously painful to carry that around when we're doing our best to work on changing our racial programming.

I never asked Jason why he trusted me enough to pose his question. Maybe, in the course of our interactions over the weekend, he saw I was open to that kind of discussion and believed I wasn't going to automatically get defensive. As a fellow Bahá'í, he knew I was committed to eliminating racial prejudice, and we had both been present in conversations about the specific roles and tasks that both white and black Bahá'ís have been given. So he did know something about me before he asked.

I had already acquired some understanding and skills before the night we sat together in the kitchen. I'd learned how to receive my black friends' expressions of pain and anger without letting myself be triggered, and I was deeply committed to staying open to further learning. More than anything else, though, I wanted to form close bonds of friendship, and I think that desire is something others can see. I think it's more important than the actual words we say.

Another point that came up in this story is the parallel between racism and sexism, and I want to take this opportunity to mention the unique role that white women can play in the work of creating racial unity—a role that grows out of our ability to understand the dynamics of race from two different perspectives.

Because we're white, we have the experience of belonging to the dominant group in this country. We've benefited from the privileges—and absorbed the attitudes and anxieties—that are part of that experience. If we are willing to be honest and to resist defensiveness, then our understanding of what it means to be white becomes an asset in the discussion of race. The same holds true for white men.

But we also have the experience of belonging to an oppressed group. We have been deeply affected by institutional discrimination. We know what it feels like to be patronized, devalued, stereotyped, and mistrusted simply because of our gender. While many might legitimately claim that gender oppression in this country is less devastating than the prejudice African-Americans face, I believe there are enough similarities to create a common ground.

Most of the women I know have little hope of seeing true gender equality achieved in their lifetime, and I hear the same kinds of comments over and over—especially from women in my age group: "I'm tired of the oppression, overt and subtle. I'm tired of trying to educate men. I have only enough energy at this point in my life to take care of myself; I'm not interested in investing any more energy helping a man raise his level of awareness." When our male acquaintances mess up—even if we know they're good-hearted and well-intentioned, with great potential for awareness—we feel sometimes like throwing in the towel. Maybe they slip and tell a slightly sexist joke, or reveal unintentionally some patronizing sense of their own superiority. I know for myself that there are days when I can't handle it, and I walk away in disgust. Then there are days when I'm more grounded, and I may draw the person's attention to the effect his remark had on me. If he gets it, I'm grateful, and my gratitude reinforces my belief that things will get better some day. If he doesn't get it, well, my response again depends on how I'm doing on that day. Maybe I can be detached, leave it in the hands of God, and continue my day without feeling diminished or resentful.

So you see, we white women understand the dynamics pretty well. We can bring our knowledge and our woundedness into situations involving race. We can be healed by what we learn and at the same time serve as healers. We can bring the positive elements of our conditioning also—our willingness to be vulnerable and our freedom to express intimacy. These are qualities we share with women of all backgrounds. May we learn how to come together and use our unique strengths to create a healthier environment for all of us. That's what I'm wishing for.

9

THAT'S A LID

Gene, October 1998
Washington

People told me the state of Washington possessed botanical beauty beyond imagination, that it was a cornucopia of nature's finest vegetation, unmatched anywhere in the entire United States.

"Why is this so?" I asked them.

"The rain. You know, it rains all the time."

"But doesn't that get to you?" I wanted to know.

"Nah. You get used to it," they assured me. And I, the naive Midwesterner, trusted those folks who claimed to have firsthand knowledge of the Evergreen State. I believed their evaluation was objective and consistent with my notion of physical comfort and that somehow, even with all the rain, it was possible for one's disposition to remain sunny and bright. But after spending the month of November in southwestern Washington, I concluded that those who had told me I would acclimate were delusional. This was not the paradise they had described. Where was the beauty? Where was the color? The purpose for living? It seemed the fog had gobbled it all up, and I felt miserable.

One morning Phyllis went shopping, and I was alone in the trailer. I was in the mood to relax and read. I opened the shades to let in some light, but the fog had pressed itself right up to the sides of our tiny home and indeed seemed intent on squeezing through a crack or an open vent to infiltrate the interior, overpower whatever living thing it encountered, and assimilate the hapless prey into the thick, gray substance that seemed to sneer at me through the window. *Let the light in? Ha! One of nature's little jokes in these parts.* My desire for solitude vanished.

I stepped outside to better evaluate the weather. The view in every direction resembled the beginning stages of a watercolor painting; no distinct shapes or lines defined objects. Buildings were fuzzy blobs, and trees looked like gestured gray brush strokes applied to a wet paper surface. People walking in the distance emerged as apparitions out of the murky haze, drifted across a two-dimensional plane of gray, and dissolved into blurry smears—transitory affirmations that other earthlings did exist out there. Everything was eerie, disorienting. I went back inside the trailer, grabbed my umbrella and a jacket, and set out to find a place to eat lunch. Surely a café or some fast food place would suffice to satisfy my growing desire for the company of other people.

Huddled under my umbrella, I found it impossible to avoid the immense puddles that covered the sidewalk. The combination of drizzle and fog was so dense I felt like I was immersed in a thin ocean. Other folks sloshed along without umbrellas, apparently not concerned they were getting soaked. Maybe this was the trick to adaptation here—get wet enough so you feel one with nature. *Who not only tolerates this weather but actually enjoys it and talks about beauty?* I just wanted to find a place that was dry.

A yellow glow ahead gave me hope there was a restaurant at the end of the block. My preoccupation with the weather faded and was replaced by thoughts of warm food and good company.

Within a few more steps, I saw a lighted globe on a post that stood in front of a door, and beyond the door there were people carrying what looked like trays of food. I hurried inside, shook the water off my umbrella and folded it, then queued up at the food counter to place my order. The other diners looked so pale. I thought that might be due to the lack of sunlight.

"One 3-piece dinner!" the cashier called out.

"Yeah, that's me," I said, waving my ticket as I walked to the cash register to pay.

In the dining area I navigated around the tiny tables propped on silver pedestals, careful not to dip the bottom of my jacket in someone's gravy. I headed toward an unoccupied table at the far end of the room, smiling at patrons along the way and hoping for something in return—a smile, a nod, or a gesture of welcome. Nothing. Each table was an independent pod of life, isolated from the others.

Suddenly a man's voice cut through the chatter in the dining area. "What the hell is that?" Everyone in the room looked out the wall of windows, and I followed their gaze to see what had caught his attention.

A large white truck was streaking through the parking lot; on its side a single word was painted in big black letters—MOVING. The truck hit a puddle and disappeared in an enormous sheet of water while I stood transfixed in the middle of the dining area, waiting to see what would happen next. The truck reappeared, headed for an empty part of the lot and skidded to a halt, taking up three parking spaces.

Two black men emerged from the vehicle and made their way toward the restaurant entrance. Inside, the shift in energy was abrupt; diners hunkered down in their tiny swivel chairs and tried not to look at the doorway through which the two men would soon enter.

Everyone in the restaurant was white. Since we'd arrived in this part of Washington, I had seen very little racial diversity, and I'd asked a new acquaintance how folks in the area viewed issues related to race. "Well, we don't really have a problem," he'd said. "In this neighborhood, about 95% of the people are white; the rest are Asian. No blacks to my knowledge. So it really doesn't affect us here."

The door made a whooshing sound as the two men entered. Now I could see details that had been obscured by the fog. They were young, probably in their late twenties. The first man through the door was of average height and casually dressed in blue jeans, a white T-shirt and white athletic shoes; no hat covered his neatly trimmed, close-cropped hair. He made his way to the counter and examined the menu.

The second man was over six feet tall and dressed entirely in black. He wore a long-sleeved black shirt, accented with a row of pearl buttons down the front and one pearl button on each cuff. His neatly pressed black jeans were held up by a black leather belt, which featured a large, oval-shaped silver buckle with an inlaid mother-of-pearl design. On his feet he wore black cowboy boots covered with silver studs. On his head sat a black cowboy hat, trimmed with a silver hatband. And tied around his neck with a neat knot was a red silk bandana—a flash of primary color.

My gaze lingered on the bandana momentarily then traveled up the short distance to the young man's face, which was partially obscured in a shadow cast by the generous brim of the hat. The expression on his face was not quite aloofness, but more like detachment. Certainly aware that a black man wearing cowboy attire in public would draw attention, he seemed indifferent to the white patrons sneaking peeks at him, and unconcerned if they were coping with fear or stifling amusement.

The young man was like a heroic fictional cowboy come to life, stepping off a page of a comic book right into this restaurant to order lunch. And his demeanor matched his image; he looked straight ahead, his gaze undistracted. His boots made solid clunking sounds on the tile floor as he strode slowly but deliberately to the counter to place his order.

But it was the hat—the beautiful black cowboy hat—that elicited my deepest appreciation and persistent fascination. Not too small, not too big, it was a perfect fit. The dome had a smooth, deep dent on top, and on each side of the dome were shallow, scooped-out depressions. The brim was wide, and it curved gently upward left and right; the silver hatband, narrow and simple, added elegance.

The man in black was approaching his partner, and I was still standing in the middle of the dining area holding my tray, when without warning my mouth started opening and closing. "Now, *that's* a hat!" I heard myself exclaim across the distance separating us. The white customers looked on reproachfully. I panicked. *What am I doing? I don't even know these guys. They could come over here and mess me up, and none of these folks would do anything to help me. I should have kept my mouth shut.*

The tall man appeared not to have heard my observation and looked up to study the menu hanging from the ceiling. The shorter man, however, turned around and confronted me, his face contorted into an expression of consternation. "No, man, that's not a hat," he said and paused to make sure I was listening, "That's a lid!" Then he smiled broadly and nodded a few times to confirm what he had just revealed.

A customer close to the front of the restaurant gulped down the rest of his meal and left, so I took the vacated table, glad to set down my tray. The young man smiled again.

"You guys from around here?" I asked, relieved at his friendliness.

"Noo-oo. We're just making a delivery in the area."

We continued chatting until their order was ready, then the young mover grabbed the bags of food, waved good-bye, and left the restaurant.

His silent coworker, who had not interacted with me the entire time he had been in the restaurant, took a black leather wallet from his back pocket and paid for the food. He strode to the exit in the same confident, determined way that he'd entered, grabbed the door handle and pushed the door open. When he was halfway out, he stopped in mid-stride, turned his upper body around and, from under the brim of his hat, looked directly into my eyes. "Take it easy," he said, then left the restaurant.

The men got into their truck, drove away and disappeared into the fog.

When the movers were out of sight, the tension in the restaurant dissipated, and the atmosphere returned to normal. I sat alone at my table eating—and smiling.

I had walked into this restaurant in need of fellowship to soothe a melancholy brought on by the perpetual absence of sunlight. Out of the fog rode two men to my rescue.

COMMENTARY

Some who have heard this story have said it took courage to engage the young men as I did. But, as many times as I've reviewed this account, I cannot recall courage as my first response. I see myself as a guy who, for some reason, was initially unafraid and therefore able to react to the novelty of the situation with unencumbered, childlike fascination. As soon as the words were out of my mouth, however, I became concerned about my safety.

The experience could have ended there. I might have felt embarrassed, found a seat and eaten my meal in silence, hoping no one was laughing at me. But the men recognized something I was only dimly aware of. My unguarded behavior exposed a fissure in my armor, so to speak, and I was for a brief moment vulnerable—and accessible. My longing for social contact was so insistent it forced out of my mouth words that grabbed their attention. They saw a flash of rapport and acknowledged it, liberated it, encouraged it to emerge (Ah, there's the courage!) and find expression. They did this for me so easily. I wonder what they typically got in return from people who look like me. What must it be like to live in a society where the majority of citizens regard you with suspicion and are closed and withholding?

Looking back at my brief encounter with the men, I feel they had seen in me something of value, a spark of life shining through the haze that enveloped me and distorted my perception of things. That interaction filled me with energy I could not ignore, that I would in time come to crave. The experience taught me a lesson that was re-inforced again and again as we traveled throughout the country and met folks from diverse backgrounds. I've learned I can initiate social encounters with complete strangers—wherever they're from—and what usually results is a connection not only to an individual but to a body of universal kinship that is nourished by the same life-giving energy that fed me that day in the restaurant.

The young men resonated with something in me and reflected it back so I could see it. That gesture affirmed my worth as a person. Can those of us who are white do the same in return? Can we see black Americans' generosity, compassion, intelligence—indeed all the characteristics we share as humans? Can we then embrace those characteristics and reflect them back? Just think of the transformative power released with such a simple act.

10

THE PROMISE

Phyllis
Prologue

I cannot think of a finer way to spend my time than sitting around a cozy kitchen table with my girlfriends, drinking good coffee, sharing bits of ourselves in that wonderfully intimate way that women have when they're feeling safe. It was in just such a setting that I found myself late one October afternoon in a small city on the East Coast. Next to me at the table, sipping at their freshly brewed cups, were Kathryn and Georgia—intense, funny, passionate women whose company I couldn't seem to get enough of. We were still new friends, but a sisterly feeling was washing over us in great waves of laughter and companionship. The three of us were fairly close in age and had much in common, although their children were younger than mine. Their two teenage sons were inseparable friends. Gene and I had gotten to know the boys a little over dinner; they had a respectful and straightforward way of relating, and the more I talked with them, the more admiration I had for their mothers.

But now the two young men had left, and Gene was in another room hanging out with friends from the community who had gathered at Kathryn's house. I can't remember how the conversation took this turn, but somehow the two women began telling me of the agonizing decisions they had to make as mothers of black teenage boys. Their sentences came out fast and overlapping, the images and the pain interweaving until they formed one common experience spoken from two mouths:

"... inevitable encounters with the police ..."

"... stopped just because they're black ..."

"... even if they weren't doing anything, just driving along ..."

"... doing nothing wrong ..."

"... I had to teach him exactly where to put his hands ..."

"... Show me your license! ..."

"... Your registration! ..."

"... how to move his hands so slowly ..."

"... think he's reaching for a weapon ..."

"... how he should look ..."

"... and what to do with his eyes ..."

"... exactly what words to use ..."

"... and which words he should never say ..."

"... otherwise he might get shot ..."

"Can you imagine what that feels like, knowing you have to teach your son those things?" one of them asked.

Their expressions had become emotionless as they spoke—rigid and tough—as if any softness in such matters, even speaking them to me, could be deadly for their children. When the final question lay on the table, their faces turned weary; it seemed the sharing of their burden had not lightened it but served only to remind them of their pain.

I struggled to empathize. I closed my eyes for a moment and tried to swallow my horror, tried to imagine their experience so I could stand in solidarity with them, tell them yes, I could relate to the picture they'd laid out for me. Instead the outrage began to rise, acidic in my throat, and I longed to purge it by screaming out my shock and disbelief. *"Here?"* I wanted to shout. *"That happens here? In New England?"* What did I think, that it happens only in the South? Or did I on some level believe it happens only in the movies? *"Those two sweet boys? How could that be possible?"*

But any of those questions would have diminished their gift, so I gave them back the only thing I had of equal value—honesty. "No. I cannot imagine it," I said. What I didn't say was, *"And not only can't I imagine it, I don't have to imagine it. I will never have to teach my son those things."*

A couple weeks after my coffee with Kathryn and Georgia, Gene and I were ready to leave their city for our next destination. We decided to say good-bye to Miss Evelyn, a friend of theirs whom we'd met a few times, and stopped at her laundromat on our way out of town. She was really excited to see our trailer parked across the street, so I suggested that she go over and ask Gene to give her a tour; I'd stay with the kids for a few minutes. She was babysitting four of her grandchildren while she ran the laundromat. Two were toddlers; one was about five or six; and the youngest, Bryce, was six months old. I had my hands full, and Miss Evelyn was obviously having a good time touring the trailer because she stayed longer than I'd expected.

I was OK with the rambunctious play of the older kids, but Bryce's behavior bothered me.

He just lay there motionless in his playpen, arms at his sides. I'd never seen a baby lie so still like that. His eyes were alert, though, and followed my face, his look so penetrating it appeared he was asking me a question. And then, as if I'd suddenly turned telepathic, I was sure I could hear his thoughts. He seemed to be saying, "What are *you* going to do to make this world a safe place for me?"

We hadn't been traveling very long, but I had learned some things already. I knew that as an African-American male, Bryce was going to have a lot of trouble to deal with in his life. I knew that his chances of making it to adulthood without being hurt in some way were nearly nonexistent. What I didn't know was how I could do anything about that. So when I sensed his question—what was *I* going to do to make this world a safe place for him?—and when he looked at me so intently, I had no answer. And that was unacceptable. You don't leave a question like that unanswered. But the best I could do was to make a promise that I would find an answer by the time I saw him again. Miss Evelyn finally came back and found me staring into the eyes of her grandson.

"Kinda gets to you, doesn't he?" she asked.

July 1998

A suburb of Chicago

About ten months after our visit to the East Coast, Gene and I were having dinner in a restaurant with our son Erik, who was twenty years old at the time. We were mellow after a busy day together and thoroughly enjoying our interaction with Randa, the woman who was waiting on our table. She was African-American and probably in her thirties, vibrant and talkative, the kind of person who makes you feel like you've been friends forever. I'd wondered during our meal if she had a hard time in this predominantly white community, but if she did, she brought no trace of suspicion or coolness into her relationship with us.

At the next table over, an African-American man was having dinner with two young children, and they were also having a great time with our waitress. In fact, they received such special attention from her that I suspected they knew each other well. After overhearing bits of their conversation—and watching Randa lean over and kiss the man while setting down his salad—I finally realized they were husband and wife, and that one of the children was their daughter. The woman carried the conversation so effortlessly between our two tables that I began to feel like we were members of her family too. Perhaps it was that very level of comfort that set us up for what happened.

Near the end of our meal, another customer walked over to greet the man. When he asked the little girl how she was doing and offered his hand, she crossed her arms and turned her head, unwilling—in spite of her father's coaxing—to interact with him in any way. The moment he left, Randa sprang into action. She took her daughter by the hand and led her toward the restroom, scolding her as they walked.

"Now you know that's no way to behave when someone greets you. I don't care if you didn't feel like talking, you speak politely to people. You need to mind your manners, young lady . . ."

She continued the lecture in the restroom, I assume, because the girl was properly repentant when they returned, and she sat back down next to her father with a sigh.

Randa came over to our table to pour more coffee, letting out a big sigh of her own and rolling her eyes at the frustrations of parenting. Our conversation took a new turn as we shared our experiences as mothers and the challenges of raising kids in these chaotic times. As she stood near my chair, coffee pot in hand, she grew quiet. I felt she had something more to say, so I stopped talking too.

"You know, it's not really my daughter I'm worried about," she finally said. "I have a teenage son, and I'm very concerned about him. There's so much he has to deal with out there . . ."

Her voice trailed off, and her face suddenly appeared exhausted. I couldn't imagine what had changed her from the chatty, smiling woman I'd been talking to a moment before to someone who looked so terribly weighed down. There was such an unbearable sadness in her expression that I wanted to reach for her hand. Instead, I searched for something encouraging to say.

I believed I understood what she was feeling; this was, after all, an experience we had in common. I too had parented a teenage son. I clearly remembered how hard it was watching him struggle into maturity, and I realized how much easier things were now that he was older. I wanted so badly to give this woman something to hang on to and to ease the pain I saw in her eyes. When she finally returned from the images in her mind and looked at me again, I smiled and gestured toward Erik as evidence that I knew what I was talking about.

"I just want you to know that it does get better," I assured her. "The closer they come to adulthood, the easier it gets. I promise." My tone was earnest to convince her of my certainty and support.

And then everything changed; the light went out of Randa's eyes. A moment ago there had been something flowing; now a heavy veil fell between us. The connection, the trust, the warmth—all of it was gone. *She* was gone. In her place was a woman standing rigidly with a pot of coffee and blank eyes that looked straight ahead.

"Yeah, whatever," she said, her voice dull. "If you say so." Then she dropped our check on the table, turned, and walked away.

It felt like a slap in the face. What had happened? It was as if everything bright and joyful had withdrawn and left me sitting there, chilled and stupid. What did I do? Did I say something that upset her? In my mind, I went over every word, every gesture and expression. Randa's abrupt departure had rocked me. I looked over at Gene and Erik to see if they could offer some insight, but they had been deeply engaged in a conversation of their own and apparently hadn't paid attention to what was happening on my side of the table. They were finishing up the last of their coffee and getting ready to leave. While Gene was calculating the tip and counting out his money, I searched through memories of conversations with other black women, hoping there I would find something that might explain Randa's reaction.

It took only a moment, and I was back on the East Coast, sitting at the table with Kathryn and Georgia, listening to their anguish as they wished their sons could stay young forever, hearing their fear of sending those gentle young men out each day into a society that perceives every black male as a criminal. And then hearing again my own admission—that I would never know what that felt like.

So now I knew what I'd said that had shattered the relationship between me and a woman who had hoped I was different. My promise was a fraud; things would not get better for her son as he got older, they would only get worse. The closer he came to adulthood, the more frequently he would be perceived as dangerous. And the worst thing was that I knew this truth already, but in that moment I had forgotten it. How is it possible to forget such a truth? Is this one of the elements of white privilege—having the option to know the truth and then forget it because it doesn't apply to my life? And because of my forgetting, whatever hopefulness she might have felt had been replaced by the inescapable reality that I was just one more ignorant white woman who actually thought I understood what she faced. Certainly she must be asking herself why she had risked such openness with someone who would inevitably hurt her. But it was not simply the realization that I was no different from all the others that had caused her to pull away; I felt sure of that. She had opened up to me, trusted me, and I had stabbed her unprotected heart with a promise that would never be honored.

OK, so I knew something. Now what? As soon as I asked myself that question, Georgia and Kathryn came to my assistance. I could see and hear them as clearly as if they were sitting at the table finishing their coffee.

"Get up off your butt, girl, and *do* something!" they urged me.

"Yes, I will. *I will!* But what?" I asked them.

"You know!" they chorused.

They were right; I did know. I would have to talk to her, apologize for hurting her, for betraying her trust, for my ignorance, for letting my privileged life leak out and burn her, for holding my son up as an example of what hers would never have. I knew I risked making a fool of myself or being rejected, which would be even more painful. But no matter what happened, nothing could be worse than imagining disappointment and resignation in the faces of those two women who had loved me enough to tell me their truth.

"I'm ready to go." Gene's voice shocked me out of my reflection.

"Would you guys mind going on and waiting for me in the car?" I asked them. "I have to talk to our waitress."

They left without further discussion; maybe they realized something was up, or they were just content to share some more time together. Either way, they went out the door and left me sitting at the table wondering exactly how I was going to make this happen.

At first I waited patiently, assuming Randa would eventually return to clear the table and pick up her tip. But when she didn't come back after several minutes, I felt a pit in my stomach. I walked around the dining room, then looked in the lobby, the restroom, and the smoking section in the back, but she was nowhere. My next destination was the kitchen; I was determined enough that even if someone had tried to stop me, I would have brushed passed him to find her. Fortunately I didn't have to go that far. Randa was walking out through the kitchen doors, carrying a large tray covered with plates of food.

She stopped when she saw me, and I stood in front of her, waiting for inspiration. She waited too. Finally I just opened my mouth and let the words fall out, ineloquent and awkward.

"I want to tell you that I'm sorry. I really do know that things are not the same for your son as they are for mine, that life will only get

133

harder for him as he gets older. I knew it, but I forgot. I know I hurt you, and I'm sorry."

My apology sounded pitiful and inadequate to my ears, and I could see no clue on her face of how she felt. She remained very still and looked into my eyes for a long moment, then stepped to the side, and I thought she was just going to walk away. But instead she set her tray down on an empty table, turned back to me, then reached out for me and took me in her arms. For a while we hugged each other tightly. Then she put her head down on my shoulder and started to weep.

It seemed like several minutes that we stood in the embrace—crying, rocking, consoling each other—each of us giving and taking comfort at the same time. The activities of the restaurant bustled unheeded around us. Finally, her tears spent, she stepped back and managed a small smile.

"It *is* going to be OK," she said softly. "With people like you and me working together, and with the help of God, things will be all right. We'll do it with His help."

I couldn't speak; the most I could do was dumbly nod my agreement. I don't remember who looked away first, how we parted, or how I got out the door and into the car. I don't even remember the details of her face. I would not recognize her if I passed her on the street. All I remember is the rocking and the tears and the comforting, and feeling the web of connection being rewoven as we stood there. And I silently made a new promise—to Randa and her son, to Miss Evelyn and Bryce, to Kathryn and Georgia and their sons—to never stop working for unity. This promise is one that, with God's help, I think I'll be able to keep.

COMMENTARY

Every time I've shared this story—I believe without exception—someone says that it was very brave of me to find the waitress and apologize. My actions had nothing to do with bravery. What drove me to look for her initially was loneliness; the abrupt cutting off of the relationship was painful, and I wanted somehow to heal that pain. Then, once I remembered the conversation with my two friends, I was compelled by their faces in my mind—faces of mothers with sons like my own, faces contorted with a pain that I couldn't even imagine—to find Randa and apologize. To have left the restaurant without addressing the severed connection would have been the same as saying to my friends, "Thank you for sharing, but I don't care. Your pain doesn't touch me; it's not relevant to my life, and I am not changed by its expression." Their sharing required a counterpart, a balance, a willingness to be vulnerable and take a risk. They planted seeds that germinated underground and eventually yielded new growth—seedlings that were then watered by the tears of the waitress. Once those shoots had broken through the earth, there was no going back to a time when I could have walked away unconcerned. The "freedom" of ignorance was gone, replaced by a sense of being a part of something much larger than myself. It was quite simply not possible for me to let them down.

And had it not been for my friends' willingness to tell me about their fear for their sons, I would never have had even the vaguest idea why our waitress withdrew. They chose to make themselves vulnerable to teach me. If we had been at that restaurant a year earlier, I would have watched the woman walk away and wondered what happened. Then I would have gone home.

Every interaction we have, every person we meet is potentially the source of some insight we'll need at a later point. Since Gene and I have been traveling, I've learned to take in everything to the fullest extent possible. I trust that it's being integrated into me and growing into the fruit that I'll be reaching for down the road. These intimate exchanges frequently provide not only information but also the motivation and power to act on it. They leave me with an image I can hold in my mind.

And speaking of the power to act, that's the motto of this story: *When you see the look, act.*

If you're engaged with a person—anyone really, but since this is a story about racial healing I'll say with a person of a different ethnicity than your own—and if in your conversation that person suddenly goes cold, and you see that look in his or her eyes, then say something, do something. Take the risk. I once told this story to a group of people after reading *Leap of Faith* for them, and when I urged them to take action if they see that look on someone's face, a twelve-year-old boy in the audience raised his hand and said, "Yeah, if she's leaping into your arms, don't drop her!"

The women I called Kathryn and Georgia are still in our lives. One of them is a particularly close friend; I have thanked her for her gift and will probably thank her again many times before I'm done.

I wish I knew how to find the waitress whose courage and acceptance touched me so deeply that night. I would tell her that when I look up at my audience after reading this story, I see women of every color wiping their eyes. I would explain that her generosity of spirit has moved the hearts of hundreds of people all over the country. And I would reassure her that I have found many, many more who are willing to do the work with us. Maybe she'll read this book, remember that day, and know that she's the one responsible for so much hope.

I'd like to end this commentary with the words of an African-American woman I met several years ago at a Bahá'í conference in Tennessee. I know the words are accurate because I wrote them down as she spoke. This is what she asked of me: "Would you carry a message from myself and my black sisters to other whites you meet who are engaged in race unity work? Please tell them this from us: if you are doing this work and you become afraid for any reason, come to us and you will be protected; we will hold you in our arms and protect you like a newborn infant."

11

PHOTO RETOUCH

Gene, February 1999
Texas

With three envelopes of freshly printed photographs in hand, I left the department store film counter and headed toward the pharmacy to meet Phyllis, who was picking up a prescription. I couldn't wait to sit down, open the envelopes and reminisce about the times we'd spent with new friends from the West and Southwest. But I was walking slowly; I was tired and my leg muscles hurt. We were on the Gulf Coast, and for the first time in our travels, we had found a campsite right on the beach. That morning, in fulfillment of a long-held wish, we had stepped out of our trailer onto the sand and hiked for hours along the beach, zigzagging around driftwood and washed-up vegetation, listening to the waves roll in, breathing the Gulf air.

Now, as I negotiated the store's narrow passages from one department to the next, dodging customers, shopping carts and children, I felt as if the joy of walking had somehow been used up for the day and that my only pleasure would be sitting and resting. I passed the hair care products, turned at the end of the aisle, and saw Phyllis still waiting in line with several customers ahead of her. I located a bench, but to my dismay it was occupied. In the middle of the bench, which appeared to be long enough to accommodate two adults, sat a young African-American man. There was clearly not enough space for me to sit on either side of him.

He looked up, and when our eyes met, I flashed back several years to a day in Illinois when I took a lunch break at a fast-food restaurant. I had been savoring my meal and enjoying a brief respite from the office routine when a group of black teenagers entered. They were laughing, full of energy, pushing and shoving. I was unnerved, concerned one of them would land in my lap, and I fretted about how I would respond to such disrespect. And they were so loud! The sheer volume had shattered my peace. I was sitting alone at a large table near the cash register and wished I had found a more secluded spot. I wanted to move, but all the other tables were occupied. My distress escalated to panic. What would the youngsters do when they received their food? Leave the restaurant and eat outside (my hoped-for preference!) or—the unthinkable—join me? They paid for their food, scanned the dining area, saw nothing available, and eyed my table enviously. They could see that the bench that wrapped around my table would easily accommodate all four of them, except for one problem—an older white guy—me. One of the teens, who was taller and seemed more sure of himself than the others, sat down with me uninvited and started eating his food, stuffing a triple-decker burger into his mouth. Over the top of the bun his eyes found mine and asserted, "Sorry, man, that's just the way it is." I glared at him with my best "what the hell do you think you're doing?" look. He was unfazed and smiled defiantly as he continued chewing. I wrapped up the remainder of my meal, and as soon as I got to my feet and turned to leave, the other teens rushed over and pushed and shoved themselves around the table.

The memory of this last scene in the flashback has haunted me and developed into a mental snapshot of that experience. I've examined it frequently over the years in an effort to determine what was missing. What could have enabled me to reassess the needs of the situation?

Now, years later, in a department store a thousand miles away, I recalled the powerlessness I felt to invoke the right to sit at "my" table alone and send the teen on his way.

"Can I sit there?" I asked. The young man moved over to one end of the bench. I sat down and immediately opened an envelope of photos. A feeling of well-being came over me as I studied the smiling faces of my friends. I had met them on reservations in the Dakotas, in cities along the Pacific Coast, in the mountains and on the desert. They comprised a diverse sampling of humanity, of many hues, from many cultures and ethnicities. As I continued thumbing through the photos, I felt my right shoulder becoming increasingly warm. I turned my head to identify the heat source and nearly pressed my lips on the cheek of the young man peering over my shoulder. Startled, he pulled his head away. I smiled and handed him a stack of prints. "These are my friends," I said. "This guy is from El Paso. She's from San Diego." I told him we were traveling and that I thought this area on the Gulf was pretty nice.

"Oh, yeah?" he said. He didn't seem to have the same opinion, and I could only guess what his experience had been. Every now and then, he would ask me about one of my friends—what state did he or she live in? How did we meet?

We had been enjoying each other's company and were almost finished with the last envelope when a shrill voice jolted us out of our camaraderie. A young woman with her arms full of bagged purchases stood in front of us, tapping her foot impatiently. "Let's go!" she snapped at my companion. She had apparently been trying to get his attention, but neither of us had heard her.

"That's my wife," he said. I nodded at her, and she nodded back.

The young man reluctantly stood up, reached over and shook my hand, and said, "Nice talking with you." He took some of the bags from the woman and the two of them walked away.

As I watched the couple disappear around a corner, I thought how easy it had been to connect with the young man. I had been the one needing a place to sit down, and he shared the bench. He was attracted to the photographs, and I shared them with him. *I'm different since that experience in the fast food restaurant. Why have I changed?* The pictures of my friends were stacked on the bench; I glanced at each one as I returned it to an envelope. *Of course. People I've met. My friends.* I remembered things we'd shared: conversations, prayers, laughter, pain, hope, and—*oh, yeah! Food.* I realized that the mental snapshot from the restaurant required editing. If only I could upload it to my computer and retouch it a bit. Cut and paste the teenagers. Put them around the table sharing a meal with me. And I am smiling, comfortable. No distress. No fear.

142

COMMENTARY

Over the years, Phyllis and I have added hundreds of photos to our album. It is, in a way, a record of personal growth, like a baby book that begins with pictures of a newborn and follows the infant's growth stages. When I look at photos taken early in our traveling, I remember numerous interactions with African-Americans in which I was inept, clumsy, and ignorant; but I can't change the past. If I could edit my experiences in an effort to delete mistakes, what would I accomplish? I wouldn't alter the record of the baby's first attempts at walking to somehow create the impression that the baby had strolled right out of the womb. Each of our photos has a story about people we've met, and like the baby book that documents milestones in an infant's development, our album reminds me of relationships that provided new possibilities for growth. Every encounter, whether it resulted in a failed effort or success, has brought about change. Looking through the album, I realize I'm not the same person I was when I encountered the black youth in the fast food restaurant. I've developed.

12

DELICATE BEIGE

Phyllis, May 1999
Alabama

I was taking an evening walk in Dothan, a small city that rises rather unexpectedly from its rural surroundings in southern Alabama. My walking companion was an African-American woman in her mid-seventies whom we had met two weeks earlier. Gene and I had spent many hours in intimate conversation with her, her husband, and their granddaughter Alycia, and in that short period of time we had developed a strong connection with their family. As we walked to-gether, talking about how sad we felt that Gene and I were leaving the next day, I remembered something I wanted to get before we went back on the road.

"You don't by any chance know of someone who sells *Mary Kay* cosmetics, do you?" I asked her. "I'm out of my make-up, and I'd like to see if I could buy some before we go tomorrow."

"Well isn't that just the strangest thing? You know, Alycia used to sell those products. It's been some time ago, but I'm sure she still has a whole bunch of it sitting around somewhere. You should give her a call tonight and let her know what you need; I'll bet she'll have it. My goodness!" And she continued to chuckle for a while at the unlikely coincidence.

I couldn't believe my good fortune! When I got back to the trailer, I phoned Alycia, who assured me that she had several boxes of stuff left over from her days as a cosmetics distributor.

"What exactly do you need?" she asked. "I've got all the cleansers, skin softeners, lipstick, eye shadow . . ."

"I just need a bottle of Day Radiance."

For those readers who may be unfamiliar with *Mary Kay* cosmetics, "Day Radiance" is the liquid foundation that matches a person's skin color. There was quite a long pause, and then Alycia said, "Um, well, uh, I'm not really sure I'll have the color you wear."

What an odd thing to say, I thought. *My skin color is about as average as it gets; surely if she has a whole box, there will be at least one bottle of my shade.*

"Oh, don't worry. It's a pretty common color; I'm sure you'll have it." I was so confident.

"Well OK, if you're sure," she said. I heard a little something in her voice, but it wasn't confidence; it sounded more like skepticism. Or maybe amusement. Truthfully, the whole exchange baffled me somewhat. Was there a joke that I was missing? We made arrangements to meet the next morning outside her office where I would look through the bottles of make-up and take, as a gift, whatever I found that met my needs.

The following day we arrived at the agreed time, and Alycia came out to the parking lot carrying a carton slightly bigger than a shoe-

DELICATE BEIGE

box. I looked over at Gene and pointed at the box, then clapped my hands like a kid being offered a whole plate of cookies.

"You can't imagine how great this is," I said in response to his questioning look. "This stuff is not cheap. I can't believe she's giving me some for free."

It did seem almost too good to be true, which should have been an indication that there was indeed something I was missing. I stepped out of the van and into the moment, naive and unsuspecting, totally unprepared for the lesson awaiting me in that box.

I took the carton in my hands and looked down at maybe thirty bottles of Day Radiance—all brown. There was light brown, medium brown, and dark brown, everything from a deep tan to a rich chocolate color. And I was caught completely off guard; it had simply never occurred to me that all of her customers had dark complexions.

Not one to give up easily, I started rummaging through the little bottles that now seemed to condemn me for my ignorance. I heard Alycia begin to laugh.

"I didn't have very many white customers," she finally said, a little apologetically but with growing amusement.

Still unwilling to concede defeat, I continued my search, pawing somewhat frantically in the box, plucking up and then discarding one Day Radiance after another. By now my friend was laughing so hard she could barely speak.

"What is your shade, exactly?" she managed to ask.

Suddenly deflated, I looked at her sheepishly and mumbled, "delicate beige," which only served to fuel her mirth.

I suppose it was her laughter that knocked something loose in my mind, and her eyes filled with equal measures of love and delight

147

that helped me finally get the joke. Only it felt painful rather than funny, and I couldn't understand why she was laughing so hard.

What had I said to her on the phone—that it was a pretty common color? That I was sure she would have it? Here, where most of the people I saw around me were African-American? What made me think she would have my shade? But I knew what made me think that. In my world, I was the definition of "average." My mom had put "flesh-tone" bandages on my scraped knees since I'd learned to walk; my girlfriends and I chose "nude" pantyhose in the winter and "suntan" in the summer to match the skin on our legs. I had spent my entire childhood filling in the faces of the people in my coloring books using that peachy-beige crayon named "flesh." What else would I think?

So I'd come to what many would call a fairly harmless assumption—that most people in the world look like me. And assumptions are often accompanied by comments that might not be so harmless, the kinds of comments that can cause so much pain for people of color.

Certainly she had heard all of this beneath my offhanded assurance. Had my words been the cause of pain for this woman who in two weeks' time felt like a lifelong friend? I looked into her eyes and opened my mouth to express my embarrassment and regret, but her giggles were so contagious that all that came out was a snort. Soon we were both doubled over, laughing helplessly while Gene looked on in bemusement.

"*Delicate* beige?" she gasped. Tears were streaming down both our faces now.

"Yes . . . yes . . . delicate . . . beige," I managed.

"Oh I must have something in here, *some* kind of beige," she said, and she grabbed the box out of my hands. "Yes! Yes, I knew it!! Here it is!" and she triumphantly produced a bottle of light brown make-up. I took it from her and looked at the label. It said "cocoa beige."

"I'm sure this will do just fine," she said, snatching the bottle back. She was still having a hard time speaking through her attacks of hilarity. "You just come on over here and we'll give it a try." Then she deftly applied that cocoa-with-milk-colored foundation to my nose, dabbing at it a few extra times for effect.

"I'll bet, if we blend it in just right, no one will ever notice," she reassured me, stroking the rich color across my tear-streaked cheeks. "And you go right ahead and take this bottle—my gift to you."

After we finally got our laughter under control, Alycia hugged me and Gene one last time before we got into the van and drove out of Dothan. I knew I was taking with me something much more valuable than a lifetime supply of free cosmetics. I was humbled but grateful as we headed out on the road, with Alycia's gift of make-up clutched in my hand and her gift of love fortifying my heart.

COMMENTARY

This is the first story I wrote down, long before we had any intention of authoring a book. I love reading it in racially diverse groups because it's fun to watch the faces of the women of color; they usually know what's coming after the first few paragraphs. And almost every time I've read it for an all-white audience, there's been at least one woman who wants to defend me by asking, "How were *you* supposed to know she didn't have white clients?" Then the next thing she will say is, "Well she should have had shades for everyone! That's reverse discrimination! Just think how angry a black woman would be if I sold cosmetics and I only had makeup for white people!" In fact, folks can get pretty riled up when I suggest we're just distancing ourselves from the real issue.

I want to be clear about this. The issue in this story is *not* whether she should have had my color. That is beside the point. The point is about my conditioning as a white person and the assumptions—innocent and naive as they seemed to be—that go along with that conditioning. If this were a book about how to make a small business more successful, then we could debate whether or not she should have stocked a wide variety of hues. But it's a book about healing—healing myself from my own brainwashing, and healing the connection between my friend and me.

This past fall I was attending a convention, and at lunchtime I sat briefly with a group in their mid-twenties, all of whom were white, and none of whom I knew personally. My friends were waiting in another room for me to join them, so I didn't intend to stay long with these young folks, but I wanted to give them some information related to a question one of them had asked earlier. When I got to the table, they were involved in a discussion, so I sat down to wait for a break in the conversation. One of the young men was talking about how a crayon manufacturer had changed the name of the red-purple crayon to "raspberry." He said that his mom was an artist and was unhappy with this change because those colors were a standard—a sort of icon that shouldn't just be changed arbitrarily. Besides, red and purple were pure color descriptions; why did they have to abandon that for the colors of fruits? I was wearing a raspberry-colored shirt, and at this point the young man pointed to it and asked, "Look at her shirt; is it really red-purple, or is it raspberry?"

And as is my habit, I kind of fell into the conversation.

"I remember it being called red-violet," I said, ever the know-it-all.

The group agreed that red-violet was correct. Someone else said, "Maybe the problem is that the idea of red or violet is not a standard in most people's minds. Maybe artists have a shared concept of what color red actually is, like there's a pure hue that all artists would agree on; but others—the rest of us—might each have different ideas of what red or violet really looks like. And these ideas are not consistent from one person to the next, whereas a specific *object* that people are familiar with, like a *raspberry*, well, we would all agree on what color that is."

That seemed like a plausible enough explanation. Thinking I might have an opportunity to get a little discussion about race going before I moved on to join my friends, I said, "Yeah, for example, how they changed the crayon called "flesh" to "peach."

Quickly the young man whose mother was an artist objected, "Well I don't know why *that* was necessary. Everyone knows what color flesh is; that's a norm, and when we hear the word "flesh," we all envision the same thing. There's a common understanding."

I was shocked speechless at the casual, matter-of-fact way he made this proclamation. I really had a hard time accepting that those words came from the mouth of someone who was so young and must have known plenty of people whose skin was not the color of peaches. Yet he seemed truly unconscious of what he was saying and of the repercussions of his convictions.

I didn't take advantage of the opportunity to challenge his statement, something I regret to this day. It seems, looking back, that I could have found a way to make this young guy aware of his faulty assumptions. But the conversation was interrupted when some newcomers joined the group, and then I saw one of my friends standing in the doorway, gesturing at me to hurry up. So I simply got up and left, giving myself the excuse that there wasn't really enough time to address the issue thoroughly, or that I didn't have the right to disrupt their discussion, or some such nonsense. Cowardice, actually, if I'm honest.

I tell myself that by leaving, I gave up my right to be upset by the young man's comment. That hasn't worked; I'm still upset. It seems to me this assumption that our pale skin color is the norm creates an insidious belief—on some unconscious, cellular level—in our superiority. I'm thinking again about the crayon box. Imagine if, from the beginning of our school years, people of all colors were taught that humanity originated in Africa and that our original color had been dark, dark brown—almost black—and that this had been the standard, normal color of human beings for a long time. And that as people migrated to climates where there was less sunshine, they lost some of their pigmentation and adapted so that they could survive physically. These lighter-skinned people would then be exceptions, a kind of aberration or deviation from the norm. Imagine if this concept had been taught at schools in England, Sweden, and Germany, and that the Northern Europeans who came to this country had brought this knowledge with them. What if this concept were taught today in cities with large African-American populations like Chicago, New Orleans, Detroit, and Los Angeles? What if it were taught in states like Wyoming, Oregon, and Maine, where an overwhelming majority of the people are white? How would that change things? Would white people then look at themselves as other than the norm? And now imagine we were all taught that the darker a person's skin color was, the closer she was to the original design; and the lighter her skin color, the farther she has adapted away from the norm. What would that do to the way we perceive our relative value in society?

I ask you, my reader, when you were a child and you were drawing a picture of yourself with your family and friends, or with your classmates on the playground, what color did you pull out of the crayon box? If it was sepia, raw sienna, or mahogany, imagine that instead that crayon had been named "flesh." Or if you're like me and your skin is the color of very unripe peaches, suppose you found a crayon named "flesh" that was brown and didn't match you at all. How would you feel?

I don't mean to get carried away here, but I was really distressed by this young guy's statement, and it just got me thinking. I had assumed—or rather hoped—that each new generation of kids would have more friends of diverse ethnicities (or if not that, at least more exposure from TV and movies), and that this idea that pale skin is the standard would disappear completely. Why did it still exist deep within the unconscious of this youth?

This perception of our color as "normal" has been quite efficiently programmed into us, it appears. And when we're not paying attention, it will rise to the surface and do a lot of damage to our relationships. The good thing is that when it does rise to the surface, at least then we can recognize the programming for what it is and make some adjustments.

I've been blessed to have people like Alycia in my life. She was particularly generous that day, or maybe she just really needed a good laugh. She says she knows my heart, and that's why she wasn't offended. Whatever the reason for her patience and understanding, I am exceedingly grateful. Unfortunately I couldn't keep the make-up; it would have made a nice memento, but it's hard enough in an RV to find space for things I use every day. I actually ended up giving it to a *Mary Kay* consultant in Tennessee. I did, however, keep the friend, and there is limitless space for her in my life.

13

TWO AND A HALF HOURS

Gene, February 2000
Texas

Journal entry: Driving through town we passed block after block of run-down houses. Roofs falling apart, siding coming off like peeling dead skin, doors hanging off hinges, windows broken and boarded up or covered with plastic sheeting. The poverty of this town and the stories of a hard, painful life here have sensitized me afresh to the injustice associated with racism. We are often in poor areas, but for some reason, the meaning of the poverty I'm seeing lately is penetrating to new depths.

In towns or cities with an African-American population, there are often borders—specific streets, a river, or a railroad track—that mark off a neighborhood where the majority of black residents live. For white citizens, comfort generally lies outside of these borders; the area inside is regarded as a potential threat to their safety. When we asked a white man for directions to the address of someone we wanted to visit, he asked, "Why do you want to go *there*? Everyone around here knows it's a high-crime area."

In fact, people in towns all across the country had warned us about "bad areas." Experience had taught us, however, that if we expected to connect with people, then we would—regardless of where we were. The attraction to those new connections was the force that pulled us across the tracks and drew us along the streets. The prospect of flirting with danger and, at the end of the day, leaving the "'hood" unscathed seemed unreal, melodramatic. The real adventure for us was journeying into the unknown realm of relationships, finding family members we hadn't yet met, and sharing precious moments together.

I drove slowly as Phyllis studied the list of names and addresses attached to her clipboard and then ran her finger across the city map until she found a matching location.

"Here," she said. "Turn here. He lives down this street."

We hoped Raymond would be available this weekday afternoon. Raymond was one of several black residents in this vicinity who, after seeing a cable TV program at two o'clock in the morning about the Bahá'í teachings on racial unity, had called an 800 number for more information. Local Bahá'ís had given us a list of viewers who'd responded and had asked us to visit as many people on the list as we could find. We parked in front of a house that we supposed was Raymond's; we weren't sure because the address tacked on to the siding next to the front door appeared to be missing a number.

I studied the surroundings through the window of the van while Phyllis double-checked her information and gathered some literature to give Raymond. Like other homes in the neighborhood, Raymond's was a small, single-family dwelling that sat nestled under mature elm trees and that needed paint and roof repair. In the front yard was a lawnmower nearly hidden by overgrown grass. On the porch were several large cardboard boxes bulging with household items. I saw the curtains in the living room window part briefly and thought how conspicuous we must be. Two white people sitting in a big blue van, examining a street map and making notations on a clipboard probably made residents nervous.

We got out of the van and made our way up the crumbling sidewalk that led to the front door. I knocked. The curtain parted again, and I caught a glimpse of a young woman's face behind the window before the curtain was quickly drawn closed. We waited, and then I knocked again. Finally the door opened slowly. "Yes?" asked a young voice through the narrow opening.

"Hi," I said. "Is Raymond home?"

"Uh, I don't know," she answered.

"We're members of the Bahá'í Faith," I said. "Raymond called an 800 number and asked for some information; we brought some literature that we'd like to give him."

"Oh, uh, I'm his niece. I'll go see if he's home. Wait there, please."

After several minutes, a man stepped out onto the three-by-five slab of concrete that served as a porch, and closed the door behind him. He glanced at the clipboard in Phyllis's hand. "I'm Raymond. Can I help you?" he asked.

Raymond looked to be in his mid-forties. He was of average build and height. The expression on his face was a mixture of caution and weariness; he looked like he was ready to defend himself but hoped he didn't have to. I could only guess what kind of life experiences had prepared him to deal with two white people standing on his porch with a clipboard. Phyllis and I introduced ourselves, made reference to the cable TV show, and told Raymond that we had brought him some literature and would try to answer any questions he might have.

Raymond relaxed a bit. "Yeah, I remember seeing that on TV. I was impressed. People from all different backgrounds enjoying each other's company—you don't see that every day," he observed with a grin. We talked about the cable show, the principle of unity in diversity, and the possibility of a world without racism.

"Phyllis and I have been traveling around the United States," I said, "and our experience has convinced us that folks from all ethnic and cultural backgrounds hunger to connect with those from other groups. People are realizing that separation is a liability to our well-being and they're sick and tired of it."

Raymond nodded, clearly warming to the topic. As we continued talking, his muscles relaxed as if he had just taken a heavy load off his shoulders and set it down on the tiny porch. It seemed he no longer saw us as a threat, and an expression of receptivity replaced the suspicion I had first seen in his eyes. "I'd invite y'all inside," Raymond said, "but I'm moving, and the place is a mess. I haven't even had time to cut the grass, I've been so busy." He gestured at the lawn.

"I'm so glad I don't have to cut grass anymore!" I said. Phyllis explained to Raymond that we didn't have a lawn because we decided to travel across the United States in an RV. We shared stories about the places we'd been, the people we'd met, and the race unity workshop we'd developed. Raymond listened with great interest, asking questions and making a comment now and then.

"So what did y'all do before y'all started traveling?" he asked.

"Well, I worked twenty-five years as a graphic artist . . ." I began.

Raymond's eyes opened wide. "Just a minute!" he said excitedly. "I want to show y'all something. I'll be right back." He hurried into the house and returned shortly with three framed paintings. Raymond carefully lined up the paintings along the side of the house. When he was finished, he stepped back and smiled at us. "I painted those," he said.

I asked if I could pick one up to get a closer look. The style and technique were impressive. They were nature scenes; the one I was holding was a forest setting with a stream running through it. I assumed that Raymond had studied art. "Where did you go to school?" I asked.

"Oh, I didn't go to school," Raymond said. "I learned from a show on TV."

I was incredulous. I told Raymond how I respected not only his painting and composition skills but also his ability to elicit a feeling for the beauty of nature. I wanted to share my art with Raymond, but I didn't have any of my paintings to show him. Then I remembered our photo album.

"I'll be right back," I said and walked quickly to the van.

I returned to the porch with the album and flipped the pages to the nature shots I was most proud of, and I was gratified when Raymond showed his appreciation. We talked about art for a while, and then he turned his attention to the photos of people. Phyllis and I frequently pointed to one or another person and related the circumstances under which we had met him or her. We shared numerous stories, many of which had to do with overcoming our own racial conditioning.

After looking at our photos for a long time, Raymond closed the album and handed it back to me. He was silent for a moment, staring at the ground. "Can I share a couple of stories with you?" he asked, looking into our eyes for permission.

We listened quietly as Raymond shared some episodes from his life in which he had suffered racism. One took place when Raymond was a child; another when he was a teenager. The last incident he related had happened more recently. This is how I remember that story.

"I was driving home from work about three years ago," Raymond began. "I had just gotten off the night shift, so it was about one o'clock in the morning. I was coming down this street that was pretty dark—no streetlights. The street really needed repairs. All of a sudden I hit a huge pothole, and my car was thrown out of the lane I was in. The car swerved this way and that, until I finally got control of it again. I was just calming down when I saw the flashing lights of a police car behind me. I pulled over and parked on the side of the street. The police parked on the opposite side and shined a spotlight at my car. I had to look away, it was so bright. They stayed in the squad car for a long time. I waited. I knew better than to get out of my car.

"Finally, they walked across the street. Two white policemen. 'Get out of the car!' they yelled. When I opened the door, they yanked me out, turned me around and told me to put my hands up on the roof. The one guy kept banging my forehead into the top of the door opening, yelling, 'Keep your head down, N . . . !'

"One of them took me across the street, while the other guy searched my car. My forehead was bleeding. The blood was dripping down my face. I said, 'I haven't done anything! I just hit a pothole, that's all!'

"After a few minutes, the one searching my car finished and started walking across the street. He held up a plastic bag with white powder in it and said, 'Look what I found!'

"I panicked. 'Oh, no!' I yelled. 'You're not doing that to me! I don't use that stuff; take me in and test me. I don't have a record. I've never been arrested for anything! Check my record! My record's clean!' I made a real fuss, and finally they called in and checked my record.

"Then the two of them walked a little ways off to talk; I couldn't hear what they were saying. When they came back, the one with the bag of white stuff stuck it in his pocket. 'OK, get in the car,' he said. I had to leave my car on the side of the street, and they drove me to the police station.

"They booked me for reckless driving. I was outraged, and I proceeded to make a stink. One of the cops said, 'Watch yourself, now. We could make it a lot worse for you.' The night clerk was a black woman, and she was watching the whole thing. I asked her if I had any options, but she just shrugged her shoulders, said she wished she could help me, but there was nothing she could do. I spent the night in jail and had to go to court. That night in the jail cell was the worst night of my life. I had never even been in a police station. I felt like a caged animal."

Raymond paused and took a deep breath. "To this day, whenever I'm in traffic and I see a police car coming along from behind . . ."

He stopped and put his hand—the hand that so adeptly captured the beauty of nature—he put his artist's hand on his chest and continued, "my heart starts pounding so hard I can't stop it. I have to wait until I get home; then I sit quietly and do nothing for an hour or so until I calm down."

The three of us stood in silence on the little porch for several minutes, reflecting, absorbing the import of Raymond's experience. I kept seeing the image of my fellow artist's bleeding head, and hearing the powerlessness in his voice when he said, "I felt like a caged animal!" I felt his indignation.

We had been talking, laughing, and sharing for two and a half hours. I realized that I had changed in that short amount of time. Raymond's sensitivity, compassion, honesty, generosity, and pain were now in some measure part of me. It's not that I took something from him and that now he was missing pieces of himself. But rather that his expression of those character qualities quickened in me a desire to care. I could feel my own heart struggling to break free of its emotional restraints.

"How long y'all staying here?" Raymond asked.

"Only a few more days," Phyllis said. We chatted a while longer, and then Phyllis and I decided we should push on.

Raymond looked at us, his eyes bright. "Y'all take care of yourselves," he said, then stepped over and hugged me.

I thought, *This doesn't feel dangerous.*

Raymond hugged Phyllis, then stepped back and said, "Drive safely, now."

Phyllis and I walked back down the crumbling sidewalk to our van. Before we pulled away, we waved to Raymond standing on the porch waving at us. As we headed up the street, Phyllis put the map and the clipboard with the list of names away in a box between the seats. In a couple of days we would be leaving, and I wondered what my relationship with Raymond might have become if we'd stayed longer.

I envisioned us, fellow artists, sitting in his living room, each with a canvas propped up on an easel, pallet and brushes in hand, learning together from the master painter on TV. Maybe another time we would leave the city and head out into nature. We would sit on canvas folding chairs by a stream in the forest, watching the sun's golden light filter through the trees. Sketching and painting, both expressing our reverence for the Creation.

And now, years later, when I think about justice, I remember my brother artist. The gift he gave me on that spring afternoon has somehow permeated my heart and strengthened my resolve to strive to be just.

COMMENTARY

Over the years since meeting Raymond, I have told this story from memory, typed it up so I wouldn't forget it, and read it a number of times. It's been almost a decade now, and I'm immersed in the editing process and revising this account for inclusion in our book. I wasn't going to add a commentary because I felt I had adequately expressed my understanding of the experience and called attention to my insights. But there is a point that needs to be emphasized.

This is not just a narrative about a black man who can paint and suffered racial indignities. What grabs me every time I reread and relive this experience is Raymond's capacity to display an innate nobility. If my story hasn't made this point, then I don't think I can make it here. But if the reader has felt that nobility, then the purpose here is to give it a name so that it is more easily retained in the mind as well as in the heart.

I have related an incident about meeting a man who is unique. But I have seen nobility in the faces of too many black men to think that Raymond is the exception.

14

EVE'S LITTLE SERPENT

Phyllis, August 1999
A city in the South Central states

"I can't believe you're so racist!"

Long, long silence. *Huh? What?* Then out loud I said, "What?"

"I said I can't believe you're so racist. You, of all people! I mean, we were just talking about this stuff a few minutes ago. We were talking about this exact same stuff, and now you say something like that." He was speaking pretty calmly—sort of detached and bemused. But beneath the sound of his voice, I fancied I heard a kind of ripping noise, something being opened up.

Again, all that came to my mind was, "What?"

"That was so racist. Don't you see it? You didn't want to consider my suggestion because I'm black. You believe what those other people told you, even though it's exactly the same thing *I* told you, but you rejected *my* idea because I'm black."

Excuse me? Excuse ME? What the hell is he talking about? "What . . . what are you talking about?"

165

"Don't try to deny it. You know perfectly well what I'm talking about!" Now he was working up a steam, his calm demeanor beginning to unravel as he started pacing around the dining room.

"OK, just hang on a minute." *This is a test. This is most assuredly a test. Remember all those things you're always saying in your workshop. "If a person of color says you're being racist, you should throw him a party." Did I really say that? Please tell me I never said anything that dumb. What else have I said? "Be glad it's been brought to the conscious level, etc., etc., etc." Just breathe. Listen to what he's trying to say.*

"What are you trying to say?"

"I'm not *trying* to say anything! I *am* saying that you discounted my suggestion because I'm black. Stop pretending you don't understand what I'm talking about."

"Look, I'm not pretending. I don't get it."

"How could you not get it? We were just talking about this same dynamic a few minutes ago!" His voice got louder. I hoped his wife and daughter were sound sleepers.

"Don't get upset. Please." *Damn, that's not what I'm supposed to say. It's alright for him to be upset, remember?*

"Well I wasn't getting upset until you went into this *denial* thing. But now . . . Listen, why don't you just apologize, and let's get on with our planning. It's really late, and we've still got a lot of work to do here tonight."

"Apologize for *what*?"

"Don't do this to me, Phyllis." A warning. Said lovingly, like a parent, but a warning nonetheless.

"What? Don't do *what* to you?"

166

"Just admit it, and this will all be over. Just admit to me that you're still racist. Don't try to hide it—that's not like you." *How does he know what's like me and what isn't?*

"OK, I'm still racist."

"Now you're just saying that to placate me. That's condescending. How about some honesty?"

Dear Lord! What's going on here?

What was going on was a scene that felt like it belonged in the "practice scenarios" section of our race unity workshop manual. So I should have known what to do, given that I coauthored that manual. But I couldn't seem to make any sense out of what my friend was saying. For one thing, I was having a hard time breathing. I felt like I'd been sucker-punched, and I don't even know what that means. I'm a sucker; I've been punched. In the gut. The word "racist," though he had flung it without taking direct aim, had hit me just below my diaphragm. Hard to think when you're not getting enough air. I had no problem admitting that I've been programmed by racial conditioning. We all have. That's a given. But racist? The word is so . . . intentional. And for another thing, he *really* wasn't making any sense.

And this is what puzzled me the most, because Nathan was a very no-nonsense sort of guy. We hadn't known him long—just over two months—but we'd all felt an instant affinity. It seemed that we agreed on every topic we discussed. He'd been excited about the race unity classes that Gene and I were facilitating and had expressed the desire to collaborate with us. So when we'd been asked to return in a couple months to conduct a workshop, we knew right away that we wanted him to present one of the sessions. It was perfect; he was a powerful speaker, passionate and straightforward. Not only would an interracial team of facilitators be more effective, but the group would benefit greatly from Nathan's insights. We'd been anticipating spending time together preparing our materials.

That's how we'd come to be sitting around his dining room table on this particular night. Since morning, we had consulted, planned, and practiced our presentations. As part of our consultation, Nathan had shared some of his very personal experiences with racism. We were honored by his trust and conscious of our responsibility to meet it with absolute honesty. It was heartbreaking but confirming to hear the same stories from him that we'd heard from black friends around the country since beginning our race unity work. As with many of these friends, a point of considerable pain for Nathan was that frequently in a meeting, he would make a suggestion that was ignored by the group, only to have the same suggestion embraced later when it was offered by a white member. That was something I could empathize with. I knew that pain intimately, having worked for years in a company dominated by men. I also knew that if I had felt it a hundred times, he had felt it a thousand. And so why, how was it possible that this—of all things—was what he seemed to be accusing me of?

But that was his claim—that I had rejected a suggestion he'd made, then agreed with the same suggestion when it was made by a white person. White like me. Because he's black. Which would mean I think black folks are stupid. And that is racist. No doubt about that. Only there were a couple crucial pieces of information he was not taking into account.

The question on the table was whether we should use a particular handout in our workshop the following day. We all thought the information was valuable, but it was Nathan who felt most strongly that it should be presented in one of our sessions. My problem was that Gene and I had gotten the handout from an acquaintance, and we didn't know who created it. Because of this, I was not comfortable using it in public without permission. I stated my feelings clearly, and it was agreed that I would try to reach Jennifer, the woman who had given it to me, and track down the author. My second and bigger problem was that it was late at night, and Jennifer was not answering her phone. I called someone who was on a committee with her, but he didn't pick up either.

At that point we were all quite frustrated. My failure to reach someone was aggravated by the lateness of the hour and the fact that we still had so much to do for the next day. Nathan was particularly frustrated because he thought my concerns were unreasonable and that it was foolish for us to waste valuable time trying to get permission. He put forth his suggestion. *The* suggestion.

"Why don't we just restate it in our own words, and we'll use it that way. No one will mind. Then we can get on with our work here."

I was not at all happy with that suggestion. I knew I didn't want people using pieces of our workshop materials without permission, and I had no intention of doing it to someone else. I said so, forcibly.

"No way. Not gonna happen. I'll keep trying."

I called our daughter, who lived in the same community as our acquaintance; she knew lots of people and gave me several more phone numbers, one of which finally bore fruit. The lady who answered not only knew Jennifer well but also served with her on the task force that had printed the very handout that had caused all this trouble. My relief was enormous.

"So may we have permission to use this material in our workshop tomorrow?"

"Oh sure, no problem. We didn't write it. I'm not really sure where we got it; I think we took it from a book or something and just put it in our own words. Go ahead and use it however you want. You could just kind of restate it, you know, put it in your own words. No one will mind."

This is not an exaggeration or enhancement for the sake of a good story; this is what the lady said.

"Alright, it's a go!" I hung up the phone and rejoined my husband and my friend at the table.

"What did she say?" This was Gene asking. Nathan didn't really care.

"She said their group created the handout but that she didn't know the source of the material. She said we could just restate it in our own words."

"And you're OK with that?" This was Nathan speaking now. His voice was flat.

"Sure. They're the ones who printed it up, so her permission is good enough for me."

How is it I failed to see what was coming?

Suddenly Nathan cared; he cared passionately. He called me a racist.

Because it all seemed so absurd, it had taken me several minutes to realize what Nathan was talking about. He couldn't really think it made any sense. The reason I'd rejected his suggestion was obvious.

"But Nathan," I whined, "come on! Give me a break. I didn't give your suggestion any credibility because you had no authority.

You didn't write that thing. I didn't want *your* permission, I wanted theirs. *They* wrote it, you see?"

"Don't try to talk your way out of this." I couldn't believe he said that.

"You've got to be kidding."

"I'm dead serious. I said the exact same thing. *I* said we should rewrite the handout. You said no. Then *they* said we should rewrite the handout. You said thanks. I'm black; my opinion has no value to you."

But wait; there's more.

"But they're all black too!" I nearly shouted this, sure that it would solve everything. "All of them! Jennifer, the other committee member, in fact the woman I just talked to on the phone. She's black!!" I was practically dancing in my urgent desire to clear this up, to make it go away. *They're all black! They're all black!* I must have appeared insane. *Will this be on my life's review? When I get to heaven, will I have to watch a video recording of myself dancing around Nathan's dining room shouting "They're all black"? Good God, whatever made me think I wanted to do race unity work?*

"That's beside the point."

"It's *what?* How could that possibly be beside the point?"

"Listen, Phyllis. You and I both know what happened here; I don't know why you're being so stubborn about it."

"It's just not what you think," I persisted. *I'm pretty sure I do know what's happening here. This is really about that little snake, isn't it—the one that's in every white guy. The one that will rear its ugly head and sink its fangs in you if you're black and careless enough to trust that this time you won't get hurt. I've heard about that snake, the symbol of betrayal. You've been bitten, my friend, bitten so often that you're just waiting for it, bitten so many times that you can't conceive of a white guy—or a white girl—who is snake-free.*

Filled with confidence in the accuracy of my analysis, I said again, "It's just really not what you think."

"Then you're in denial." Such a dreadful word.

"I'm *not* in denial!"

"You're in denial because you think you know what happened, but you don't. In fact, I know you better than you know your own self."

Long, long silence. Longer than the first time. Gene, who'd been watching our exchange without comment, seemed to realize that anything he said would only make things worse. Besides, he knew enough to let me fight my own battles.

I want to tell you that up to this point, I was still in control of my own mind. True, I was upset, but I was lucid. Then the words were spoken that changed this from a story about Nathan's inability to get past his pain to a story about me and my struggle to become a more authentic human being. "I know you better than you know your own self," he had said. And bam! I was hooked.

I am not a fragile person. I have opinions and feelings, and I can express them powerfully. I know who I am, what I think, and how to take care of myself in most situations. But I have acquired these strengths only after a lot of work. I was raised by a father who loved me and who evidently thought it was his job to keep me from getting too cocky. His method for making me humble was to tell me, over and over, in all kinds of situations, that he knew me better than I knew my own self. He claimed to know what I was thinking, what I was feeling, and what my motives were—as if he were psychic and could see right into my mind. It was a subtle but effective form of disempowerment, and it enraged me. It reduced me to tears or goaded me to screaming, every single time.

So when Nathan spoke those words, I checked out. Inside, I became maybe twelve years old, and my choices were limited to screaming, crying, or withdrawing. I stayed there physically, continued to participate at a minimal level, but emotionally I was gone. And oddly, although I remember everything else about that evening with such clarity, I cannot remember what was said at that point. Maybe Nathan interpreted my silence as acquiescence, or maybe he realized I'd had enough; I don't know. In any case, we finished our preparations around midnight and finally went upstairs to bed.

The bed Gene and I went to was king-sized with a comfy mattress in a large, beautifully decorated guest room. Gene was exhausted from our long day of work and fell asleep quickly. He was unaware of the intensity of my emotions, and I chose not to burden him with my private demons. Besides, one of us had to be coherent the next day. So I kept my struggle to myself and lay awake all night trying to sort things out.

Now I've used the expression "I lay awake all night" figuratively in the past to mean that my sleep was fitful or troubled. This time, however, it's meant to be taken literally. I was awake all night. The birds were well into their songs when I finally closed my eyes for a little sleep before the alarm went off.

In the hours before I slept, though, a great purging took place. I tried to lie still so I wouldn't wake Gene, but my insides contorted with the effort. I did all my weeping and hollering in imaginary scenarios, blasted Nathan with my feelings about his absurd opinions, dumped enough righteous indignation to bury the falsest of accusa-tions. How dare he call me racist? I had worked so hard to become sensitive; I was making such an effort; I was trustworthy; I was ac-countable; I was . . . finally spent. Which emptied out some space for reflection. *Let's look at the facts. I'm way more angry about his claim to know me than about his accusation of racism. I'm clear where that anger comes from, and it has nothing to do with race. I can set that aside and focus on my relationship with Nathan.*

Now I was getting some clarity. *What do I propose over and over as the solution to separation, prejudice, injustice? Relationship. Connection. So even if I am right, and he is wrong, and all my feelings are justified, is it possible the relationship is more important than proving my point? Even if his reaction was not about me at all but about his own stereotypes of white people, can I forgive that? Do I not want to be forgiven for my own screw-ups? While defending my integrity seems essential, is there something else that's of higher value?* The purging had taken most of the night; the realization came to me in the last few minutes, just before I fell asleep. *The relationship is the highest value. And today, at this moment, I am capable of letting go of my hurt feelings and my need to be heard, my need to be believed and validated. My need to be right. I can do this.*

Just a couple of hours later, I headed back downstairs to the room where it all began. Nathan's cheery voice met us before my feet touched the bottom step.

"Good morning, Sleepyheads! Did you sleep OK?"

I was quiet. I was really tired.

Gene said, "Yeah, man. Comfortable bed!"

"I'm makin' eggs for breakfast. You guys like eggs? I make some pretty good scrambled eggs."

"Yeah, thanks. Eggs are great."

"Bacon? It's turkey bacon. You like it chewy or crispy? Coffee's done; help yourself."

Nathan had been up for a while, making sure everything would be ready for us when we came down. The table was set, the juice had been poured, and slices of bread were sitting in the toaster, waiting for the right moment to be pushed down so they would pop up just when the eggs were finished. Nathan's wife and daughter were awake too, and we sat down together to enjoy a nourishing breakfast prepared by loving hands.

I'd assumed there would be lingering bad feelings in the morning, and Nathan's good spirits left me doubting my memory. Had I in my sleepiness and anger created high drama out of a simple expression of frustration? For a moment, I considered just dropping the whole thing, but some insistent part of me needed the resolution I would feel only if I followed through with my intention. When he got up to take some dishes to the sink, I stepped into his path.

"Nathan, I want to tell you something." I took my time; it was important to say exactly what I meant to say. "I want to thank you for trusting me enough to be honest last night, for taking the risk of speaking your feelings like that. And I want to thank you for giving me a lot to think about."

"You're welcome! You are very welcome!" As he spoke, he hugged me tightly with one arm while in his other hand he balanced the stack of plates he'd cleared from the table. "That's what I love about you so much, Phyllis—your willingness to grow and learn something new about yourself."

I'll take that. If I can just keep doing that, I'll be alright.

COMMENTARY

In case you're wondering, our workshop the following day was a great success, in spite of my sleep-deprived state. And Nathan and his family are still our dearly loved friends. We've never talked about that night; he may not even remember it. If he does, his memory of what happened is probably quite different than mine. But that's OK, because what happened in the dining room is not the point of this story. What happened in the guest room is, and it was my own private struggle.

Before I talk about that struggle, though, I want to say something about conditioning. It's not inherently a bad thing; it's just a type of training, and whether the results are good or bad depends on what we're being trained for. We can be conditioned to perform well in a marathon and to have nice table manners. Or we can be conditioned to eat a snack every time we sit down in front of the television. The first—and thankfully only—time I was bitten by fire ants, I became so anxious that for an entire summer I was afraid to walk through tall grass. A long time ago, maybe twenty-five years, I was involved in a car accident. I entered an intersection, and a driver approaching from the right ran a red light and hit me broadside. She was going about sixty miles per hour. Amazingly, neither I nor the people in the other car were seriously injured, but my car was totaled. Now, a quarter-century later, when I'm driving and a car appears suddenly from the right, I flinch and feel a painful sensation of adrenaline shooting through my body. This never happens when a car approaches suddenly from the left—only from the right. There is a cellular memory at work here, preparing me for an impact on my right side.

I think the memory of emotional pain, especially pain that has been inflicted over and over, has the same function. It sends surging through the body, mind, and heart a substance whose purpose is protection—a shoring up of the natural defense systems a human being inherently possesses. It puts a person in a state where he's expecting to be hurt and preparing himself for the strike. It's a natural human process, and it's difficult for someone who's been hurt repeatedly to unlearn that conditioning. All too often, the process just continues functioning as it was designed to. In this state of preparedness, the person is easily triggered by words or actions that would otherwise seem insignificant; the reaction may seem irrational or "oversensitive" to others, but to the one who's been triggered, it makes perfect sense.

Intentional racial conditioning is a malicious form of brainwashing; it is specifically designed to create expectations about people based on their skin color. Ever since the first African slaves were brought here, our institutions have methodically used racial stereotypes to manipulate our attitudes, stirring up fear and hatred to achieve their own ends. All of us in this country have been subjected to intentional racial conditioning; its pernicious effects dictate the way we relate to each other. When that racial conditioning and a person's natural defense system work together, the result is often anger, separation, and feelings of betrayal.

But while these explanations might apply to Nathan's behavior, as I said before, that's not what I want to focus on with this story. It's not my responsibility to fix his attitude, nor should I have any stake in whether or not *he* fixes his attitude. Besides, there's always the possibility that he was right about my denial and that there's still something I'm not seeing about my behavior that night. Either way, I've got my hands full dealing with my own conditioning. My responsibility is to make a choice about my behavior, to assess at any given moment what is the higher value, and then to be willing and capable of sacrificing the lesser value—in this case my righteous indignation, my understanding of justice, my "right" to be heard and believed—for the greater value, which is the relationship. This process requires me to exercise forgiveness and to detach from my own triggers. And that is extremely difficult for me. Because of my history with my father, the feeling that I've been unjustly accused is an inevitable hook.

In order to make an authentic choice in my conflict with Nathan, I needed clarity about my goal, freedom from any habits of thought that might prevent me from assessing the situation accurately, the motivation to sacrifice, and the ability to compare relative values. This last piece often requires that I consult a standard outside myself for help with identifying any inauthentic priorities. When I turned to my source of inspiration, the teachings of the Bahá'í Faith, I found that help. My internal dialogue sounded something like this:

What is it that I need to do first? "Let the white make a supreme effort . . . to master their impatience of any lack of responsiveness on the part of a people who have received, for so long a period, such grievous and slow-healing wounds."[1] OK, that's pretty clear. I need to be patient with him. What's next? "Let not your heart be offended with anyone. If someone commits an error and wrong toward you, you must instantly forgive him."[2] That's not so easy;

forgiveness means to cease to feel resentful, and I'm not sure I can let that go. Especially when I *know* I was right. "Blessed are they who are the means of making unity among the friends, and pity on those who *in the right or wrong* [emphasis added] are the cause of discord."[3] I prefer not to be in the category of those who need pity; I would much rather be blessed. And what was the higher priority again? "We declare that love is the cause of the existence of all phenomena and that the absence of love is the cause of disintegration or nonexistence."[4] No ambiguity there!

So my final question was: Can I love not only Nathan but also myself and my Creator enough to let this go? When I heard my own answer, I was finally able to sleep.

How do we do this consistently? I mean actually, keeping it real, on a normal day when we may not be feeling noble or virtuous in any way—how do we pull this off? It's such a difficult thing, this tug of war between what I know is authentic and what I think will make me feel good. On the long night of no sleep, I had to help it along a little. Once the priority was clear, that little voice kept wheedling at me—*but that was so unjust what he said, so unfair!* So I reminded the voice that if I make a decision based on my understanding of the highest value, and if I then choose to sacrifice something of lesser value, and (here's the hard part) *if* I'm truly detached and not resentful, then it is a manifestation of justice. Isn't that what I wanted?

I'd like to be clear that I'm not proposing, with any of these stories, a permanent solution that should be applied in every case. The task of building unity has a slippery element to it; what works this time might not work the next time. Each situation will require its own assessment, and while I believe that unity is always the highest priority, what that entails and what has to be sacrificed to promote it will be different each time.

I've related this story not because I feel I deserve any gold stars for my success in overcoming my own pain and anger. If that were my reason, then to be completely fair I would have to tell hundreds of stories about the times I was not successful. I share this account of my experience with Nathan to show you my personal struggle with the process and how it works—when it works. Will I be able to pull this off every time? Certainly not; I'm nowhere near that spiritually evolved. But as a work in progress, I know that it can happen with increasing frequency.

A final word about that little snake. The snake can be a symbol of evil and betrayal, or it can symbolize rebirth and transformation. Maybe it's the second one we should be looking for in each other. Unhealthy conditioning is like a skin that restricts our growth, both individually and collectively. Can we split it open, step out of it, and leave it behind to become something transformed? Will that not then allow us the freedom and the space to grow into the skin that God created for us? Just imagine how it would be if that's what we anticipated when we looked at each other.

15

ELECTRIC FLY

Gene, December 2000
California

Ragtime, Dixieland, The Blues, R&B, Funk, Jazz—a legacy rooted in the creativity of African-American composers and musicians. I have listened to the truth from all of these since I was a child. Who I am—a white American man—has been shaped to some extent by the music of black Americans.

Before we started traveling, I had often felt as if I were looking at the black community as a spectator. Even though my mind had been filled with negative and frightening images of African-Americans, somehow I was still able, in spite of that conditioning, to perceive qualities that attracted me. I found myself observing a lifestyle full of artistic creativity and other cultural contributions I hold in high regard—and yet, because of racial separation, they were accessible only secondhand through TV, movies, and music recordings.

When I attended a black church for the first time in 1998, I was all too aware that I would no longer be a bystander on the outside but rather a visitor on the inside being observed. Some white folks believe that if the playing field is leveled and black people acquire more social and political influence, they will do to whites what we have done to them. I wondered how they would treat me—a white man in their midst. "The Man." Would I stick out as an icon of white supremacy, a reminder of all they and their ancestors had suffered at the hands of people who looked like me? Would they be inclined to teach me a lesson?

As we entered the AME Church in South Carolina, I noticed that Dr. Martin Luther King Jr.'s statement—that eleven o'clock on Sunday morning is the most segregated hour in this nation—still appeared to be true some thirty years later. Phyllis and I were the only whites in the church. Heads turned. A man walked quickly over to us.

"Can I help you?" he asked.

Maybe he thought we were lost or that we had not noticed the "A" for African in "AME" on the sign outside.

We told him we had been invited by an acquaintance.

"Oh, well, welcome. Follow me, please. There's seating over here."

Our acquaintance sat in front with other church leaders. When he saw us, he rushed over, embraced us, then returned to his seat just as the service was beginning. A man stood up and asked if there were any guests visiting for the first time.

Again heads turned in our direction; we stood up and introduced ourselves.

"Welcome," he said. "We're blessed to have you here with us today."

The church members were then asked to extend a warm greeting to someone sitting nearby, and hands reached out to us from all directions. A few more items on the program were attended to, then the minister stepped up to the pulpit to deliver his sermon.

Although we had been warmly received, I was still a bit nervous, and I wondered what would be expected of me. My experience with the black church was limited to watching African-American ministers and gospel choirs on television. The hard wooden pew was a stark reminder that I was not nestled in the comfort of my recliner at home, remote control in hand, passively watching a screenplay unfold. I was touching, breathing, hearing, and seeing real life. Waves of heat radiated from bodies around me and carried a mixture of perfume and aftershave into my nostrils. The minister's voice filled the church. The rhythm of a piano and bass guitar combined with the harmony of the choir to quicken in me unfamiliar emotions. Everyone around us responded to the minister and choir on cue. People were moving! Sitting and rocking. Standing and swaying. They did a two-step, while simultaneously clapping and singing, which I couldn't quite manage. I heard expressions of "Amen!" during the sermon. "That's right!" Hands reached heavenwards. "Yes, Lord! Oh, yes, Jesus!" Young and old, everyone was involved. I did my best to respond to the spirit of it all, wondering what impression I made on those who might be watching me.

After the benediction, Phyllis and I stood up and moved toward the exit with the rest of the congregation. Many church members pressed forward to shake our hands or clap us on the shoulder and to tell us they were glad we had visited them. The minister stood at the front door greeting people as they left, and when we introduced ourselves, he invited us to come back.

Outside, we waited in the parking lot for our acquaintance. After quite a while, he finally appeared with another member of the church. Both men, we learned, were active not only in the church but in the community as well. Here we were, two white northern suburbanites and two black leaders in a small rural South Carolina town. What did we have to talk about? Four hours later we parted, and I felt I had two new friends.

In other communities across the country, we met African-Americans who invited us to church services where we always felt welcome. People made efforts to ensure our comfort in an environment they knew was different and challenging for us. In Tennessee, when we entered a black Baptist Church, we were greeted by the minister, who felt it necessary to caution us, "It's gonna get loud in here." We assured him that was OK by us. And it got loud!

In California we met Don and Linda, members of a gospel choir that performed at a Bahá'í center on Martin Luther King Day. Phyllis was moved by the way Linda directed the choir and introduced herself after the celebration. The next evening the four of us went out to dinner, and when we parted several hours later, we were excited about the potential of our new friendship. "I feel like we've known you guys for years," Don said.

Phyllis and I sang with Linda's choir, attended their church services, and went to Bible study classes. As our friendship developed, we went on shopping trips and met their kids and grandkids; they, in turn, met members of our family. Before we left California, we got together for dinner and talked about activities we could do during our next visit.

About a year and a half later, we were in Tennessee and were just finishing breakfast when Phyllis's phone rang.

"Of course. Of course, we would be delighted. Just a second; I'll tell Gene." Phyllis turned to me. "It's Linda. She and Don are renewing their vows, and they want us to be in the wedding."

"Cool!" I said.

While the two women discussed details about the date, a rented tux for me, and Phyllis's bridesmaid dress and shoes, my mind wandered. I envisioned Phyllis and me dressed up in wedding finery, hanging out with the folks we had met in the church. *We will probably be the only whites.* I got a little heady; I felt privileged. *After all, how many white folks do I know who have been part of a black wedding? In a black church. Where everyone else is black. Socializing after the ceremony and—uh oh!* I hadn't thought about the dancing. *Good grief! What am I going to do? I can't dance. Now I'm not so sure I want to be in the wedding. I'm doomed. I am going to look so bad. Everyone at the reception is going to laugh at me.*

"Phyllis. Let me talk to Don when you're finished with Linda."

A few minutes later she handed me the phone.

"Hey, Don! How ya doin'? Hey, thanks for including us in your wedding. I'm really looking forward to it. Say, by the way. Uh, at the reception? Uh, there'll be (gulp) dancing, right?"

"Oh, yes, my friend, we're gonna have some fun."

"Uh, what kind of dancing?"

"We'll definitely be doing the electric fly."

"Oh, great, cool. OK, man. Take care. We'll see you when we get out there."

When I put down the phone, I was hyperventilating.

"What's wrong with you?" Phyllis asked.

"There's going to be dancing. At the reception."

"Of course. That's just part of a wedding. Are you worried?"

"I'm terrified. You know I can't dance."

"Well, you don't have to dance. Nobody's going to mind if you don't."

"No. I've got to. How will that look, the only white guy, and I'm not dancing? And Don said they're going to be doing the electric fly."

"What's that?"

"No idea. Some kind of dance, I guess."

"Maybe we can find a video that teaches it."

The next day we went to one video store after another looking for a recording of dance lessons.

"We're looking for a dance instruction video that includes the electric fly. Do you think you might have one?"

"The electric fly. Hmmm, let me see." The clerk checked the inventory. "No, I'm sorry. Nothing. Have you tried the video store on the other side of town?"

At the last store we checked out, the clerk said, "The electric fly? Are you sure you don't mean the Electric Slide?"[1]

Phyllis and I looked at each other. "Maybe," we said.

The store had one video that included, among various dance steps, the Electric Slide. We were saved, or so we thought.

Back home in our tiny trailer, we put the videotape into our 13" TV/VCR that sat on a corner cabinet just inside the door. We had about three square feet of floor surface on which to practice. The Electric Slide, we quickly learned, involves a lot of movement, side to side, front to back, and an energetic kick and spin so one is facing a different direction. While we bumped into each other and sent household items flying, Phyllis encouraged me to move my hips more. "You're just moving your shoulders, and your neck is sticking out like this . . ." She flexed her shoulder muscles like a wrestler and stuck out her chin to demonstrate, for my benefit, just how hopelessly uncool I looked.

An RV is a vehicle on wheels and springs. Every time we attempted a dance move and stopped, the trailer continued to bounce. What might our fellow campers think was happening inside? Neither Phyllis's enthusiasm nor my fear of ridicule could sustain our effort to learn the Electric Slide under those conditions. And we could not bring ourselves to practice in any of our friends' family rooms. There had to be another solution.

On our way west, we stopped to visit family in Arizona. One afternoon while Phyllis was shopping, she discovered a dance studio that advertised three lessons for twenty-five dollars.

"What do you think? It's not that much money. Should we do it?" she asked.

"Yes!" I said.

When we entered the dance studio, we told the woman at the reception desk that we were visiting in the area and were only interested in the three-for-twenty-five-dollars deal. "We just want to learn how to do the Electric Slide."

"You're in luck. We have a dance instructor who is an expert at that. I'll go see if he's available." She returned in a few minutes accompanied by a young African-American man. "This is Gerard. He'll be your teacher for the three sessions."

Phyllis explained to Gerard that our friends were renewing their wedding vows, we guessed we would be the only white people, and we didn't want to stick out too much, especially when the dancing started at the reception. "They're going to be doing the Electric Slide."

Gerard looked from Phyllis to me and then back to Phyllis. "You're in big trouble. But don't worry; I'll take care of you. Let's get started."

During our three one-hour sessions, Gerard's encouragement was unflagging. "Looking good, Phyllis. Great movement. You're a natural. Gene, loosen up in the shoulders, man. Get those hips moving. That's right." When he finished with us, we were ready. During the remaining time until the wedding, we practiced diligently. Finally, the day arrived.

At the church, the bridesmaids filed in and lined up near the altar. I scanned the row of women from left to right. They were stunning. The various shades of brown skin tone in contrast to the light colored dresses they wore created a rhythmic effect, as if one were looking at a human representation of a musical score. Dark, medium, darker, lighter, medium . . . .whoa! What's that? Oh, yeah. Phyllis.

My rented tux was too large and hung loosely on me. But our friends looked happy, and the ceremony was beautiful. Still, I was glad to get out of the tux and put on my own clothes that fit.

On the drive to the reception, the good feeling I had from the wedding faded as I began to obsess over dancing. By the time we arrived, I had lost my nerve and was quiet during dinner. Apparently Gerard hadn't imbued me with a permanent positive mental attitude.

After dinner the tables were cleared, the music started, and people wandered over to the dance floor. I was watching the other guests moving with grace and dexterity and wondered how I could possibly leave the security of my chair and join them, when I heard the beginning notes of the music we used when we learned the Electric Slide. I looked at Phyllis.

"Whatever you want to do," she said.

"Well, we did shell out twenty-five dollars. Let's go."

On the dance floor, we lined up with the others and, after a brief adjustment to the novelty of the situation, we were doing the Electric Slide! It was such a relief—like being back in the dance class—but this was the real deal. We danced for three or four more songs, and I did the two-step I had observed so often in church. It seemed good enough. I didn't care. I was having fun. As we stepped off the dance floor, one of the men we knew from church walked over to Phyllis and said, "I saw you up there. You're one of us now!"

Long after the wedding, whenever we visited Don and Linda's church, people would walk up to us, point and say, "I know you. You were in the wedding." And, to this day, I love to dance. Funk is my favorite genre. I do my modified two-step I learned in church; it works just fine. I can even get my hips moving.

COMMENTARY

I love music. It created a cherished bond with both of my parents. Mom loved ragtime and jazz standards, and Dad loved classical music, especially opera. I grew up appreciating all types of music. What was missing, however, was moving and dancing to the music I loved, with one exception—the polka. Although in this story I lamented my inability to dance, there is actually one dance I do well. I can polka. I learned as a child when we took our annual vacation in northern Wisconsin.

The big event up there was the weekend dance that attracted folks from the community and the surrounding farms. On the night of the dance, we took the main highway out of town and drove for miles before turning off onto a smaller road that led into the woods. I remember the excitement of driving through the darkness, anticipating what lay ahead. Soon we saw the glow of yellow light filtering through the trees, and finally the dance hall—a big, white, rectangular building with people from the area streaming in the front door to literally kick up their heels and have a good time.

The interior was a large space set up for one purpose only—dancing. The room was arranged with the band at one end, refreshments at the other, and folding chairs lining the walls between. Everything else was dance floor. The music started, and in short order, almost everyone was bouncing up and down, 1-2-3, 1-2-3. I felt the beat, and my parents encouraged me to try. The music made my muscles itch, and the only relief was to dance until I was exhausted.

Had I grown up in Germany fifty years earlier, I would have been considered a good dancer. I can just see myself as a young man, bopping up and down on the dance floor with my rosy-cheeked girlfriend, losing control to the wild beat of a polka. In that era, I would have learned a trade and practiced it all my life, maybe the work my father and his father had done. I would also have remained in the same village, probably in the house my family had lived in for generations, and I would have adhered to social customs that today would be considered rigid and old-fashioned.

More than likely my grandparents held on to remnants of their former lives even while establishing new habits as American citizens. But my parents were born here, and it seemed the old ways held less importance for them as they worked to attain the "dream." For me, the old world was alien. Bratwurst and sauerkraut were already part of Americana. The polka and traditional German songs, still enjoyed at family celebrations, had been the only vestiges of a distant origin that still elicited a feeling of belonging to something not strictly American.

Now, as adults, we don't sing the songs anymore. I feel a bit of a loss—more than missing a certain kind of food and entertainment; maybe the loss has something to do with the vanishing of an ancestral sense of community, bonding with others who share similar physical characteristics and cultural traditions including language, humor, and of course music and dance. I remember the pride I felt as a youngster when I thought, "That's the way we Germans are. That's the way we do it." But a commitment to preserving the German way of life seems to have passed with the elders, and it doesn't evoke the same charm for me now as an adult. I am an American.

By the time the United States reached its bicentennial, it had already attracted people from many countries—a trend that has since resulted in the representation of probably every nation on earth. This diversification, according to the Bahá'í writings, is part of a larger global process in which the United States has been given a special task: to demonstrate to the rest of the world that it is possible to create a just social system with the strength to unify the disparate groups of humanity.

Yet the goal of achieving a cultural mixture—where diverse traits associated with ethnicity and national identity are blended into one integrated whole—presents challenges. As this blending process unfolds, customs and traditions we have held dear for generations might seem to be slipping through our fingers. Many of us who are white wish we lived in an earlier historical period because it seems that in the past, those customs and traditions were still intact and provided a sense of stability.

What is the American way of life? Who is an American? The global migration of people from place to place has radically impacted national identities across the world. "American" does not elicit the image of someone with particular physical characteristics and cultural habits. The people we meet in our travels usually understand that our country represents all the citizens of the world. They are proud of this fact yet concerned about the repercussions. They ask, "If this continues, will we have to give up our language? If my child marries someone of a different race, what difficulties will my grandchildren face? How will we reconcile the differences that have historically separated us and caused friction?" Blending our differences into one harmonious entity seems to be one of the greatest challenges facing us today.

Belonging is a basic human need; group membership helps us understand who we are. But because of the universal process that is reshaping societies around the globe, we have to redefine what it means to "belong." Today it means being connected with people who are different and not only with people who are just like us. My loss of a German identity is compensated for by the benefits of belonging to a bigger group—the human family.

In this story, I was so eager to fit in that I learned the Electric Slide. Folks at the wedding reception appreciated my effort and welcomed me. But I wasn't expected to act black, walk a certain way, dress differently, alter my speech, or shake hands in an unfamiliar way. And while I, a white man, was being accepted, I knew that all too often the acceptance is withheld when the tables are turned. Today if any group is made to feel it doesn't belong, we have failed.

16

THE MOOR
AND THE MINSTREL

Phyllis, December 1999
Arizona

During the year before my father died, he began a gradual process of sharing parts of his life story that he'd kept secret, at least from me. The first of these revelations happened before he found out he was sick, although it's likely that the disease was already present in his body; maybe on a subconscious level he knew.

On this particular day, my parents and I went to pay our respects at the grave of Dad's sister Peggy; she was his only sibling and had passed away several years before. On the way, we picked up Peggy's husband, returning to his house for coffee after our visit to the cemetery. As we were getting ready to leave, my uncle said to Dad, "Wait, Lou. Before you go, there's something I'd like for you to take. Peggy had all these boxes of old photos, and I just haven't had the energy to look through them. I'm sure they're pictures of your family; you should have them."

So we hauled several large, dusty boxes out to the car. Later that evening, after dinner and a round of cards, Dad dragged them all into the living room, vacuumed off the dust, and began looking through the photographs. Apparently in some continuation of a past sibling rivalry, Peggy had acquired the pictures long ago and had kept them to herself. At this very late point in his life, my father was seeing some of them for the first time. There were newspaper clippings of his parents' wedding and his dad's funeral, and a print of his paternal grandmother that he'd never seen before. His voice was soft with nostalgia as he sorted through the memorabilia, sharing scraps of his past that I—at this late point in my own life—was hearing for the first time.

I was most interested in the photos of his father. I'd been very close to my grandmother growing up; she had lived to see the birth of our first child and had been a source of encouragement and spiritual insight for me throughout her life. But her husband had died when my dad was only fifteen, and I'd heard very few stories about him. So now I listened closely for clues about this mysterious man that had departed this world long before I was born. As a firm believer in knowing one's roots, I hoped to learn more about myself by understanding something about how my dad had been raised.

"My father was an entertainer, you know."

"No, I didn't know that! An entertainer? What did he do?"

"Oh, he used to sing and dance. He was a performer."

"Where did he perform?"

"I don't remember exactly. Just around. I used to go watch him sometimes." He kept sorting through the photos as he talked. I was fascinated. I'd had no idea Grandpa was musical. He'd passed only a part of that on to his son, who loved to entertain us but always sang off-key.

"He did those minstrel shows, you know?"

"Minstrel shows?"

"Yeah. He'd make his face black and then dance and sing those . . . you know, those songs."

"Blackface? Your father performed in blackface?"

"Yeah. I went and saw him once."

"You mean your father—*my* grandfather—danced in minstrel shows in blackface?"

"Sure. That's what folks did back then. That was their entertainment."

Oh-so-casually he dropped this bomb; it exploded so quietly, in fact, that my mom, sitting just across the room, didn't even hear it go off. I think all the noise was contained inside my head. White guilt—that vague sort of theoretical concept—suddenly took on a very personal face.

Scrambling frantically through my mind for some thread of redemption, I finally came up with a memory that just might wipe this stain from my image. Years earlier I had discovered another family secret. This one had been hidden not by a person, but rather by the passage of time . . .

"Oh, that doesn't look good."

Terrifying words, coming as they did from the mouth of my dermatologist, who was examining a black mark on my body. She peered at it for a few more seconds from different angles, first close-up, then further away, finally scraping at it a little with a shiny, sharp instrument.

"That looks dangerous," she said. She seemed to be avoiding my eyes.

I was lying on my back on the examining table, lifting my head off the hard cylinder that posed as a pillow so I could watch my doctor's expression. Beyond my foot, past the quarter-inch wide black stripe that ran the length of my toenail, I could see her head shaking slowly back and forth worriedly. Having ascertained everything she could from her inspection, she finally stood straight and looked me squarely and bravely in the eye.

"No, I don't like the looks of that at all. I'm going to send you to a specialist in the city."

And the next day I was on the crowded expressway, heading into Chicago for an appointment with a dermatological specialist at a prestigious university hospital.

When you grow up in a suburb, there's something magical about "going downtown" as we used to call it. There were school field trips that got us out of class for the entire day and family outings in summer to visit the museums, aquarium, and planetarium. It was always great fun. My Aunt Peggy (yes, the same one who would later squirrel away my dad's photos) worked as a secretary in the city and loved going in on the weekends. In December we would take the bus downtown to look at Christmas lights and window decorations. Once when I was eight, we made the mistake of sitting all the way in back for the hour-long trip; between the bouncing and the cigar smoke from the man in front of us, I got quite sick and threw up all over myself, much to the dismay of my aunt and everyone else on the bus. My clothes were unsalvageable, so the first order of business on our arrival was to buy me a new dress at the huge Marshal Fields store on State Street. I wanted to linger in front of the giant Christmas tree and begged for a photo of me on Santa's lap, but for some reason my aunt was in a huge hurry to get me into that new dress.

It was what we used to call a sailor dress; it had a blue and white striped skirt and a navy blue top, a square collar with white piping, two rows of brass buttons down the front, and a bright red neckerchief that had to be tied with a special kind of knot—a sailor's knot—which my mom (probably a sailor's wife in some other incarnation) executed perfectly each time. How I loved that dress! I wore it long after it should have been handed down to my sister, the waistband riding just below my armpits and the white piping around the edges of the sleeves squeezing my pudgy arms. Throwing up on a bus was a small price to pay for a dress like that.

On this trip, driving by myself into the city, I was just as nauseous as I'd been on the day of the sailor dress, and it required some effort to keep my lunch down. I'm fairly brave when it comes to disease; I subscribe to an odd combination of fatalism and eternal optimism, which normally leaves me confident that whatever will be will be, and whatever does happen will surely turn out just fine in the end. But this scared me.

I'd never heard of cancer of the big toe—if that was in fact what I had. Nor did I know what might be involved in its treatment, but I knew it couldn't be good. Or maybe it wasn't cancer; maybe it was the beginning of gangrene, a delayed result of toes frostbitten in childhood, possibly requiring amputation. One of my imagined scenarios involved removal of the toenail in a hopefully anesthetized version of a Chicago mafia boss trying to extract a confession from a traitor. My metabolism is normally extremely slow, my resting heart rate so low that I once set off a warning alarm during a routine EKG. Now my heart banged rapidly in my chest, making it nearly impossible to consult the map and navigate heavy freeway traffic at the same time.

Somehow I made it to the medical building, found a parking spot near the entrance, and rode the elevator to the doctor's office. The big-city dermatologist was a fatherly figure, concerned and reassuring yet confident and professional. He did not ask me to take off my shoe and sock, but removed them gently himself. He leaned down and took a long, close look at my toe, then sat up straight and laughed. This distinguished doctor in the very diverse city of Chicago, whose patients included people from every conceivable background, was for some unfathomable reason amused.

"Why that's nothing to worry about, Sweetheart," he said in his most fatherly voice. "I see this all the time in my African-American patients. That's just your African heritage coming out."

"My *what*?"

"Your African blood."

"*I* have African blood?"

"Well, we all do really, but yours is just a little more recent" (than other white folks', I assumed he meant). "You see, there are small deposits of pigmentation—melanin—that sometimes accumulate at the base of the toenail. Then as the nail grows, it drags a black stripe along with it. It's common in people of African descent. You're fine. Don't be alarmed."

"Oh, I'm not alarmed." *I'm amazed! I'm ecstatic! I'm . . . African!!*

My relief was great, but my curiosity was even greater; the first thing I did when I got back home was call my mom, the family genealogist. While I waited for her to answer, I kept thinking of all the photos I'd seen, even back to my great-great-grandparents—pictures of recent immigrants from Denmark and Germany, and the English and Scottish ancestors that had been in this country for several generations. Where, in all this Northern European mix, had there been an African?

After consulting the family tree and adding a great deal of speculation, Mom and I decided that the most likely link was my dad's maternal grandfather. He'd been born in Germany (and according to family lore was Kaiser Wilhelm's personal barber at one time), but my grandmother said his family had come from Spain during the Inquisition. Spain—home of the Moors for hundreds of years! When he came to the United States in 1893, was my great-grandfather carrying African blood in his veins?

The theory gained credibility when my mother told me about the castle. Long ago—when I'd been too young to have any say in the matter—Grandma had received an official-looking letter from an embassy or government agency in Spain. According to this letter there was an unclaimed estate, and its ownership had been traced to her deceased father. The stipulation however was that she must come to Spain and claim her manor—or castle, or whatever it was—in person. If she failed to do so, the property would revert to the State.

And evidently Grandma had no desire to own a castle in Spain or even to fly over for a look, so that was the end of it. The letter was eventually lost, along with any hope of easily tracing my heritage.

But I didn't mind; I had my proof. The stripe on my toenail was enough for me.

And so it was the memory of my little melanin deposit that soothed me as I sat across the card table from my dad, staring at the picture of his father, the minstrel. Grandpa had dressed in a suit and tie for the photographer, but his face wore only its original skin. He looked gentle and intelligent; the old black-and-white print revealed nothing of the man's special talents.

When my dad passed away, Mom gave me several of the photos from that big dusty box, including the one that rocked my world that evening. I stare at it from time to time, trying to imagine how my grandfather would have looked made up to portray a caricature of a black man. Too bad I don't have a picture of my Moorish ancestor; I would place them side-by-side to remind me who I am and where I come from, and that I am a child of God from head to toe.

COMMENTARY

Many of our stories have been shared publicly over the past few years, but this one is recounted here in its entirety for the first time. I have, however, told people about my toenail, and it's always interesting to watch their reactions. White listeners usually look skeptical and smile indulgently at my flair for a good story. I often wonder if they go home that night and inspect their nails. I tell it to African-

Americans only in more private settings, and the response is usually a lot of laughter, particularly from the women (although I don't know how to account for this gender difference). What I wonder then is what's going on in their minds. Perhaps, if they love me already, they find it endearing that I'm so pleased to have a blood connection with them. But I'm sure there are others who are cringing inside; that's probably happening more often than I realize, and people are just too polite to roll their eyes in front of me. Maybe they're saying to themselves, "*this fool thinks she's so clever with her toenail; she's got no clue what it would mean to have that melanin distributed evenly over the entire surface of her skin.*"

And they would be right. I have no clue. The good Lord, in His wisdom, chose to hitch my soul up with a fair-skinned body, and that's what I've got to work with. My best explanation for my delight is that I was thrilled to be walking around, for a short time, with physical proof that we are, in fact, related. It's great to agree that we all come originally from Africa and claim Lucy as our common mother, but it's far more exciting to look down and see evidence of that truth with one's own eyes.

I didn't have that particular evidence for very long, though. Within a year my stripe, officially known as *longitudinal melanonychia,* disappeared as the doctor had predicted. It was clearly a very small deposit of pigmentation, maybe just one Moor and one Spaniard getting together. As the nail grew, it dragged the melanin-influenced cells with it—depleting with every passing day the little deposit of blackness—until it dragged them right off the end of my foot. Each time I trimmed my nails, I cut off more proof of my African heritage and threw it in the wastebasket with the other nail clippings. Finally it was gone, and there was no way to tell, looking at my feet, that I was a descendent of the Moors.

It's actually a good thing it disappeared, and not only because that proved it was benign. When we were pitching our diversity training workshop, people frequently told us they needed an interracial facilitation team. It would have been nearly impossible for me— performer that I am—to resist the impulse to excuse myself for a moment, bend over nonchalantly in my chair, remove my shoe, raise my foot in the air, dramatically rip off my sock and then place my bare foot on the desk, revealing my black stripe as undeniable proof that . . . what? That I can speak for black people? I can claim to understand the black experience? Bring the black perspective? Or be the person of African descent their black employees could relate to? I, who with the simple act of putting on my sock could hide that tiny strip of evidence and go about my day taking full advantage of all the perks of being white? No, it's a good thing it grew out.

In order to write commentary on the story of my less distant relative, I did some research on blackface performers and minstrel shows. The Encarta online dictionary defines *minstrel* as "any of a group of entertainers who wore black facial makeup and sang and performed in variety shows, a form of entertainment now usually considered racist and highly offensive."

I found web sites that defended the value of minstrel shows, pointing out that they were the first true American theatrical form, the precursor to variety and vaudeville shows, that they introduced African culture to white audiences and paved the way for black performers. And how bad could they be? After all, blacks did it too—they themselves rubbed burnt cork or black greasepaint on their already dark skin and sang in exaggerated dialect. So where's the harm? I even read that this form of entertainment was beneficial because it helped whites cope with their fear of these Africans who were suddenly everywhere.

It's not my purpose here to debate the validity of such claims. My own claim, however, is that regardless of anything positive these performances may have contributed, it is certain that they reinforced racist images of black people. They also allowed white audiences to laugh in relief, secure in their belief that they were smarter, more re-fined, more beautiful—in fact, better in all ways—than the characters portrayed on stage. Minstrel shows perpetuated two of the most crucial elements of racism—stereotypes and a sense of superiority.

Given the purpose they served, I can see why these shows were so popular; by the time my grandpa was rubbing shoe polish on his face—and then washing it off with great relief before he stepped out the stage door—this form of entertainment had been around for a century. I went to my hometown library and searched back issues of the local newspaper for some reference to his show—hoping I wouldn't find it, dreading that I would. After several days in front of the microfiche monitor, I did find a review that raved about the lovely minstrel show performed for everyone's pleasure at a PTA meeting, of all places, in 1933. But there was no mention of Grandpa's name. He died in 1941, so I still have several years of articles to scan.

My goal, now that I know about my grandfather's pastime, is to enjoy the good things I inherited from him; obviously he was at ease in front of an audience, and he must have loved singing and enter-taining. I won't gain anything by being judgmental of his choices.

Nor do I buy the notion of heritable guilt, although it's an interesting idea to play with in the context of a story. Does the fact that my grandfather performed in blackface diminish my wisp of African ancestry? Or does my Moorish heritage immunize me against the virus of Grandpa's unconscious sense of superiority? These questions are designed merely to stimulate reflection. To actually feel guilty about the behavior of a man I never knew is not only illogical; it is a luxury I cannot afford. In fact, if I indulge it, guilt quickly becomes a distancing behavior, something that distracts me from my real work, undermines my credibility, prevents me from being honest with myself, and skews my reasons for engaging.

So if I don't use Grandpa's behavior to fuel guilt, of what value is it? Why did I write a whole story about it? For me, it acts as a symbol of the cultural conditioning I have absorbed as a white person—the sense of superiority, the stereotypes, the irrational fears that have come from outside myself and have injured my health just as surely as an inherited but undiagnosed disease harms the body. This conditioning is a part of me whether I want to acknowledge it or not, and it influences my own behavior in subtle or overt ways.

And what about my toenail stripe? It may have come from a mole and not had any connection with my ancestry. But again it serves as a symbol; it represents the spiritual knowledge I have as a human being that we are all family. This knowledge may come from science or religion, or it might be deposited in each one of us at the moment of our creation. Wherever it originates, it is required for our survival.

I struggled for a while to identify the actual point of this story, to combine these two parts of my personal history into a coherent whole. Then I realized that I am the point. I am the fruit of my father's parents, and I am a typical white American. Like all of my light-complexioned compatriots, I am constantly being molded by two forces. On one hand, we are biological children of Africa, descendents of dark-skinned people. On the other hand, we have inherited this pernicious social conditioning. We are walking paradoxes, carrying around within ourselves a mental construct that is at odds with our biological truth, and the contradiction keeps us in a state of unbalance. At any given moment, both of these forces—the urge to separate and the urge to connect—are exerting their influence and have the power to determine our choices. It is our job to ascertain which force is acting on us in every situation, whether it involves race or not.

As I was writing this commentary, I had a strange thought. For several years I have been playing the djembe, an African hand drum of the Mandingue people. I've studied with a master drummer from Guinea, learning not only traditional rhythms and songs, but also a little about the culture of the people who created the djembe and use it in their daily lives. I want to learn the dances that go with each rhythm, and if I can work up the courage, someday I will dance them inside a circle of drummers. My teacher has told us that as djembe players, we are representatives of the Mandingue culture and have a responsibility to present it with accuracy and respect. I've been drawn by the drum since I was a young child. So who is it that draws me—the Moor or the minstrel? The line between honoring a culture and exploiting it is very thin.

I call on all my ancestors to help me follow the right voice.

17

THE PITCH

Gene, October 2001
Illinois

The sound of my footsteps on the tile floor galvanized my resolve. I was wearing new dress shoes and the popping of hard rubber heels on linoleum vibrated through my body. My stride took on a deliberate cadence. I was grounded, ready for battle. The opponent was neither an individual nor a group, but rather a centuries-old false notion about who we are and who others are, and the idea that one group of people is inherently superior—a myth that has spread like a toxic cloud poisoning souls, concealing the truth, and obscuring the lethal nature of discrimination and separation.

Our victory would be setting a date for a workshop with students to discuss racial unity. As Phyllis and I made our way down the hallway, I felt confident and prepared to pitch our workshop.

I had called the college a few days earlier and asked if the school had a diversity committee; the receptionist had recommended we talk to Jim Miller, the faculty advisor for a newly-formed Cultural Diversity Club.

On the phone, Jim had seemed curious about the people we'd met during our travels, and he had made an appointment to hear our proposal. I was hopeful that our meeting with him would result in an opportunity to talk with students and listen to their thoughts and feelings about how racism affected their lives.

"Oh, before I hang up," Jim had said, "I, uh, well I hope you don't take this the wrong way. Well, uh, you don't sound . . . Mmm, what I mean is that from the way you speak, uh, you sound to me like, uh, you're white, I mean European-American . . . are you?"

"Yes, I am."

"Your wife, too?"

"Yes. Is that a problem?"

"Well, no, not really. I was just wondering what you as white folks can offer about racism that others would find useful."

"I'll be happy to explain what we can offer when we meet you next Tuesday. OK?"

"Alright. See you then."

Now Phyllis and I stood at the door to Jim's office, one of a series of small boxes that bordered the periphery of a large box, Building D. I adjusted my tie, then knocked. We heard drawers closing, someone grunting, the clatter of an object hitting the floor, more grunting, and finally, the door opened. Jim greeted us and invited us in.

He pulled a chair from the corridor into his tiny workspace, placed it next to one already in front of his desk and, after Phyllis and I sat down, somehow managed to close the door behind us. He then squeezed between the desk and a filing cabinet to get to his chair, sat down, and quickly scooped up papers and folders and plopped them on top of two teetering stacks on either side of the desktop.

Jim's office was now stuffed beyond capacity, not only with three adults, three chairs, a large desk and file cabinet, bookshelves, a wall calendar and schedules, but also with his personal items: trophies, several model boats, pictures of boats, family photos, and children's drawings.

When he finished his housekeeping, Jim looked at his watch, folded his hands and placed them on the cleared area in front of him. "So, whaddaya got for me?"

I looked at his hands resting on the shiny wood grain surface in an attitude of routine duty I'd seen before, then glanced at the towers of paper that threatened to collapse at any moment and bury everything in the little valley between them with administrative rubble. I wondered if Jim or the college had any space left for a workshop devoted to racial unity.

I pulled one of our four-color brochures out of my attaché bag and, glancing nervously at the stacks of paper, cautiously slid it across the desktop for Jim to examine. Ignoring the cover design I had labored over, he opened the tri-fold, glanced at it, closed it, and then set it on the desk. "I had a black friend in college," Jim announced, and went on to proclaim how "tight" he and his black friend were. "I'm not sure where he lives now; sort of lost touch over the years. But, well, let me tell you about our Cultural Diversity Club."

Jim explained that in the past, the college had made efforts to address challenges resulting from some "racial incidents" on campus but that there hadn't been enough support for an ongoing program.

More recently, the college had been pressured by students of color to create some kind of forum to discuss the difficulties they faced in a predominantly white school environment, and the administration had decided to form the Cultural Diversity Club. "We're getting more and more minority students every year," Jim said. "I had some gaps in my teaching schedule and was asked to be the faculty advisor. I was happy to take it on. I feel that there's a real need for something like this."

I asked Jim to tell us about the goals and activities of the club. "Well, we're still getting organized at this point, but in general we want to have a place where students can come together and get to know each other. And we invited an African-American professional from the community to talk to the students. He did a great job. I think we all learned something."

Jim looked through our photo album with interest and listened attentively as we presented the features and benefits of our workshop. We emphasized the merit of two white people talking to a group of students about race. We told Jim that in our experience, whites were more likely to freely express their concerns about racial issues when the facilitators were also white, but they tended to hold back when the facilitators were people of color, out of fear of revealing unconscious racism. We had also found out that participants of color were encouraged when they heard whites talking about racism and making an effort to understand their role in eliminating it.

After half an hour, Jim looked at his watch again and said, "Well, this has been really interesting. Unfortunately I'm on a tight schedule, and I've got other fires to put out." Holding up our brochure he continued, "But I'll run this by the other committee members. I've got your phone number; I'll let you know what happens. Thanks for stopping by."

That was the last time we talked to Jim. I tried a couple of times to reach him by phone without success.

We had hoped that a workshop would help prepare the students for the work of building better communities for themselves and their children. Over a decade has passed since our visit with Jim, and we still read about racial hostility and hate crimes on college campuses.

COMMENTARY

I often wonder why we did not get that opportunity to speak to the students. Was our presentation inadequate? Did we lack the necessary credentials? Or was it that people of color are considered the experts on racism and for that reason the preferred educators? Does the fact that we're white mean racism is not our problem and that we therefore have nothing to offer?

When presenting a proposal for a race unity workshop, we always suggested that sufficient time be allotted, so that we would be able to present all of our information and establish conditions that supported open and honest dialogue. But we found that administrators often seemed to want a quick fix to address a current predicament, and for them, a lengthy workshop had no appeal. And when we were able to give a workshop, we saw that the participants frequently wanted a "drive through" approach to the issue. They wondered how fast they could get the material, ingest it, and get on with life. I finally realized that a workshop about race can be intimidating if one senses that one has to abandon certain cherished ideas, go beyond the abstract, step into the practical, and have a change of heart. Eventually, we had to accept that people are busy and have difficulty clearing time in their schedules to sponsor or attend a workshop that would address racial unity on a deeper level. So along the way, we adjusted our approach and welcomed any span of time for a discussion.

The diversity club was formed to address issues raised by students of color; presumably if those students had remained silent or if the student population had been 100% white, the administration would have perceived no need for a club. Perhaps the problem was a failure to recognize that the United States has become a society made up of people from every conceivable background. The changing student demographic should have been appreciated as an enrichment of the college community—not as a problem—and even before the increase in the enrollment of students of color, the college should have prepared to welcome them. White Americans have to accept that racism is our issue, and it is irresponsible for us to minimize the extent of its damage, simplify the solution, or assume that people of color are responsible to do all of the work. Protecting the dignity and liberty of everyone in this country is a commitment inherent in our concept of citizenship. If we fail to embrace diversity, how many hate crimes will it take to motivate us to honor that commitment?

18

HANDS

Phyllis, 1997–2006

This is a hypothetical incident—a sort of parable I suppose—something that never actually happened to me. I call it *The Little Girl and the Cookie.*

A white woman and her young daughter are walking together along a busy sidewalk, holding hands. Coming toward them is a man with dark-colored skin. As the man approaches, the child becomes keenly aware of changes in her mother's body, and she begins to feel anxious. Mother's breathing quickens slightly, and the child notices that they are walking just a little bit faster. Now she is conscious of the pulse pounding in her mother's fingers. The girl looks around to see what has frightened the one she relies on for protection, but she finds no indication of danger. She is confused and looks up at her mother's face for reassurance. But Mother looks straight ahead, her expression giving no clue about the nature of the threat. She just squeezes her daughter's hand so tightly that it's starting to hurt. The child's own body is shaking now as she runs to keep up with her mother's lengthening steps; she has stopped trying to figure out what's wrong and is focused only on getting to safety.

In the next moment, they have passed the man with the dark-colored skin; he continues walking down the sidewalk, going farther and farther away. Slowly Mother's grip relaxes; her breathing and pace return to normal, the throbbing in her fingers subsides. The little girl's body relaxes too. She is very relieved, not only because her mother is happy again, but also because now there is no more confusion in her mind. She received the message loud and clear.

You see, no words were necessary. The squeeze of the hand contained a highly concentrated dose of all the mother's conditioning from her birth up to the present, transmitted in an instant directly into the child. The fear shot along the girl's nerves, from her hand to her brain, where it bonded securely to the only other sensory input available—the image of a dark-skinned man. Because she was so young, the child did not have the capacity to evaluate this transmission. And because the message was sent by someone she trusted implicitly, it lodged in the deepest places of her mind, those most resistant to change.

Some have called it "the poison in the cookies"—the transfer of unwarranted fear disguised as a legitimate urge to protect. Fortunately every poison has an antidote, and our story is not yet ended. Perhaps the little girl can be healed by the very thing that delivered the toxin in the first place; perhaps she can be healed by the touch of a hand.

The following are true anecdotes, adapted from my journal entries. The events took place in five different states, over an eight-year period in our travels.

<u>December 1997; North Carolina</u>: Gene and I met today with Lawrence, a member of the local Bahá'í community. We'd learned from my sister that he was a professional diversity trainer, and we called him a few days ago to introduce ourselves and ask him to have lunch with us this afternoon, hoping he could give us some advice on how to conduct our race unity workshops. During our meal we talked mostly about the skills required to facilitate a discussion of race; we described some of the challenges we'd encountered, and he told us how he handles sensitive situations and deals with hostile workshop participants.

I couldn't take my eyes off his hands—dark brown, long-fingered hands. They punctuated his sentences with forceful gestures, then rested briefly on the table, then flew back into the air to underscore a point. I was hypnotized by their movement and unable to focus on what he was saying, which is rare for me; I'm normally attentive to verbal detail. But even though I couldn't seem to stay with the discussion, I felt the intensity of his sharing and wanted to give something in return. So when he paused for a moment I told him a story about myself—about some pain that I had endured long ago. When I finished, I suddenly felt embarrassed for disrupting the conversation with comments that were self-centered and irrelevant. But he was silent for a while, taking in what I had told him. Then he reached across the table and touched my face with that beautiful hand.

<u>April 1999; a city in the Deep South</u>: People have been urging Gene and me since we got here to drop in on the youth program at the local Bahá'í Center. They've told us about Andrew, who goes out

into the neighborhood every Friday, gathers young men in their late teens, and brings them to the Center for an evening of recreation and discussion. He plans activities for them—organized around the principles of Kwanzaa—that promote physical, mental, and spiritual health. We wanted to support Andrew's service, and I thought I might get some ideas to pass along to our son, who also mentors teenagers through the Boy Scouts. So tonight, after our meeting, we drove to the Bahá'í Center. It was fairly late when we arrived; the young men were just leaving the gym after a game of basketball. We sat in our van and watched them swagger out the door, into the parking lot, hollering at each other, pushing and laughing. Everyone except us—maybe everyone in the whole neighborhood—was black.

I was so far out of my element that I actually felt a little unsteady. This wasn't the first time we'd been the only whites in a group of African-Americans; since we'd come to the Deep South we'd had that experience many times. But somehow this felt . . . unpredictable. Gene and I got out of the van and then just stood there in the corner of the parking lot, wondering what to do next. When the young men saw us, their playful energy drained away and was replaced by a quiet but palpable concern—something that was more than curiosity but less than alarm. And we just stood and smiled.

"Hey!" Andrew broke away from the group and jogged over to us. He was sweating and out of breath, and tall enough that he had to bend down to hug us.

"Welcome! Welcome! How great that you stopped by!"

I don't know if someone had alerted him to our visit or if it was just obvious to him that we were Bahá'ís, but he acted like he'd known us forever, and his response was an instant catalyst. The young men gathered closely around; Andrew introduced every one of them by name, and each one in turn extended his hand and grasped first mine, then Gene's, in a powerful, sweaty, respectful grip. They told us a little about their evening, and we told them a little about our journey. Then a few minutes later they dispersed into the night.

Take any sheltered, northern white woman and dredge from her subconscious mind the most frightening racial scenario she can imagine, and I'd nearly guarantee it involves a group of black men. I'm sure I must have felt threatened by such an image once, although I don't remember it clearly. The details are foggy. What I see instead when I close my eyes is a circle of hands outstretched in welcome.

<u>December 2002; Alabama</u>: Twelve-year-old Larissa was fascinated with my hands. She reached across the small kitchen table and took hold of my left one, drawing it closer to her without a word. I assumed she was trying not to interrupt the conversation I was having with her mother, Adele, but my attention wandered from the discussion to Larissa's intent expression. She held my hand palm up, running her fingers slowly along the lines like a fortune-teller assessing my future love-life. Next she turned it over and studied the back, holding it first close to her face and tilting her head back and forth to better see it from all angles; then she laid it on the table and rubbed the skin, as gently as if she were soothing a frightened kitten. Finally finished with her inspection, she traded, returning my left hand to me and taking my right, making it a little harder for me to pick up the coffee that steamed in a heavy clay mug in front of me. Adele resolutely kept up her end of the discussion until her daughter reached over again, this time taking her mom's left hand and placing

it on the table next to mine. My skin, although darkened by several months' exposure to the southern sun, was so very pale in contrast to the deep brown color she and her mother share that the image was visually quite striking.

All pretense of conversation stopped then, and Adele and I watched as she arranged our two hands, squinting her artist-eye to get the composition just right. She brought them together into a clasp with the fingers intertwined, but not perfectly alternating; she was apparently going for a natural, unposed look. When she had them positioned exactly the way she wanted, she sighed, "So beautiful."

Then, tightening her own fingers around our wrists so we wouldn't move and undo all her hard work, she turned slightly in her chair and called across the room to my husband.

"Mr. Gene! Mr. Gene! Please come and bring your camera!"

She had watched him taking pictures since we'd arrived and knew it was unofficially his job to record on film our new friends and new experiences. Adele and I obediently kept our hands still until Gene arrived to photograph her living sculpture.

"I love how their hands look together," she explained as he found the best angle for his shot. "Don't you just love how they look?"

Gene agreed. Our two hands—clasped and entwined, contrasting, bonding, foretelling years of friendship—were truly a work of art.

November 2005; a suburb south of Chicago: Gene and I drove forever trying to get back to the RV park last night. Torrential rain accompanied us out of the city, and heavy clouds obscured any light that would have illuminated the street signs. I suddenly realized I'd been detoured by the endless construction into a lane that bypassed my exit and merged me, against my will, onto the toll road going north. I was already tense from navigating the slick highway; now that tension was compounded by worry about how far it was to the next exit. So when I saw flashing yellow lights and the words *Pay Toll 1 Mile* I was greatly relieved. I steered into the far right lane, knowing a human being waited in a tollbooth somewhere out there in the fog and that there I would find shelter from the driving rain for the few moments it took to pay my toll and get directions.

The attendant was African-American, probably in his mid-sixties and surprisingly cheerful on such a gloomy night. He wore a clear plastic shower cap stretched over his hat; I assumed he occasionally had to go out in the rain to push open an obstinate toll gate in one of the automatic lanes. He also wore a raincoat with sleeves that were far too short for his arms, one of which was extended toward me through the door in his booth, hand cupped to receive my money.

"Good evening, ma'am. Nasty weather out there this evening. You driving safely on those wet roads?"

"Safely, yes. But in the wrong direction." I explained my predicament and asked how to get to the southbound highway that would take us home. As he answered, I placed the correct change in his open hand but realized I was reluctant to let go of the coins and relinquish the human contact. So I let my fingers rest there on his palm. We stayed like that for a moment, until he'd finished explaining the route, and then he closed his large hand around mine, enfolding my fist in long, rough fingers. Several seconds later he opened those fingers very slowly, as though setting free a butterfly. My hand returned to its place on the steering wheel and I closed the window, getting in a final "Goodnight" before it shut all the way. Then we drove out from under the shelter of the toll plaza into the rain. I felt indebted to this man in the toll booth because it wasn't a fair exchange at all; I gave him only sixty cents, and he gave me enough strength to drive home through a storm.

I think I've figured out the problem we suffer from in this country. I think fear has made us stingy with touch, and in our withholding we have inadvertently cut ourselves off from the very energy we need to feel unafraid. The cycle is self-perpetuating, but not irreversible.

February 2006; Florida: At the post office today, when I'd completed my transaction, the African-American woman who had served me said, "Thank you for placing your money directly into my hand. It means a lot to me that you made physical contact between your fingers and my palm."

I don't know what kind of day she'd had that left her in a place of such vulnerable honesty, but she went on to tell me how normally her white customers just drop the money on the counter, refusing to touch her. I've heard from so many of my black friends that they experience this touchless exchange of money constantly and that every time it hurts. So at one point I began to consciously place skin on skin, hoping to ease the pain of others' aversion. Apparently I believed my touch had magic healing powers. I could never figure out though how to warn the people who were causing that pain. Clearly they didn't realize that by hastily dropping coins on the counter and snatching away their uncontaminated hands, they were actually jabbing their fingers into an open wound.

Over the years I've changed a lot of the ways I relate to people of color; I still make sure to touch when exchanging money, but now my reason is hopefully less pretentious. I do it now because I crave the contact and love the sight of beige on brown; I am soothed by the flow of energy that tells me something is being given and received on a cellular level.

19

BODY LANGUAGE

Gene, January 2002
Tennessee

I jumped out of the car, dashed into the trailer, and turned on the television. My favorite show was about to start, and as the picture came into focus, the 5:30 newscast was just ending. I noticed a community service announcement that was briefly displayed on the screen: "*Invisible Man.* Ralph Ellison. Tuesday. 7:00 p.m. City Book Store." Then it was gone. I wanted more information, but the news anchors were already smiling and bidding the viewers a "good evening," so I jotted the information on the calendar and sat down to watch my show.

The following Tuesday I was excited about the event at the bookstore. At six o'clock I called and asked the person who answered the phone, "Could you give me information about the event tonight with Ralph Ellison, author of *Invisible Man?*"

"I just started my shift and don't know what's scheduled this evening," he said. "Hold on, and I'll find out." A couple of minutes later the man reported, "Yes, that's happening tonight at seven o'clock."

"Will he be reading from his book? Is Mr. Ellison a former resident of this city?" I asked.

"I really don't know anything about it."

Forty minutes later, I was on my way to meet Ralph Ellison. I dimly remembered reading *Invisible Man* at some point in my education, and I knew Ralph Ellison was African-American, a literary giant of the twentieth century. Because his appearance at the bookstore occurred during our brief visit in this city, I was going to meet him. I brought a notebook. This was history.

During the drive, I chided myself for running late. I worried that the parking lot would be full and that seating—and possibly standing room—inside the bookstore would be unavailable. I pressed harder on the gas pedal. When I arrived, the lot was nearly empty. I had anticipated balloons and big signs welcoming Mr. Ellison, but there was no indication that an event of such import was taking place. Inside there was no throng; in fact, there were very few people. I walked to the information desk and inquired about the program.

"Oh," said the clerk, gesturing indifferently to the furthermost part of the store, "That's back there in the corner."

What? In a corner? How could they put Ralph Ellison back in a corner? As I hurried toward the area set aside for the event, each disinterested customer I passed only served to increase my annoyance. And everyone was white. Where were the African-American citizens of the city? Wasn't black literature taught in public school?

When I made my way around the last of the tall bookshelves, which seemed like walls set up to isolate Mr. Ellison's reading from the rest of the bookstore's activities, I stood dumbfounded in front of those who had gathered. Before me was a long wooden table around which were seated six white people, two men and four women. Ralph Ellison was not there. *I'm glad I didn't miss anything*, I thought. *He's late; maybe his flight was delayed.* At one end of the table were two empty chairs; I sat in one of them and realized, *Oh, man! When he gets here, he'll sit right next to me!*

The man to my left suggested that we all introduce ourselves. After introductions, we waited in silence.

A couple of minutes later, he said, "Maybe we should get started."
What? Get started with what?

Taken aback by the suggestion to start without our guest, I retreated to a daydream and fantasized about meeting Ralph Ellison. I peered through a gap in the wall of books to catch sight of him as he approached our little corner of the world to share a slice of reality I was hungry for. In my reverie I saw him, unruffled and smiling, as he came around the barricade of shelving and stood before us. He walked over to the chair next to me, set a worn leather satchel on the tabletop, and greeted us. Now, I was ready to get started!

My vision evaporated when the guy on my left said, "I've read *Invisible Man* numerous times." To make his point he held up his dog-eared copy. "As some of you know, I'm a retired literature teacher."

These folks know each other?

"So, what were your impressions of this book?" he asked, waving the beat-up paperback.

Everyone had a book except me.

"Well, I really liked the battle royal!" said the other man. "It was really interesting." His contribution was followed by silence.

"How about the rest of you?" the teacher asked.

"I liked his writing style," said a woman at the far end of the table.

"Ah! Great!" said the teacher. "You know, he incorporates a lot of surrealism in his writing. Did any of you notice that?"

Silence.

"How about symbolism?" the teacher asked, coaxing the group to respond.

Symbolism was a literary concept that seemed more accessible to the folks gathered around the table. Each of them had a contribution to make about his or her favorite symbol in the book. I thought, *This is crazy! Why don't we just wait for Mr. Ellison to get here? He'll answer all of our questions about surrealism and symbolism and . . .* All of a sudden, it hit me—Ralph Ellison, esteemed literary giant of the twentieth century, was not coming to the bookstore this evening. I glanced around at the six white people. This was a book review group! Suddenly my desire to sit at the head of the table waned.

As the discussion continued, I felt frustrated because I didn't recognize any passages that were cited from the book; I was beginning to doubt I had ever read it. Did I really know who Ralph Ellison was? *He was African-American, wasn't he? I thought* Invisible Man *addressed the challenge of being black in America. Have I somehow gotten it wrong?* The group had been talking about *Invisible Man* for over half an hour, and I had not heard one reference to the protagonist or any other character in the book that identified them as black. The word *black* seemed to be irrelevant—or taboo.

I was just about to confess my ignorance, excuse myself and go home, when the woman at the far end of the table suggested, "Maybe he was treated that way because he was black."

Everyone turned and looked at her. I leaned forward in my chair.

"I mean, life wasn't that easy for them in the '50s," she said.

228

Hallelujah! Now I felt I could contribute something. "Do you think the patterns of racial prejudice that were common in the '50s have changed since then, or have they been perpetuated into the present?" I asked.

Now everyone turned and looked at me.

"Well, in some ways things are a lot better for African-Americans today," offered one of the other women at the table.

"Yeah, but some things are still tough for them, like racial profiling," another woman added. Our conversation now focused on the race issue in the United States, and several references were made to the stylistic way in which the author wrote about racism.

The teacher was clearly not comfortable with the direction our book review had taken. "What do you think is the meaning behind the title *Invisible Man?*" he asked, in an effort to get us back on the "symbolic" track.

"I know!" I answered, in a countereffort to keep the conversation focused on the content of the book.

The teacher looked annoyed, but the others seemed interested, so I continued.

"The protagonist in the book isn't literally invisible. The title is a symbol"—I paused and smiled at the teacher—"that expresses how a black man feels white America treats him—like he's invisible," I said, nodding at the empty chair next to me. "I'll give you an example."

I told them about an African-American man I had met at an event in the city about a year earlier. Phyllis and I had arranged to meet him at a local restaurant the following week. An hour into our dinner conversation, he grew quiet, reflective, apparently picking his next words carefully. Finally he said, "You know, I can always tell who lives here and who doesn't."

"How?" I asked.

"When I'm walking downtown, in the middle of the day mind you, with pedestrians everywhere, I make an effort to look others in the eye and say 'good morning' or give some kind of greeting. The only white people who respond are obviously tourists. Other white folks, those who live here, just look through me like I don't exist, like I'm invisible."

This real-life story elicited empathy, especially from the women. We started talking about how we relate to one another, white to black, and how we need to learn skills that will improve understanding and cooperation.

Suddenly, the other man in the group—the one who liked the battle royal—declared, "It's all about body language!"

I let out an involuntary "Huh?"

"Let me tell you what I mean," he said. "Last year I picked up my son from school to bring him home for the holidays. We had to drive through a big city on the East Coast, and somehow I took a wrong turn, and we got lost. Next thing I knew, we were in the . . ." he hesitated and looked at the six of us sitting around the table, then continued, "well we were in what people call 'the ghetto'—you know, the inner city where blacks live mostly. Anyhow, my son got really nervous, said we were in a high-crime area and had to get out quick. I told him I had no idea how to get out, that I had to stop somewhere and ask for directions. He pleaded with me to just keep driving, but I told him I had no choice; I didn't have a clue which way to drive."

"So, eventually, I saw a convenience store and parked," the man continued. "'Don't worry,' I told my son. 'You just gotta have the right body language. Watch what I do.' My son followed me into the store; we were the only white people in there. Everyone else was black—uh, African-American. I walked up to the counter, told the guy there that we were lost, and asked him for directions back to the freeway. I just kept calm, like everything was all right. And I had the right body language that communicated I wasn't afraid, that I could take care of myself." As the man said this, he rocked back and forth in his chair with a sort of sitting swagger. "The guy was real friendly, though. He gave us directions, and we left. Nothing happened to us. We got in our car, found the expressway, and drove home."

The man thrust out his arms, hands extended, palms up. "Body language!" he exclaimed, as if he were concluding a motivational talk. "It's all about body language!"

"All right," said the teacher. "We should probably wrap things up for tonight. Thanks for coming everyone. And feel free to join us next month," he said to me. "We'll be discussing *The Hunchback of Notre Dame*." I thanked him for the invitation but doubted I would come back to the next book review.

I was pretty sure Victor Hugo wouldn't be there.

COMMENTARY

"I am an invisible man. No, I am not a spook like those who haunted Edgar Allan Poe; nor am I one of your Hollywood-movie ectoplasms. I am a man of substance, of flesh and bone, fiber and liquids—and I might even be said to possess a mind. I am invisible, understand, simply because people refuse to see me."[1]

By the time I attended the book review group, Phyllis and I had already met many African-Americans who told us about the racial challenges they face. Everything I shared at the meeting I learned from them. I went to the bookstore to meet Ralph Ellison,[2] and when I realized he wasn't going to show up, my first impulse was to leave. But I lingered, hoping there would be an opportunity to discuss a topic often met with discomfort or indifference in white circles. African-American friends have asked me to always speak up when other whites are unaware of racial issues.

"You're white. They'll listen to you," these friends have said.

I've considered their request a personal mandate, but it isn't always easy to carry out. I am white. And while I continue to wrestle with my own racial conditioning, I feel I have the responsibility to talk with other white people about our role in mending the rip that racism has caused in the social fabric of our communities. Tact is required, and compassion. I'm not always successful. But on the night of the book review, I felt some of the folks were open to talking about race and to hearing my thoughts. I offered what I could at that point in my own developing awareness.

We learned that the city in which this story takes place was split after slavery ended. The absence of industry based on the farming of cotton, tobacco, or peanuts meant that there were fewer field workers in antebellum times. Because geography in this area made land unsuitable for crops, most slaves had domestic jobs that required some degree of education; instead of laboring in fields, they learned skills that prepared them to earn wages as trades people and professionals after slavery was abolished. Although blacks and whites had worked together for generations, when slavery ended, each group went its separate way. The result was two thriving business communities—one black and one white. Black citizens created a social and economic structure in which the educational, medical, and financial needs of the black community were met without dependence on whites.

We also learned that in time, whites got irritated seeing people they had regarded as property now independent and successful. Whites still had the upper hand economically and politically, and evidently it did not occur to white businessmen and politicians that a golden opportunity had emerged to collaborate and tap into the real potential of the black community. Instead, as has been the case in cities and towns across the country, whites used the power that comes with controlling resources to reestablish a dependency relationship. The separation—both physical and psychological—between black and white apparently became so entrenched that some outsiders we spoke to have a palpable feeling of it when they visit the city. It's not just that black folks aren't acknowledged and greeted in public. Their contributions as fellow citizens remain invisible.

In many cities, the invisibility of African-Americans can extend to entire neighborhoods. The man who shared with me his experience of feeling invisible in broad daylight was hesitant when Phyllis and I offered him a ride home after dinner. He said he was concerned about our comfort, but we assured him that it would be OK.

On the way to his apartment, we drove under a freeway viaduct—a boundary separating two realities—into his neighborhood, an area isolated by surrounding industry. There were no streetlights, and the darkness was relieved only by lighted doorways and windows, which generated an eerie glow. The car's headlights exposed vacant lots littered with debris. Adults and children were still outside socializing at 11:00 at night. Our acquaintance was apologetic. "This is a place the city has forgotten," he said. "Nobody on the outside knows what goes on here. Even the police don't come in."

Such conditions are evidence of an intractable social problem that cannot be solved by simply assuming "the right body language," a tactic that might reasonably be used in some situations to protect oneself. What will it take, then, to find and implement a realistic and effective solution?

Maybe the first step should be to acknowledge one another with a greeting and body language that reveals our longing to see the reflection of God's image in everybody's face. The Bahá'í writings offer the following guidance: "Thus should it be among the children of men! The diversity in the human family should be the cause of love and harmony, as it is in music where many different notes blend together in the making of a perfect chord. If you meet those of different race and color from yourself, do not mistrust them and withdraw yourself into your shell of conventionality, but rather be glad and show them kindness. Think of them as different colored roses growing in the beautiful garden of humanity, and rejoice to be among them."[3]

What happens after we take the first step? We won't really know until we stand up and start moving. There are choices to be made at every stage of the journey, and our strength increases when we practice the principle of unity in diversity in real-life situations. By mastering the skills developed in taking the first step, we'll strengthen the spiritual muscles needed to take step two, and then step three, and eventually we will be making unimpeded progress and wondering why we were stationary in the first place.

PART 3

2005–2009

Our patterns of traveling began to change during the years between the second and third sections of this book. Because of educational and family needs, we spent less time driving from place to place, although we did make extended visits to New England and through the southeastern states and Texas in 2002, then back into the South in 2003. That trip ended with the purchase of our present RV, a fifth-wheel trailer that was actually big enough for us to live in together. By then it was clear we were not going back to any kind of normal lifestyle.

People had been telling us for a while that our personal stories— which served to illustrate concepts introduced in our workshops— were the most effective part of our presentations. At some point during 2002, we decided to stop using a workshop format and instead to tell stories in the communities we visited. Each time we shared these personal accounts, we would get feedback from our listeners, which helped us better understand the incidents we were relating. Before long we started writing the stories down so they would be consistent from one telling to the next. Then people began encouraging us to put them in book form.

Although none of the stories from those interim years were included in this book, we continued during that period to have experiences and build relationships that affected us deeply. The things we learned prepared us for the incidents you will read about in the section that follows.

The stories in Part 3 relate events that took place between spring 2005 and summer 2007. By this time, it had become too expensive for us to maintain a pattern of continuous traveling, and we began staying for longer periods of time in each location. In 2006, we spent several months in Florida but after that moved mainly between Illinois and California, with stops in New Mexico and trips to New England and the Southeast to be with family. All along our routes, we would visit friends we'd met previously and share our stories in their communities.

We realized we'd begun to consolidate knowledge acquired during our more intensive periods of travel. It also seemed to us that the racial conditioning we uncovered in ourselves was more subtle than the stereotypes and anxieties we faced when we first started on our journey. Our experiences began to build on each other in ways we hadn't anticipated; every time we thought we'd learned something about race, that learning was tested in some situation or relationship. All of this new awareness impacted the way we presented our stories.

As in the previous section, the narratives are not presented in exact chronological order because we wanted to alternate between Phyllis's and Gene's stories. Also there is no seamless transition between chapters; they relate separate events that took place at various times and in different locations. The thread of continuity is our ever-increasing awareness of how we'd been affected by separation from our brothers and sisters of color.

In the summer of 2008, aware that we needed to stay in one place while we edited our stories and prepared this book for publication, we traveled to the Oregon coast. This is where our last three chapters were written.

20

SNOWBIRD

Phyllis, May 2006
Florida

It was so hot. Florida in May, while not as oppressive as Florida in August, is still really hot. It's not the kind of heat where you break an egg on the sidewalk just to see if it will actually fry. It's more an egg-poaching kind of heat. I would much rather have been at the air-conditioned health club, doing my aerobic workout on a tread-mill. But for some reason that I can't remember now, I was walking outside in the RV park where we'd been since December. This was a very large, luxury resort, open only to people age fifty-five and over, with nearly six hundred privately-owned sites. Most of these sites were occupied by semi-permanent living units called park models—dwellings that are really more like mobile homes than recreational vehicles—little vacation cottages that were once moveable, but were now tethered to the ground by water pipes and sewer lines. Other sites were designed for motorhomes and fifth-wheel trailers like ours.

Some site owners rented out their fancy cement pads on a monthly basis, with very reasonable rates. This is how Gene and I came to be at a place that otherwise would have been beyond our means. It was a beautiful setting—right across the street from the beach—and we felt fortunate to be there. But we were definitely "temporaries," not regarded by the more permanent residents as members of the community.

To get the full impact of this story, you need to know about my outfit, for the things that happen later will make sense only if you can imagine how I looked. You also need to know that I've struggled with body-image issues all of my life. So be kind. I'll begin with the basic attire: spandex shorts and a tank top. I know—but like I said, it was really hot.

The first accessory was the heart rate monitor, a device that allowed me to stay in the optimal "burn zone" and keep track of the actual number of calories destroyed. The apparatus consisted of two elements: an oversized, powder-blue plastic watch with random numbers blinking frantically on its easy-to-read face; and a monitor strapped around my ribcage that, according to the box, should not have been visible under my shirt but that nevertheless created a strangely shaped bulge just above my diaphragm.

Next came the ipod—nestled in its special little case on a strap around my waist—from which extended a long cord connected to my earphones. Then there was the fanny pack, turned around so it really did ride on my fanny and therefore did not interfere with the aforementioned ipod-holding case. This pack contained everything I needed to survive on my walk: keys to our trailer, travel-size sunscreen, and a miniature bug spray to deter mosquitoes the size of hummingbirds.

The final touch was my special water-bottle carrier net—complete with a deep purple no-spill thermos—that was also somehow strapped around my waist. It was positioned so that the bottle hung off my side, where it wouldn't interfere with either the ipod belt or the fanny pack, but where it bounced oddly as I walked. This chic ensemble was topped off with a large-brimmed straw hat and trendy tortoise-shell sunglasses. When you add the sweat streaming down my face and dampening my shirt, you have the whole picture.

Thus attired, I strode along to the beat of my Celtic music, pumping my arms energetically to keep my heart rate in the maximum fat-burning zone. As I sped past row after row of park models and RVs, I smiled and nodded a greeting to my neighbors. Sometimes I got a nod in return; more often I was not acknowledged at all—not even a mildly interested glance.

This RV park was a winter roosting place for the ubiquitous snowbird. By definition, a *snowbird* is a retiree who lives in the North during the warmer months and then migrates to the South in the winter, flocking together with others of its species in hot, sunny places like Florida, Arizona, or Texas. Unlike the snowy egret, which is named for its color, snowbirds come in many shades and are named for their highly developed survival instinct, which prompts them to flee south as soon as the temperature dips below forty-five degrees (if you ever tried to drive an RV in the snow, you'd understand why).

I know what you're wondering. If it was May and already so hot, why hadn't Gene and I headed back north? The explanation in our case is that we are not true representatives of the species. We don't actually migrate; we wander, following some call that is more elusive than Mother Nature's. I can't answer for our fellow RVers, who complained loudly about the heat but showed no signs of leaving.

In the five months that Gene and I had been staying at this particular park, we had found no neighbors of African descent. I can't really say we were all white folks, as the intense Florida sun had turned most of us some shade of brown. But though my fellow RVers apparently thought dark skin was attractive on their own bodies, it seemed that some of them didn't appreciate it nearly as much on people who were born with it.

Just a week before the events related in this story, we invited an African-American friend over for lunch. The visitor parking spaces were located next to the office at the entrance to the park, so I met him there, and we walked together to our trailer—a distance of about an eighth of a mile. Our progress along the avenue was marked by the flicking open of blinds in one unit after another. As we passed a light-green park model, a woman actually stepped outside her door and stared, furrowing her brow and shading her eyes with her hand to get a clearer look. If it had been possible, I would have split myself in two and walked on both sides of my friend to shield him from the peering eyes of my temporary neighbors. I apologized for their behavior, as if elected to speak on their behalf, and vowed next time to have lunch in town to spare him the humiliation of being gawked at. Had this occurred earlier in our stay, we might have relocated. But we were due to leave in a few weeks, and finding an RV site on such short notice is nearly impossible in that part of the country.

So now the scene is set for my story. Imagine a hot, humid day; picture me—as previously described—treading rhythmically up one avenue and down the other in this snowbird haven. Now I will try to explain what happened.

Coming toward me down the lane was a pickup truck with a construction company logo; the driver was a white man about my age, and his coworker in the passenger seat was a young black man. I smiled and gave a little wave as the truck passed me, but both men were looking intently at lot numbers on the other side of the street, obviously trying to locate their customer's site; neither one of them saw me or my welcoming smile.

A few minutes later, I rounded a curve in an outlying, secluded area of the resort next to the river. This was where the biggest lots and most expensive park models were located. Each had elaborate landscaping and tasteful outdoor decorations; sailboats were tied to many of the private docks. Ahead of me I saw an older African-American man who was carrying a load of lumber balanced on his shoulder; it looked as if he might be preparing to work on one of the piers. Just then the truck drove up from behind and passed me, and the man shouted, "I was wondering where you guys had got to."

"Had a hard time finding the lot," the driver called back, leaning out his window.

The man with the lumber pointed to a neighboring site and shouted again, "It's around back."

Now the driver pulled over, and the young black man hopped out of the truck. He sprinted past two park models, then turned and disappeared behind one of them. By that time, I had arrived at the spot where the truck was parked. I'd been happy to see the two black men in this homogenous place; I wished only to exchange a smile and a greeting with them, knowing this would ease the sense of loneliness that I often felt there.

Why did I think either one of them was the least bit interested in exchanging pleasantries with me? Because in my experience African-Americans, generally speaking of course, are the most receptive, engaging people I've encountered anywhere. Black folks, whether male or female, old or young, will usually look me in the eye and offer a greeting. Over the years I've come to expect it, and that's why I was in connection-mode as I approached the man with the lumber.

But he was intent on his planks and didn't look in my direction.

The white man was still sitting in the truck, but he got not even a nod from me as I walked past his open window; I had no hope of anything uplifting happening there. I assumed, based on many past experiences with white men of every age, that he was laughing at me from inside his truck, making snide little comments to himself about my appearance. I know—I'm making a generalization. I admit that my self-esteem has been wounded in the past and that I've developed a set of assumptions as a result. I am as vulnerable to this process of forming prejudice as anyone, and I won't try to pretend otherwise. The truth is that I just wanted to get past the guy as quickly as possible.

Thankfully I heard no remarks through the truck's open window as I strode by; I left both the lumber-carrier and the driver behind and was now intent on encountering the younger man, who had gone behind a two-story park model just ahead. I was walking fairly quickly and in a few seconds reached the spot where he'd veered off the road. I watched for him without slowing my pace, hoping he would be in view as I passed the space between the trailers, hoping he would look my way, grin, raise his hand, and call out a "how ya doin'?" And I would respond with a "good afternoon," a casual wave, and a grin of my own, then continue on my way, feeling refreshed.

But the young black man was not in sight; I assumed he'd gone down by one of the docks along the river. I kept looking, but it was hard to keep up my burn-zone pace with my head turned to the side. Finally I accepted that there would be no exchange of greetings on this day and gave up trying to spot him.

I was doing OK, pumping purposefully down the road, when a thought occurred to me. It was more than a thought, to be perfectly honest. It was an entire scene out of a play that was being written just then in my head, complete with dialogue. My own creative muse was the playwright, and she was really on a roll. She apparently had these characters all figured out. If you'd been inside there with me, you would have heard everything they said. But since you weren't, I'll lay it out for you, uncensored.

Character #1—the white guy: "Whew! Don't stop walking, lady. You've still got plenty of fat there to burn!" (we'll choose to ignore him—who cares what he thinks anyway?)

Character #2—the young black guy: (he doesn't say anything—he's in back by the dock)

Character #3—the older black guy, as he watches me walking away (this is the one that did me in):

Look at her watching for my coworker. She probably thinks he's a thief and she's going to catch him in the act, thinks he's trying to break in somewhere, steal a boat or something. Look how fast she's breathing—

she's got herself all wound up. Man that's a lot of stuff she's got hanging off of her; I'll bet she's got a cell phone in one of those bags, she's going to pull it out any second now and call security. I'm so sick of white folks always assuming the worst. There she goes again, still looking; she thinks he's sneaking around back there, that he's up to no good. She's just like all the rest of them.

I was yanked to an abrupt halt by the words in my head—stopped dead in my tracks just as surely as a roped calf, waiting in resignation for the branding that was certain to follow. I tried reasoning with the voice.

Character #4—me: *No really, those thoughts were not going through my mind at all. Please don't think I'm just like everyone else around here. MY INTENTIONS WERE GOOD!! I swear. I just wanted to, you know, connect . . .*

I stood still, listening attentively to my internal dialogue, hoping for a clue what to do next. Anyone watching would think I had just paused in my walk to catch my breath, maybe take a swig of water from my purple thermos, or fast-forward to a new tune on my ipod. Because I'd stopped moving, my heart rate dropped out of the burn zone, prompting a harsh, reproachful beep from the powder-blue watch: *Warning! Warning! Calories are no longer being burned! You have entered fat-storage mode!! Resume motion immediately! Warning!* It roused me out of my trance. I wasn't so worried about the calories; I'd just walk longer tomorrow. The prospect of being branded, however, was intolerable, and I had to do something other than talk to myself if I wanted to put things right.

But first I needed to take a moment and examine my assumptions. They seemed solid enough. I'd gotten to know a number of African-

Americans since we'd come here; they all lived on the mainland, just across the bridge from the narrow strip of land where our lovely resort was located. Every one of them had told me of the stereotypes and prejudice that awaited them at the beach. Two had spoken of being stopped on the bridge by police, who questioned their reasons for leaving their neighborhood. And I myself had witnessed the reaction to my friend's lunchtime visit only a week before. So it seemed reasonable that this man would expect me to have the same suspicious attitudes as other whites.

But I did not *want* to be perceived as mistrustful like all those other white people! I wanted to be perceived as *different*. I believed I must take some action, but I couldn't see clearly what I should do. And my options seemed so few and so unattractive. See if you agree:

Option #1—the most embarrassing:

I could go back to the man with the lumber—just spin about and walk in the direction I just came from, making it look as if I suddenly realized it was time to go home. Then on my way by, I could strike up a conversation and prove to him through my genuine kindness that I am in fact very nice and not at all prejudiced, that I am pleasant and trustworthy in every way. But that would be so very awkward; here I am in my skimpy work-out clothes, wired, sweaty, breathing heavily, glasses all steamed up, sweaty . . . (This is the point in the story where I need you to remember the image I described earlier). . . . *surely he'd think I was nuts. And I'd feel so exposed. What could I possibly say to him that wouldn't sound pathetically phony and contrived? Plus I'd have to go by the white guy again, and I know what he's thinking* . . .

Option #2—the stupidest:

I could speed-walk between the trailers into the backyard—pretend it's just an extra loop on my walking route, just a little boost for the metabolism. Maybe the young guy is still back there; we'll exchange greetings, then later when the older guy puts forth his assumptions the young guy will set him straight, and then . . . Oh please. Get over yourself!

Option #3—the lamest, most pathetic, poorest, most pitiful, sorriest excuse for an option anyone's ever heard:

OK, just keep going like nothing happened.

That's the one I finally settled on. Back in motion, regaining my speed, I continued to look between the park models as I rapidly passed them by, trying—if anyone was still watching—to appear casual yet purposeful, as though hoping to catch a glimpse of an endangered manatee lounging in the river near one of the docks.

On my way back to the trailer, I wondered briefly what Gene would have done in my position. Then I realized that was a silly thought; he would never have been in my position to begin with. He would have simply stopped for a moment to chat with the man carrying the lumber. No need for drama; it would have been the most natural thing in the world for him.

But then again, Gene never walks around in spandex shorts.

COMMENTARY

I was pretty pleased with this piece when I finished writing it; I had a lot of fun with the descriptions, and I believed I'd addressed some important issues. Writing the commentary, though, was a struggle. I couldn't seem to identify the actual point of the story. After peeling away layers of distortion and getting down to the core, I wasn't so pleased any more. My intentions were not as noble as I would have liked to think, which was probably apparent to my readers. I avoided looking at my real motivation as long as possible—I'm guessing that's why so much humor came out as I related the incident.

First, let me put to rest the idea that this was really about connection. That's what I wanted to think, and I let that desire mask the truth. If it had been about connection, I simply would have moved on when it didn't happen. That was the first layer of distortion I had to peel away.

Then I thought maybe the story was about what the older black man—I'm going to call him Frank—might have been thinking. Let's suppose for a moment that my assumptions about Frank's thoughts were incorrect, that he was so intent on his work he didn't even notice me, or he noticed me but saw nothing wrong with my behavior. In that case, I falsely projected suspicion and mistrust on him. Not only is that exactly the same thing I thought he was projecting on me, but it is every bit as unjust as assuming his partner was a criminal. It's nothing more than another stereotype masquerading as concern; I'm expecting pettiness instead of nobility. Plus, I'm making it about race when it wasn't; racial concerns are big enough without creating imaginary scenarios. I'll come back to this topic in a moment.

Now let's suppose I was right about Frank's thoughts; after all, I had good reasons for my assumption. I've heard hundreds of times, particularly from black men, how painful it is to feel they're always being watched with suspicion. The account of our friend coming to the RV park for lunch was very real, and it was only one of several things he shared with us about how he was treated in that city. He said it's as if everywhere he goes, he sees that question in white people's faces: what the hell is *he* doing here? So it makes sense that Frank would have had the same experience. And what, then, is my role? Is it up to me to fix that for him? If I believe that, then I've made him the victim and put myself in a place of superiority over him. Suddenly I think I've got the power to ruin or redeem his day; I can protect him from this hostile environment he's in and single-handedly compensate for the shortcomings of my fellow-snowbirds while I'm at it!

So now we're finally getting closer to the core. Looking back over my story, I see that my real motivation for trying to engage one of the black men was to prove that I had no prejudice. The unavoidable truth is that I didn't want Frank to think I was suspicious because I didn't want to look bad; I wanted to be perceived as a good white person. Turns out I'm as fearful as some of my white neighbors—not of dark-complexioned people, but of being misjudged and rejected by them.

It's possible that these racial overtones existed only in my mind. Here were these two black men in a place filled with racial hostil-ity—at least, that was my assumption. So I became kind of obsessed with figuring out how to make them feel welcome—something I hadn't been able to do for my friend the week before. And I still felt very angry about that incident, which certainly impacted how I saw things.

Over the course of many years talking with white people about race, I've come to the conclusion that the majority of us go through the same process: when we first become aware of the dynamics of racism, we can swing from not seeing it at all to seeing it everywhere. First we see it "out there"—in the media, in our schools, in all the institutions of our society—and especially in *other* white people. Then we realize *Oh no! It's in me too!* and we think all our words and actions are tainted by some subconscious racist attitude. It's an inevitable part of the process of finding balance, which eventually allows us to perceive the truth but makes us do some crazy stuff in the meantime.

I remember once being at a party, talking to a friend and referring to the *only* African-American in the room. "You see that man over there? The one near the corner, leaning on the table? Tall guy, wearing the green shirt?" I described everything about him except his skin color, terrified that if I said—or even noticed—he was black, it would mean I was a racist. And even though that was a long time ago, I don't claim that I've found balance in every situation.

It's also possible, or even likely, I was so self-conscious about my appearance that I felt defensive the moment I stepped out of my trailer and assumed everyone who saw me would be judgmental. And as I've had no personal experience with African-American men rejecting me because I'm overweight, I had to project a different reason onto the guy with the lumber. Race just made sense.

I guess I could analyze this story till the cows come home, as my great-aunt Minnie used to say, and there'd still be no guarantee I got it right or uncovered all the layers of meaning. I'll leave it to my readers to identify anything I've missed.

Besides, not all my thoughts in the story were self-delusional. The attraction between people who have been artificially separated is a very real force, and my expectation of connection with African-Americans is based on genuine experiences. But just as love makes us do stupid things, we don't always know how to respond to the attraction in authentic ways. If I'm turning myself inside-out in an attempt to do everything right, never upset anyone, and make sure no one misjudges me, that's not racial sensitivity, it's just plain code-pendence. It's very different from being sensitive to others' feelings and choosing my actions accordingly.

I almost decided not to put this anecdote in the book, because after all the analyses I didn't come out smelling so sweet, and it's not my goal to bash anyone, including myself. But in the end I decided to keep it because it serves as a cautionary tale of sorts: one of the things we have to watch out for is being tripped up by our egos. Maybe that's the lesson of my story. If any of my readers can relate to this, or to anything else I've struggled with, then perhaps there's some value in including it.

Ultimately I had to remind myself that wanting so badly to be rid of racial conditioning is a good thing, and wanting to avoid hurting people is a good thing. But my most authentic response, if I think someone's feeling pain over an issue of race, is to continue cleaning up my own act. So I say we celebrate the little victories yet try not to let them distract us from uncovering the big stuff hiding beneath the surface.

Postscript: I wrote that last sentence and went to bed, still not sure if I'd evaluated the story accurately. This morning when I turned on my computer, I was greeted by this quotation from William James that had been randomly selected by a widget on my web browser and displayed on my home page: "A great many people think they are thinking when they are really rearranging their prejudices."[1]

Now I know I'm finished with it.

21

MAGIC

Gene, April 2005
California

It was in South Carolina that we discovered what Phyllis and I referred to as the "magic," something we were reluctant to talk openly
about because, well, we didn't know how to talk about it. Typical
of things magical, it was shrouded in mystery. All we knew is that it
was real, not a gimmick. When the circumstances were right and we
conducted ourselves in a certain way, "magic" happened. Although
we were not in control of the process, we were learning the skills
necessary to participate in summoning the "magic" as often as possible. All we needed were other willing souls.

At the beginning of our traveling, we spent a few days—a week
at most—in each community we visited. We learned that we had to
compress the period of relationship-building if we hoped to have
heart-to-heart exchanges with folks in the places we were passing
through. The reason we were able to establish quick rapport with
people was what Phyllis liked to call the "taxi driver / hairdresser /

bartender syndrome." We were strangers. People could share their feelings with us risk-free, and they'd never see us again. But often they did; many of our connections developed into lasting acquaintances and friendships. My conclusion (by *conclusion* I mean my understanding at the present time) was the following: If I reach out to someone, most of the time that person will respond.

When we first got to South Carolina, we were trying to figure out how to invite people to our workshop. A friend who lived in the area told us that the best way to connect with folks was to just go into town and start talking to them. It seemed so simple, yet terrifying. I felt as if we had landed on an alien planet—a rural town of about ten thousand residents, the majority of whom were African-American. My mind was full of notions and images that made the prospect of walking into stores and engaging black employees and customers in conversation seem overwhelming.

But our friend's advice was sage. To my surprise and delight I found that it was easy to talk with black townsfolk. They had an openness and a readiness to respond that challenged my preconceptions about them. And that's how we discovered the "magic."

Back in the Midwest, we were eager to share our discovery with our white friends. We attempted to describe the "magic" and encouraged people to venture beyond their comfort zones and find it for themselves. The "magic," I felt, had the potential to bring about social change because it released a cohesive power that could unite black and white community members. Phyllis and I struggled for words to convince our listeners that what we were attempting to describe was real and valuable. Our explanation boiled down to this:

We have connected with African-Americans down South; we have felt an energy that we have never experienced before, and we think we've discovered something important.

"What you're describing is friendship," someone said. "I feel that energy you're talking about when I am with my white friends. Why do I have to go out and find black friends?"

"It's different," I said. I didn't know what else to say.

We continued to talk about our trip—and the "magic"—in other communities around the Midwest. In one meeting, where two black women were present, we again attempted to explain the benefits to whites of interacting with African-Americans. One of the women became agitated as our presentation progressed. Finally, unable to contain herself, she lost her composure.

"What do they get from you?" she blurted. I was taken off guard. Then, with controlled vehemence, she demanded, "What—do—they—get—from—you? As a black person, I don't want to be patronized!"

I had no answer and sat silently, looking to Phyllis for help. As I stated, we had no words to describe the "magic." I had never even thought about what *they* were getting from us; now I was forced to think about it. It felt like the thing we were describing—a good thing—was somehow flipped around and now sounded like a bad thing. Were we somehow exploiting African-Americans, getting an energy rush from our encounters without giving anything in return? How could we legitimize our claim? After all, the good feeling—the "magic"—might simply be an illusion that we were good-hearted, well-meaning white folks, doing the right thing. For weeks after the meeting I thought about that question. I had to. We hadn't been able to give the woman in that meeting a satisfactory answer. What if someone else asked? This is what I finally came up with.

When we connect with people belonging to a group from which we've been historically separated, we actually gain greater access to the body of humanity. The "magic" is a life force that flows both ways once the connection has been made. *They* get what we get— the same nurturing energy we all hunger for. It *is* different from the energy we get from others who are like us, because it establishes bonds between individuals who have been separated and creates new pathways through which it can carry healing to the whole body of mankind. I think most people of African descent have been willing to make this connection from the beginning.

Once I found the words, it was easier to talk about the "magic." But I have come to another conclusion: If you haven't actually experienced the "magic," it remains abstract, theoretical, remote. Only when it touches your heart does it become real.

After one of the meetings in our home town, a man approached me and stated, "You have a natural ability to interact with different kinds of people. I could never do what you do." He was sincere but really didn't know me very well. Prior to my involvement in race unity work, I could be found in gatherings, not interacting with different kinds of people, but sitting far away from the center of activity, maybe engaged in a private conversation with somebody I already knew. The man's evaluation of my natural capacities was far from true, and this has led me to yet another conclusion: We change. It's the nature of our design. We are spiritual beings, and we are all born with the capacity to express compassion, justice, forgiveness, trustworthiness, and assertiveness. As we express justice, for example, we become fair in our dealings with others, and with the passage of time we are different, transformed into advanced versions of ourselves. To resist change is to thwart the growth and development of our true selves.

We are born with a longing to attain our potential as human beings, to discover, nurture, and express our unique worth, but this longing cannot be satisfied in a vacuum. We need to connect with the body of humanity and take in the life force that enables us to develop our inherent excellence. How do we do that?

As the final exercise in a workshop we presented at a university, we asked participants to describe how they would like to see people from other ethnic groups contribute to racial unity. When her turn came, an African woman tearfully expressed her wish to have white students acknowledge her presence when they entered the elevator she was riding. "Just a greeting. That's all. When they don't even look at me, it's like I don't exist." This poignant request reminded me of a participant in a previous workshop, an African-American journalist who had done research in South Africa. He told us how some black South Africans greet one another. Upon meeting, one says, "I am here." The other responds, "I see you." The journalist said this greeting validates one's existence.

How do we calculate the loss caused by passing one another silently, eyes averted, not seeing each other?

Offering a greeting to people we encounter is a key to connecting with the body of humanity and accessing the "magic." A simple "Good morning" or "How ya doin'" can create a connection that can last for seconds or minutes, and can lead to a relationship that might endure for years. Not everyone will respond. But so what? For every non-respondent, there are a hundred who do respond.

Returning to our trailer late one night in New England, I stopped at a convenience store. The checkout line was surprisingly long for so late at night and most of the customers appeared to be students from nearby colleges. I got the item I needed and walked to the back of the line. In front of me stood a young African-American man—a student, I assumed. I wondered how he was getting along in this predominantly white environment, where people prided themselves on their culture of privacy. I waited for an opportunity to catch his eye and say something. It was so quiet in that store. No one was talking. Everyone in line seemed preoccupied with private thoughts. *Too quiet. It's unnatural. When is this young guy going to turn around?* I waited. The line got shorter. Finally he turned his head so I could see his face in profile. "How ya doin'?" I asked. (Sometimes my efforts to connect have been pretty awkward. But the urgency of eliminating separation impels me to continue trying.)

He turned his head a bit more, looked at me scornfully and said, "Fine." Then he abruptly faced forward again.

Wow, I thought. *What has this place done to this young man?* I had expected him to be much more socially accessible because he was black. Later, at home, I was thinking about what had happened and realized that obviously not all people of African descent are the same, nor are all people of European descent the same. What we do have in common is an identity as human beings, but we each express that identity in unique ways.

And yet, as I said before, I believe that connecting with people from whom we've been historically separated is an important part of the work we have to do to bring about racial unity. Should we wait for some far-off event at which the country's leaders sign a document declaring an end to racism? Or is there a vital role that each one of us must play? I believe that informal, chance encounters, which provide opportunities for connecting and racial healing, are perhaps the most important events in which we can all participate right now.

In the spring of 2005, several years after that night in New England and clear across the country, I found myself standing behind two African-American men in a department store checkout lane. At one point, one of the men walked off, presumably to browse while his friend waited to complete his purchase. I smiled at him as he left. His expression seemed to ask, "Why are you looking at me?" I hoped the other man would turn around. The line was long, and as we moved gradually forward he kept his back to me. *How can I connect with this guy?* I wondered. He was wearing a baseball cap, and on the little adjustment strap on the back of the cap were the words, "Chicago Bears."

"You from Chicago?" I said to the back of his head. He turned around, his face beaming.

"No. I just like the team," he said. "You from Chicago?"

It seemed he was as eager to connect as I was. We talked about football as we advanced in the line. His friend returned, saw us chatting, smiled at me, and joined in the conversation. We continued talking while his purchases were scanned, and after he paid, we shook hands, he wished me well and walked away with his friend.

I consider these ten-minute exchanges to be important events in the work of eliminating racism. These brief encounters enable us to reduce the tension that generally exists between people from different ethnic groups and to replace it with a feeling of trust. These mini-events support my belief that the majority of people want to abandon the dysfunctional ways of interacting that have pitted us against one another. I think people just want to get to know each other at a deeper level.

While I am committed to the racial healing that results from encounters like this, my hunger for connection has become indiscriminate.

Not long after my exchange with the Bears fan, we left the West coast and headed back to the Midwest. I was sad to leave our friends, and after two days on the road, I was lonely. We stopped to over-night at a campground in the Texas panhandle. It was still daylight when we walked next door to get dinner, and as we approached the restaurant, I noticed two people sitting in a pickup truck close to the entrance. I quickened my pace and walked directly to the passenger side of the truck. The window was open. I placed my hands on the bottom of the window opening and said to the passengers inside, "How y'all doin'?"

Two white faces and two cowboy hats turned simultaneously in my direction.

"Not bad. How 'bout you?" one responded.

At that moment I realized that I had better come up with some reason for my intrusion. I looked around frantically and noticed the truck had really great side view mirrors. "You got some fantastic mir-rors here," I said. "Where'd you get them?"

The driver told me where he had purchased the mirrors, and then asked where I was from. We chatted for a while before I remembered that I'd abandoned Phyllis.

"Well, I'd better join my wife. We're starving."
"Y'all take care. Enjoy your meal. Drive safely."
Magic!

22

MOOSE TRACKS

Phyllis, October 2006
Chicago, Illinois

This, I will bravely admit, is one of my most embarrassing stories. My only explanation for what happened is that I had ice cream in my mind, which always prevents me from thinking clearly.

I had driven into Chicago to spend a few days visiting our son Erik, and we had just finished dinner at one of his favorite South Side restaurants. We'd been engaged in a serious conversation and were anxious to continue, so we decided to pick up some dessert and head back to his apartment.

"What do you have a taste for?" he asked me.

"Ice cream." No hesitation on my part.

"Any particular kind?"

Again no hesitation. "*Moose Tracks.*"

"Well, we could go to the little neighborhood grocery store near my place, but they usually carry only the basics. Or we could drive to a bigger store; they're more likely to have what you want."

I really didn't feel like going all the way to the supermarket, so I chose the first option. Besides, I enjoyed visiting the small shops that line the streets near his apartment.

Before I continue, it's important for you to know something about my son. He is very different from me. For example, I am quick to speak and must constantly remind myself to listen. Erik listens by preference and uses words only when he actually has something of value to say. He has quietly eased into his life on Chicago's South Side and is one of very few white residents in a black community that is surrounded on all sides by more black communities. He is known and respected by his neighbors and recognized by those who work in the local businesses and restaurants he frequents. The owner of the little grocery store had seen him and exchanged brief greetings many times; on this particular night, she would have the rare treat of meeting his mother.

As we walked toward the store's entrance, we passed an elderly man pushing a train of shopping carts he'd collected from the parking lot. He pushed these carts as if they weighed a hundred pounds apiece. Inside the store were a dozen or more customers; two of the three checkout lanes were closed, and several shoppers were lined up at the open register on the far right. The cashier's friendly chatter with people standing in line didn't appear to distract her from efficiently scanning the groceries, and she greeted us as we entered. Although I saw her for only a few moments as we walked past, I had the impression she was keeping an eye on everything at once, taking care of the customers in her line at the same time that she watched over the market's activities. I guessed that she was the owner.

We passed to the right of her checkout lane, and I followed Erik along the outside aisle, across the back of the store, and then around a corner to the freezer section, where I examined the shelves of ice cream with growing disappointment. They had—as my son predicted—only the basics: vanilla, chocolate, and Neapolitan, none of which interested me in the least. Just enough time had passed for me to become fixated on my original idea, and I suggested we make the trip to the supermarket where I could buy what I really wanted. So we continued down the frozen foods aisle, which brought us to the front of the store on the opposite end from where we'd come in. How the cashier managed to see us so clearly without interrupting her scanning is puzzling to me even now, but she noticed that we were leaving empty-handed and called over to us,

"Didn't find what you were looking for?"

"Well, no," I called back, remembering my mother's instructions to always tell the truth. "I was hoping to get some *Moose Tracks* ice cream, but I guess you don't have any."

As I said the words, my salivary glands kicked in and took over for my brain. Are you familiar with this ice cream? Delicious, but typically more costly than less exotic flavors, it is one of those concoctions that has appeared in the past few years with unusual ingredients and highly inventive names. Imagine lots of miniature peanut butter cups and swirls of dark chocolate fudge surrounded by smooth vanilla ice cream. Surely the image evokes an idyllic north woods scene: drifts of pure white snow marked only by the tracks of the elusive moose. They say the moose is quite shy. Though one of the most powerful mammals, it lives a cautious and reclusive life in cold northern climes. It's rare to see one standing gloriously large and mighty by the side of the road, and an eager visitor is lucky just to spot its tracks in the snow.

As I answered the woman, however, my thoughts were not on the north woods but on the South Side, and most particularly on this little store on the South Side, and on the question now looming ever larger in my mind: *What could possibly make me think that a store whose shelves are filled with only the basic necessities would carry* Moose Tracks *ice cream?*

But the words were out, and there was no taking them back. I had only an instant to nurse my regret, to wish that I could push a rewind button and hear the garbled sound of language played backwards. The woman's reaction, however, was far too swift for me to exit gracefully. She scrunched up her face, peered at me in utter confusion, and said, very loudly, "Goose tracks?"

Don't laugh, I warned myself. *Whatever else you do, do not laugh.* The image of geese trying to walk through deep snow was making this difficult.

"No, no," I hollered back. "Mmmmmmoose tracks." We'd kept walking toward the door during the exchange, and at this point I was standing no more than six feet from the woman; I can't imagine why I felt the need to holler. I clearly heard the "WHOOOSH" of a dozen or more heads turning at once, as the other customers in the store reacted to my mooing.

"What d'you say?" She leaned toward me and tilted her head slightly, trying to catch my words. She had that timeless look I've seen so often in women of African descent; I knew she was older than I, but whether she was sixty or eighty was hard to tell. *Please just let me slip quietly through a crack in the floor,* I begged whoever is responsible for such feats of magic. My anxiety transformed me into a thirteen-year-old.

"*Moose Tracks*—you know, it's a kind of, like, you know, vanilla ice cream with like, fudge and little peanut butter cups mixed in." *Surely she thinks I'm talking down to her. And why am I assuming she doesn't know what it is? But on the other hand, why should I expect her to know what it is?* This was going downhill as fast as Bullwinkle on skis, and I had no idea how to bring it to a satisfying end.

Having completed my eloquent description, I stood there with the stupidest of grins on my face, waiting to see what was coming next. I still had options at that point. I could, for example, have said, "Oh, please don't trouble yourself on my account; I'll look for my silly ice cream elsewhere" and then exited gracefully, waving a cheerful good-bye over my shoulder as I left. But I didn't do that. It seemed I was paralyzed, and I saw the whole scene as if caught on a hidden camera: me grinning, my son rubbing his forehead, the old man dragging his tired feet across the floor, the woman puzzling, the customers frowning in irritation.

We were all set back in motion by the woman's voice; her baffled expression had been replaced by one of relief and pleasure.

"Oh yes! OK, OK then. I know about that." She paused, cocked her head to the other side, and then said, surprisingly, "In fact, I'm sure we have some. Did you look back there by the other ice cream?"

What? She's sure they have some? Certainly not. She's just saying that to appease me. Why does she feel she has to do that? But I know why. I'm white. I'm standing here in her store in an economically depressed black neighborhood, asking for a high-priced specialty item, and she wants me not to be upset. I wish she wouldn't feel that way, wish she would just laugh and tell me I must be out of my mind, tell me I can just take my white self someplace else to get my fancy ice cream. That would make me feel better.

"Yes. I did . . . I mean we did, look back there, I mean. There wasn't any." It seemed I'd lost all ability to think creatively and was reduced to just blurting out the simple truth over and over.

And this dear woman was either afraid to disappoint me or unusually eager to be of service; I couldn't tell which. In front of her, a thick black cord hung from the ceiling, and attached to its end was a bulky rectangular box—with two big red buttons—that housed the microphone for the PA system. It was suspended within her easy reach so that she could speak to any corner of the building without leaving her spot at the cash register. I hadn't seen one of those since I was a kid in my own neighborhood market.

She grabbed it then, and her voice boomed and crackled throughout the tiny store. "Sam? Where are you, Sam? Go in back for me, will you Sam? Go see if we've got any of that *Moose Tracks* ice cream back there in the freezer." She stopped her broadcast when she saw the old man come from behind a tall stack of canned beans and move along the aisle toward the back of the store. As he walked, he cast one single glance over his shoulder at me, then continued slowly on his assignment. I imagined I saw in that one look a deep well of weariness and resentment, accumulated over a lifetime of catering to the whims of white folk.

I wanted to run after the old man, take him gently by the arm, and lead him back to the front of the store, reassuring him the whole time that there'd been a mistake, he didn't need to go off on this wild

268

moose chase, that we'd just be leaving now so they could all get back to their normal lives. But of course I couldn't do that. Instead, I did the only other thing I could think of—I started chatting with the cashier, as though nothing out of the ordinary were occurring here.

Under any other circumstances it would have been a delightful chat. I made some reference to the fact that I obviously wasn't going to die of starvation if I didn't get my ice cream, which she acknowledged with an understanding chuckle. She participated in the banter as easily as she had with her other customers, only there was one painfully noticeable difference—as she talked with me, she stopped scanning groceries, and the people in line were forced to wait.

While all this was happening, my son turned his back toward me and the cashier, and began intently studying the cans of green beans that were stacked high on a pallet next to the door. Never before had I known him to be so interested in the nutritional content of canned beans. I knew my behavior was embarrassing him, but I could see no way to stop it gracefully.

The old man had not yet reappeared, and in the meantime, another woman opened a second checkout lane. Several customers had already lined up by her register, and now they were joined by those who weren't willing to wait while their cashier conversed with me. Finally Sam came from the far aisle and shook his head. *No,* I read in the slow gesture, *there is no* Moose Tracks *ice cream to be found—not here, not anywhere near here. Now please let me be so I can finish my work and go home.*

Instead of marking the end of the incident, the old man's silent report only fueled further speculation. The two women now talked to each other about the mysterious disappearance of the Moose Tracks.

269

"Didn't we used to have some of that back in the freezer?"

"Well I don't know. I'm not sure I know what it is."

"That vanilla with the fudge and the peanut butter. Like the lady here said."

"Maybe we had it once, I don't remember. Don't think I've seen anything like that back there lately."

"Well, I'll be. I was sure I'd seen it."

Oh dear God, please make this be over. Meanwhile all the customers waited. None of them looked the least bit amused. Desperate for relief, I took back control of my brain and spoke the words that should have come out of my mouth much earlier: "That's really OK, please don't worry about it. It's fine. Thanks so much for all your effort. I really appreciate it. We'll be going now. Thanks again." Did I reach out to shake her hand? It's quite possible, knowing me, but my memory's not clear on this point. I know I looked around for the old man, to direct my gratitude to him as well, but he was not in sight. I thanked the other cashier too, even though she'd done nothing but add to the torment.

Then we left. Our ride to the supermarket was quiet, both of us assessing our choices and feelings. The difference was that my assessment resulted in contemplating what I might do differently next time, if there were a next time. My son's options were much less theoretical; he was probably considering whether he'd ever take me shopping again.

I wasn't so scarred by the incident that it put me off my favorite ice cream, but every time I eat it, I'm reminded that it's not always easy to see what needs to be done. Sometimes the truth is elusive, and we find it only by following the tracks it leaves in our hearts.

COMMENTARY

When I read this story once for a diverse group, a debate ensued over what motivated the cashier's behavior. Several people agreed that she must have been acting out of a fear of displeasing me, while others insisted that as a business owner, she was simply doing what made sense—trying her best to satisfy a customer. There were whites and people of color on both sides of the argument. The next time I read it, a different question caused disagreement, not about the woman's thoughts but about mine: had I been correct in perceiving a racial dynamic, or was I projecting imaginary racial overtones onto the situation. The first issue, of course, is impossible to resolve, as none of us can know what the woman was thinking. The second is not much easier, because it depends on the answer to the first. So I think it would be best to start this commentary with a statement of the obvious: nobody knows what was actually motivating the behavior of the people in this story. I'm not even absolutely sure what was motivating me.

The truth is that I don't know whether or not this was about race. I was pretty convinced at the time, but I can get so hyper-alert in certain situations that I misread cues. What's interesting is that my vigilance is a direct result of having gained more knowledge about the dynamics of racism. Ten years ago, I would have waltzed my way through that situation in the store and never given a thought to the woman's behavior. But the more I've learned about race, the harder it is to be carefree. It seems that I'm always trying to find the balance between two extremes: I can be sensitive but inhibited, or spontaneous but oblivious. Neither one is effective. Maybe that's why they say that ignorance is bliss.

My assumption that this incident was indeed about race is easy enough to understand if we look at the situation from a historical perspective. Up until a relatively short time ago, a displeased white person could easily arrange to have the black person who caused that displeasure punished. It wouldn't have to be much—maybe the white person was in a bad mood that day and didn't like the other's look or tone of voice. At one time, the punishment might be death or selling a mother's children. From our more recent history, we know that all a white woman has to do is point her finger, and an innocent black man can be thrown in prison without a trial, or worse.

But the particular knowledge that made me think race was a factor has come not from books or movies but from the hearts of African-American friends. Even though times have changed and we now have laws to protect people from capricious accusations, the dynamics still play themselves out in the lives of people of color all over this country. Black women with teenage sons have told me of the fear they feel every time their boys go out; others have shared how nervous they get at work when they make a mistake, knowing that some white person in management wants them gone and that laws against discrimination are not always enforced.

We have a white friend in Tennessee who was once accosted late at night by a black teenager. She thwarted his attempt to steal her purse and called the police after he ran off. Because she has so many close African-American friends, she'd heard the same stories I have, and she was keenly aware of the potential repercussions of anything she said. So she described the boy very accurately—down to the shoes he was wearing—and a short time later the police returned with someone who, except for having dark skin, bore no resemblance to the person she described. She recounts the expression of terror in the boy's face as he looked out at her through the window of the squad car; he knew how much power she had in that situation. She had only to nod her head, and he would have been hauled off to jail. She thought about the boy's mother. If she had been confused or frightened enough to be careless in her identification, it could have changed that family's life forever. Fortunately she was neither confused nor frightened; she pointed out the officers' obvious mistake and insisted that they release the young man immediately.

But my situation in the store was so different, you might say. After all, what could I really have done to the cashier if I'd been upset with her failure to satisfy my request? She didn't do anything wrong; so what if I'd decided to raise a stink? Maybe it doesn't seem reasonable that she would have felt the need to keep me happy at all costs. But it's also not reasonable for a war veteran to drop to the ground and cover his head when a car backfires. People who have been injured repeatedly—by violence, betrayal, or oppression—will do things to preserve their safety that make perfect sense to them. If the woman had experienced enough of those incidents—and certainly at her age she had seen more injustice than anyone should be asked to endure—then it's possible she was apprehensive. It's just as possible that all the other people in that store were thinking the same thing.

My son helped me sort out the various threads in this story. While we were driving back to his apartment from the supermarket, we processed our feelings and discussed the cashier's behavior and my responses. His experience living in a black neighborhood has given him insights far beyond my own. I also turned to him for assistance as I was writing this commentary and trying to understand my responsibility. We agreed that while race is not always a factor in such situations, it's quite possible that it *was* a factor in this case. Once I know something about racial dynamics, my task is to be sensitive to that possibility and to ask myself how I want to show up in that situation, given the roles that both the cashier and I might be playing. As I mentioned earlier, the hard part is finding balance. I don't want to be paralyzed by the fear of slipping up, but I do want to be thoughtful in the choices I make.

So now the question—given that there was no way of knowing what folks were thinking—is what I might have done differently. I could have made a better choice, for example, when the cashier noticed we hadn't found what we were looking for. I asked Erik what he would have done, and he said he wouldn't have been in that situation in the first place. He never leaves a store empty-handed; if he doesn't find what he wants, he buys a pack of gum and avoids the possibility of creating that particular discomfort.

"But what if you *had* been in that situation?" I pressed him. "What would you have said?"

"Very little," he answered. "Probably, 'I'm good, thanks,' and then I'd leave."

He certainly wouldn't have made casual remarks about what they did or didn't carry, but then he wouldn't do that in a store full of white people either. Like I mentioned before, he's very different from me and doesn't feel driven to talk about everything.

And that's another issue that should be taken into account. Personality will always play a role in how each of us chooses to respond to a situation. I'm a connector by nature; according to my mother, I've been that way since I learned how to talk. And I've been embarrassing all three of my children with my indiscriminate chattiness for a long time. Possibly the cashier was like me in that respect; maybe she was really happy to see me there and pleased that I felt comfortable enough to come in. I'm sure white customers were rare—maybe she was just hoping to put me at ease and let me know that I was welcome there. The only way I'll ever know for sure is if I go back and ask her.

What I do know for sure is that these situations are often unclear. Our life experiences are so disparate that when we do come together—even in normal, simple places like a grocery store—there is an increased risk of misunderstanding. Sometimes we won't think of a better alternative until later, as the result of soul-searching or input from someone with more experience. And even that won't necessarily help us go back and change the situation, but it will prepare us to make a different choice next time.

Like I've said so often in the context of these different stories, racism has robbed us of the freedom to relate spontaneously. There've been plenty of times when I've apologized to black friends for things I was sure were racial insults, and they thought I was crazy, suggesting I was seeing race where it wasn't really an issue. I've decided that's better than *not* seeing it when it *is* an issue. I would never choose to go back to being ignorant, even if it meant spending less time trying to figure things out. Because the more I learn, the more I assess and experiment with different behaviors, the closer I come to my goal of being authentic in all my relationships. The payoff for that is increased trust and intimacy, which seems like a pretty good deal.

When I get frustrated, I remember a statement from the writings of my faith: " . . . in matter[s] where race enters, a hundred times more consideration and wisdom in handling situations is necessary than when an issue is not complicated by this factor."[1] Then I don't feel so bad about how hard I struggle to get it right.

23

IMAGES

Eeny, meeny, miney, moe. Catch a tiger by the toe. If he hollers let him go. Eeny, meeny, miney, moe. My mother told me to pick the very best one. And you are not it.

Gene, July 2005
California

When I was four years old, I named my beloved black cocker spaniel Sambo, after a favorite character in a children's story.

I was fifty when I learned that Sambo wasn't just a child's name but was a demeaning and devastating caricature of black men that had been propagated during the enslavement of people of African descent. It had meanings I wasn't aware of when I named my dog. I didn't know that at four years old. Does that make a difference? That I didn't know?

I remember the eeny, meeny, miney, moe rhyme we learned as kids to help us make choices. There were two versions. I wasn't quite sure which to catch by the toe, a tiger or . . . the other one. What confused me was that tigers didn't have toes.

I didn't know the meaning of the N-word. Since one version of eeny, meeny, miney, moe involved an animal I was familiar with, I assumed the other was a type of animal, too. How could I have known otherwise? My parents didn't tell me. My teachers didn't tell me. Does that make a difference?

The images in cartoons and movies I saw as a kid portrayed black characters either as buffoons or savages. During visits to museums, zoos, and amusement parks in the city, I saw people who reminded me of the characters I'd seen on TV. I stuck close to my parents.

There were no black children in my circle of friends and therefore no opportunities to become acquainted and to distinguish between TV images and real people. There was an African-American girl in my first grade class for a few weeks, but until I went to college where there were a small number of black students, I didn't have any interactions with African-Americans. How did my childhood and adolescence prepare me to relate to black folks as an adult?

In 1966, during the summer of my junior year in college, I set off alone in my car to explore the United States. I drove south, headed for New Orleans. The romance of travel faded the moment I pulled off our gravel road onto the state highway. I reached the "Big Easy" a lonely and frightened country boy. After a day and an evening walking around the French Quarter, I checked into a hotel in a neighboring area of the city. The elevator attendant on duty was an elderly African-American man. "Good evening, sir," he greeted me as I stepped into the elevator.

"Hello," I mumbled. On the way up to my room, we didn't speak. During the ride to the fifth floor, I clutched my duffle bag. I remember watching the attendant to make sure he didn't catch me off guard and attack me.

When the door opened at my floor, the man asked softly, "Can I help you with your luggage, sir?" Certainly he must have offered the same service to every patron and likely hoped for a tip. But all I could envision was this elderly black man entering my room, hitting me over the head with something, and robbing me.

"Hell no!" I snarled at the man, who looked shocked at my explosive reply to his gesture of courtesy.

Looking back, I am embarrassed. Standing before me was a man, and because he was African-American, I had regarded and treated him as if he were the most contemptible and dangerous person I could imagine. My line of reasoning at the time was something like this: "He's a black man. You might have to fight him—or run for your life." It never occurred to me that my logic was a manifestation of racial conditioning. On the contrary, I was certain that my behavior was justified. After all, I was out of my element, in a dangerous environment; I felt cornered. My reaction was simply an act of survival. *Show him I'm tough. He'd better not mess with me.*

I wasn't aware at the time that I was relating to a mental picture of a black man—not to a real person standing within arm's reach. The emotionally-charged images of black men from my childhood had governed my behavior toward him, and I was acting like a frightened child—not a levelheaded adult.

Does that make a difference? That I wasn't aware?

In California in 2005, I met an African-American man with whom I had a long and probing discussion about racism and the work of establishing racial unity. We had been in many of the same places in the Deep South. I brought up the issue of the "unfinished business" between blacks and whites, and he helped me better understand the ongoing process of racial healing in the South. He referred to the hostility between blacks and whites that goes back hundreds of years and said that the present generation is still dealing with the impact of the past. He told me that it's not simply about blacks and whites becoming unified. In many cases, the "unfinished business" is a family issue; second and third cousins living in the same community remember what their grandparents and great grandparents perpetrated or suffered at each other's hands.

At one point he said, "You know, there's one thing I can't get out of my mind." He paused as he sought for the words to express something, the pain and turmoil of which were already written on his face. Finally he said, "It's the idea that African-Americans are less than human."

He cited the devastating images of African-Americans that have persisted throughout the centuries and explained how those images have made it almost impossible for whites to accept blacks as equals, even in religious communities. When he finished, we stood in silence and let the gravity of what he had shared penetrate. I had heard these things before, but the pain he expressed carried the meaning to a deeper part of my being.

"How do we get past that?" he finally asked.

I can only answer his question for myself. I have knowledge now. I know that pernicious images of people of African descent have poisoned my mind. As a result, the full expression of my humanity has been compromised. Recalling my past behavior causes immediate discomfort, and I must accept that I had conformed to a widespread mindset that maligned one group of the human family.

Knowledge of the truth makes me accountable for my choices. I choose not to be incapacitated by guilt and shame. That is a luxury I can't afford. So here are choices I have to make: Who will I seek out as friends? Will I visit them if they live in black neighborhoods? How will I respond to another's pain caused by racial injustice? How will I collaborate with people who have every reason to regard me with suspicion?

Now, my question is not a defensive "Doesn't my ignorance excuse me from accountability?" but rather "How will I make a difference?"

COMMENTARY

The Sambo was an image used by whites to portray black men as simple, helpless, and irresponsible. The purpose of this characterization was to convince white citizens that slavery was a beneficent institution, well-suited to protect black men from their own incompetence.

After slavery was outlawed, the caricature of an irresponsible, violent black man replaced that of the Sambo. This image was intended to convince whites that the abolition of slavery was a mistake.

The first time I learned about the Sambo character, I thought immediately about naming my dog when I was a child. I concealed my embarrassment for years, even while I was going through race unity facilitator training. I was angry because I realized that, for most of my life, brainwashing had effectively programmed my behavior.

During my ride in the elevator in New Orleans, I had been relating to a malicious portrayal of African-American men created over a century earlier.

Friendships with African-Americans have allowed me to replace Jim Crow images—which have for centuries effectively given rise to suspicion—with new images that are proof of compassionate encounters with real people. The old images can burden our hearts with fear and guilt that impact our choices. The new images enable us to envision a life in which we can make legitimate choices for our common well-being.

24

ROBBED!

Phyllis, May 2007
New Mexico

When our grandson turned ten, his heart's desire was to have his birthday party at a skate park where he and his friends could indulge their shared passion for skateboarding. Gene and I had been out with him a few weeks earlier, and we'd found a wonderful park in the small city near where their family lives in the Southwest. It had bowls and ramps and many other features, the names of which I, a non-skateboarder, do not know. When it came time to plan his party, I told our daughter where I thought we'd seen the park, but I was unfamiliar with the city and not sure what street it was on. After looking online, we felt confident we'd located the same one, and invitations with directions to the park were given to the boys' mothers.

On the day of the party, our daughter made the half-hour drive into the city with our grandson and five-year-old granddaughter. I drove separately because I had errands to do beforehand, and told her I would meet them at the park. But as I followed the directions to the party, it quickly became obvious that we'd made a mistake. I turned off the main road and found myself in a neighborhood with a distinctively different feel from the place we'd been before. It was a severely neglected area, with garbage in the streets and boarded-up businesses. There were more adult men standing around on the street corners than there were kids playing in the park. And the words I could hear those kids shouting at each other made me wince; I don't think I'd ever before heard such young children using such foul language.

Thinking my daughter had realized the error when she arrived and that they had all left to look for the other skate park, I called her on my cell phone as I drove along the street. But they were there, she told me, at the far end of the block by the picnic area, trying to keep the children from stepping on broken glass. I said I'd park the car and join them, and then we could decide together what we wanted to do.

Unfortunately, every parking space on the street was taken. I cruised slowly so I wouldn't inadvertently pass an available spot, but I reached the end of the block without finding one. I called over to my daughter through my open window that I was going to keep looking and that I'd be back in a few minutes, then I turned around and drove back down the street.

When I was nearing the intersection with the main road, I slowed to look at a small lot on my left. I'd passed it before but thought I'd seen a sign that said parking was restricted; now I stopped the car to read the sign more carefully. It was April—a warm time of year in the high desert of the Southwest—and I'd left my passenger-side window open after talking to my daughter. My purse was on the front seat, along with bags of groceries I'd picked up for the party.

While I sat there deliberating, a man left the group he'd been standing with on the sidewalk and approached my car on the passenger side. He was older than a teenager but most likely younger than thirty; his clothes were casual but not shabby. From his features and complexion, I guessed he was Native American or Latino, or perhaps both. He was smiling as he walked toward me and had his hand held out, as if he hoped to reach through my window and offer me a gift. I hesitated for only a second, then looked away, shut my window, and drove off, staring straight ahead to avoid making eye contact with him.

The remorse that suddenly took hold of me was tangible and debilitating. But it was momentarily overshadowed by confusion, caused by the imagined words of two people—women who were not really sitting in the backseat of my car but might as well have been, so loud was their commentary in my head.

From the passenger side, I fancied I heard the voice of a dear friend, a lady of my age and complexion, a passionate and long-time worker for racial unity, and a person whose heart would be broken if she thought she had hurt someone's feelings. She reminded me in a sadder-but-wiser tone of the time she pulled up at an intersection and rolled down her car window to assist a young black man; he had behaved as though he wanted to ask a question, and she would never refuse someone who needed help, especially if that refusal served to reinforce racial stereotypes or in any way impede interracial fellowship and trust. The man grabbed her purse off the front seat and ran; he was never apprehended, and my friend lost some valuable items and experienced great difficulty trying to replace important documents. Perhaps

I'd been remembering her story when I closed my window and drove away. But why was she popping up in my mind now, after the fact? Was there something else I was supposed to learn from her experience? Or was she simply trying to make me feel better about my actions?

From directly behind me, next to my friend, came the disembodied voice of Oprah Winfrey. It calmly reminded me of one of her TV shows that aired in the mid-1990s; Gene and I had frequently referred to a segment of that show in our race unity workshops. Two of Oprah's male African-American staff members had been made up to look white and had stood on a street corner in Chicago gesturing to white drivers to roll down their windows, after which they had asked for directions or for the correct time. They'd found these folks to be extremely friendly and cooperative; the drivers had opened their windows, the two men reported, even on very cold days, and happily offered their assistance. When the staffers repeated the experiment the following day without makeup, however, the good white people of the Windy City had hastily shut any open windows, locked their doors, and stared straight ahead as they pulled away. All of this had been filmed by hidden cameras and played back for the education of the studio audience and the folks watching at home. I had no trouble remembering that show; the pain on the men's faces was devastating as they talked about how they were consistently perceived as a threat. Even though Oprah's imaginary voice was quiet as it reviewed the events on her show, it had drowned out the words of my friend the instant it started speaking.

So my confusion abated and I felt extreme remorse that refused to leave me alone. I pulled into the small parking lot and bribed the approaching security officer with the promise of a piece of birthday cake if she'd let me park there, which she happily agreed to. Then I crossed the street and walked along the rubbish-littered sidewalk toward the area where the birthday boy and his friends were trying to skateboard without engaging the neighborhood kids. The entire time I looked for the man who had approached me, but he and his friends had evidently relocated. I continued to look for him on my way back to the car, after consulting with my daughter and the other moms and deciding to pack up the kids and drive to a different park.

I'm not sure exactly how I planned to do it, but my intention if I found him was to apologize for my disrespect. Everyone deserves to be treated with dignity, even thieves and drug dealers, although I had no proof that he was either. I never found him, though, and that's all there is to say. This story has no happy ending.

COMMENTARY

I've never talked about this incident in public, but I related it to a number of close friends and family members, and most of them say it's a good thing that I kept my eyes straight ahead and did not stop to chit-chat with the man at the curb. They are apparently relieved to hear that I do, in fact, know how to recognize a potentially unsafe situation and take appropriate action. Some of them asked what I'd learned from the experience, which made me remember something that happened when I was a young teenager.

A boy had broken my heart, and I went to my grandmother for comfort. When I'd expressed my hurt and outrage at the injustice done to me, she gave me tea with milk and sugar then said, "You're feeling hurt and angry, and that's fine, that's OK. But I want to know what you learned from this experience."

I thought really hard for a long time, but I couldn't come up with anything that seemed like a lesson. So I told her, "Nothing."

Then she hugged me and said, "That's wonderful! Because the only thing a person learns from that kind of experience is that it's not safe to trust people. And I'd be sad if you'd come to that conclusion."

So that's where I'm coming from. Other people have been trying to teach me not to trust for most of my adult life, but it never took. I think that's why the incident shocked me so much; I'd never done anything like that before. My default instinct is to assume that people will behave in a noble fashion.

In this particular case, however, I did learn one thing of value, and I'm willing to state it in the form of a lesson: PUT YOUR PURSE IN THE TRUNK. Because if I drive around—anywhere really, not just in the big, bad city—with my window open and my purse on the front seat, then if a person of any color leans into my window, I will most assuredly be robbed—not necessarily of my purse, but most definitely of my freedom to relate as spontaneously as I otherwise would, according to the directives issued by my heart.

No woman wants to go through the trauma of having her purse stolen. I don't know what it's like for men to lose a bag or briefcase, but for women it's definitely traumatic. There's just too much stuff in there, and we can't bear the thought of it being in someone else's hands. It's not only the credit cards, driver's license, and all those other important documents, and it's not just the large sums of cash, which most of us don't carry anyway. I don't even begrudge a thief the use of my Starbuck's frequent-coffee-drinker card. Let him have a free cup of coffee if he's that desperate. Rather it's the irreplaceable things—a flower petal pressed between the pages of my datebook, a special stone my granddaughter picked up on our evening walk—the little tokens of my life that no one else would value.

A white friend of ours who lives in a black neighborhood has a good solution. People on his street know him, but when he goes off his block he's a potential target—maybe more so than others because it's often assumed the only reason a white man would be there is to buy or sell drugs, and either way he'd be carrying around a large sum of money. So that he doesn't have to be wary all the time, he carries an old wallet containing no credit cards and just enough money to buy his lunch. That way, if he is mugged, he has nothing material to lose and can walk through his neighborhood with his freedom intact—the freedom to look another human being in the eye and greet him without fear.

But let's give the guy at the skate park the benefit of the doubt and assume he was not a thief. Maybe he was just a drug dealer; he interpreted my slow drive-by as a signal that I wanted to purchase his wares, and he was merely a shrewd enough businessman not to ignore a potential sale.

Sometimes, when my gut tells me to flee, it's clearly basing its suggestion on an inherent drive to protect my physical life. If bullets were flying, for example, I should probably pay attention to that instinct and get out of there. If I'm alone in an elevator in the middle of the day in a busy commercial building, however, and an African-American man joins me, it's a fairly safe bet that I'm not at risk. In that case, if the voice is telling me to flee, it's most likely the result of racial fear conditioning. If I had taken just a moment in the park to look around and assess the situation calmly (and if my purse had been in the trunk!), I probably would have come to the conclusion that I was not really in any physical danger. Then I could have responded to his greeting, refused his kind offer and been on my way, minus the remorse. Taking time to assess the message my gut instinct sent me would have allowed me to choose rather than simply react.

What complicated things for me in that situation was my lack of experience; I had no knowledge to call on that would either validate or refute my first impulse and help me make a decision. The fact that I haven't been approached by someone who wants to sell me drugs since the '60s tells you something. All I had to rely on then was my gut instinct, and that's what I did. My gut instinct said I was in danger, and I responded accordingly.

The question that continues to plague me is this: was that instinct my true inner voice telling me how to keep myself safe? Or was that a voice tainted by conditioning? How can I know? What are the means for determining if the message from my "inner voice"—my gut instinct—is authentic or healthy, or even in my best interest? The only way is to check it against some external standard.

I know people will protest when they read that because we've been sold the idea that we should have the courage to follow our instincts, the wisdom to listen to that small, quiet voice that speaks the Truth inside each one of us, and the will to ignore the clamor of the outside world that tells us to be someone besides our true self. And I believe that. The issue here is not whether we have such a guiding voice but rather how we can distinguish when the voice is uncontaminated and when it's been influenced by brainwashing. I'm not naive enough to think it will be possible every time, but if we ever want to be successful in making that determination, we need some frame of reference that we can use to assess an instinctive urge. Let me give you a personal example to persuade you I know what I'm talking about.

Let's say I pick up a "this-is-not-a-diet" book from its spot among many like it on a bookstore shelf, and I read that I should listen to my body, which knows what it needs and will always lead me on the path to true health if I only have the wisdom to respect it. So I close my eyes, center myself, take a cleansing breath, tune out the distractions, and tune in to my inner voice. I listen intently, and that voice says clearly, "I need a double-fudge brownie." Hey, who are you and what have you done with my True Self? Certainly this is the voice of habit or craving. Or is it? Maybe I really do need a brownie right now. Maybe it will soothe my inner child to the point that I can learn some important lesson.

But now I'm confused, because my body also says it wants to be healthy, which means I need to lose weight, which surely will never happen if I keep listening to this impostor.

What I know for a fact is that my body has been conditioned for over fifty years to "need" or crave certain food at certain times. How can I trust what it tells me? As a result of that conditioning, I've developed relationships with food that I continue to reinforce. It doesn't matter whether I call it an addiction, an eating disorder, a hereditary pattern, or simply a bad habit, the result is not only that I'm unhealthy but also that I've been robbed of the freedom to make good choices by that insidious voice in my head prompting me to eat. I will be free to choose authentically only when I learn to identify the true nature of that voice and then ignore it. And in order to do that, I have to consider the opinion of an expert—a doctor or nutritionist—who will tell me that if I take in more calories than I use up, I will not lose weight.

We believe we are free; we cherish and defend to the death our freedom to choose, and yet our choices are so frequently dictated by an inner despot—a self-sustained inner government that has been compromised by corruption, graft, and our own personal special-interest groups lobbying for decisions that keep us unhealthy. I am not free if my decisions are made for me by some other agency or source, whether that agency stands outside me or in my own mind.

My instinct to eat is not the enemy here; it was built into me by design for the continuation of my individual life—and, by extension, for the propagation of the species. But it's been corrupted by programming and is telling me to do things that are not healthy for my body. In the same way, my instinct to flee from danger for self-protection is a gift from God; it was built into me by design for the continuation of my own life and thereby the continuing life of the species. But it also has been corrupted by programming that's not healthy for my individual soul or for the body of humanity.

So I come back to my previous question: How can I tell the difference?

For me, the standard by which I can assess my instincts, my thoughts, and my behavior is the Word of God. If I can't perform this assessment in a moment of perceived danger, which is frequently the case, then I can look back at my decision later and assess it according to the standard I've chosen. I can ask myself if the behavior moves me toward my goal of authentic physical, emotional, and spiritual health or if it contributes to moving us collectively toward the goal of a just society, the end of prejudice, the emergence of peace. But without divine guidance—which I personally find in the writings of the Bahá'í Faith—I have neither the clarity to understand exactly how those goals can be accomplished, nor the spiritual power to carry out my assessment.

There's one final question I'd like to address. Some have told me that I'm being too hard on myself because I regret my decision that day at the skate park. They say, "What's the big deal? What does it matter if you err on the side of caution? Who have you really hurt anyway?" But I can't take any comfort in that thought because so many of my friends of color—my teachers, the people I love—have recounted their resentment when a white person responds to them based on fear, how they feel disrespected and humiliated. It is my long-term goal, for the sake of my own spiritual growth and the growth of my human family, to avoid behavior that creates that kind of distress for another and retards the cause of interracial fellowship that I champion so loudly.

25

THE WORD

Journal entry: The "word," insidious agent of disintegration, is a shape-shifter. It takes on whichever form is best suited to its mission: to wreak havoc when the brain's security guard dozes off.

Gene
Prologue

I can still hear Lamont's voice as he rushed from one black friend to another and, like an old-time crier, shouted, "Unnershoots said the word!"

"What? He what?"

"Unnershoots said the word!"

"He what? Oh, no! Shit man! What you gonna do?"

I was bewildered as I watched this outlandish scene unfold. We were gathered outside at night, and apparently I had done something, or said something, that had provoked Lamont's odd behavior. *This is a joke,* I concluded. *I work with these guys. Lamont and I are friends; he's just showing his buddies how close we are.* I stood grinning as I watched him move among the men and waited for their expressions of anger and distress to disappear with a signal from Lamont and be replaced by smiles revealing camaraderie. But their grim mood intensified. All the black guys glared at me, and I finally realized that this was no joke. I was in danger.

Gradually Lamont's message sunk in: "Unnershoots said the word!" The word. The "word"? Did he mean the "N-word"? No. No! I didn't say anything like that! I did not say the "word"!

Lamont finally made his way back to me and snapped, "You said the word, man! I thought you were OK, but now we're finished! You're in trouble. You better watch out!"

They were all gathered tightly around me, pushing, shouting out their condemnation. I found Lamont's eyes and said, "I didn't say the word, man. Really. I didn't." I appealed to the group, "I didn't! I didn't!"

"Yeah, you did," Lamont growled. "Don't deny it!"

"Yeah, don't deny it!" the group chorused.

Glancing from one face to another I sought a friend, an ally, a lifeline. I found only contempt, frustration, distrust. *What's going on?* I wondered. *Is this real?* As they walked away from me, muttering, each man gave me one last shove.

I stood alone in the dark, watching the group of men from a distance. I was cut off, and I felt a sense of loss I was not prepared to deal with. I guessed they must be looking at me as they continued to rehash what had just gone down, but in the darkness I could see only obscure movements in the shadows, and now and then momentary bursts of ambient light reflecting off objects in motion: a belt buckle, a wristwatch, a cross on a neck chain, teeth.

Teeth. *I did not say the "word,"* I thought. *What I said was, "Hey, Lamont, smile so we can see where we are." That is definitely not the "word." What's his problem anyway? I thought we were friends. Can't he take a joke? I guess we really weren't as close as I thought we were. Well, I'll be careful in the future. Not going to let my defenses down. Think someone's my friend. It was just a joke! Why the hell is he so sensitive? I didn't do anything wrong. He's the one with the hang-up!*

It was 1968.

For weeks after that incident, I felt invisible to Lamont and the other black men. It was as if I had been airbrushed right out of their picture of reality.

Lamont had reached out to me, and we'd had conversations in which we listened to each other's life goals and plans for the future. It was Lamont who left the security of his group of friends to come over to me and make the connection. He took the initiative, and I was receptive. But I was ignorant of so much. I had no clue about the civil rights drama that was raging throughout the United States and absolutely no understanding about the genocide casually referred to as slavery and its relationship to raised fists. "Black Power!" was the mantra that accompanied the gesture. I thought it was simply a greeting. "Black is beautiful!" was another common expression that left me wondering, *Why do they say that? I can't imagine saying "White is beautiful"; we're all beautiful in our own way. Why is it so important to shout it out?*

My relationship with Lamont was never mended. He stayed close to his buddies and distanced himself from me. At that stage of my life, committing to relationships required a level of maturity I had not attained. My interactions with people were governed by patterns of social survival that I had acquired in grade school and junior high, a repertoire of reactions that were supposed to keep me safe in every situation but which in fact left me insecure, wary, and vulnerable.

A few years later, in the mid-1970s, Phyllis and I were invited to an African-American couple's home for dinner. I remember looking around their apartment and noting their furnishings, the graphics on the walls, the music playing in the background, the food being prepared, and thinking, *So, this is how black people live.* When our hostess announced that dinner was ready, I remember looking at her and saying, "I like black people. They're so earthy."

Somehow I made an assessment about our friends based solely on my observations of their apartment, generalized it to include all African-Americans, and distilled it all into one word: "earthy." And for some reason I had to express that to our friend, who in turn shared it with her husband as he brought in the hamburgers.

"Gene likes black people because we're earthy."

I felt I was offering a compliment. And, as dense as I was then, I was still aware of an unmistakable shift in the atmosphere. The warm glow of welcome in their eyes had vanished. Conversation during dinner was polite but sparse and stilted. I had the feeling our friends were anxious for us to leave, and probably breathed a sigh of relief when we finally walked out the door. We never saw them again.

What did "earthy" mean to the couple I referred to as friends? Was it, for them, the "word" in one of its insidious shapeshifter forms? What was their experience with whites, and how did the word *earthy* restimulate painful feelings for them?

When I was middle-aged and we started traveling, I had encounters that helped me get insights about my interactions with African-

Americans. On the East Coast, we met a black woman named Sophie, and in a conversation with her I related the experience with Lamont and my analysis of it. I had gained some understanding about race and racism and, in retrospect, I see that my purpose in sharing that anecdote was to impress her with my current awareness of the unconscious racial prejudice I had back in 1968. As I poured out my tale, I expected smiles and feedback that would assure me I was a good white man, illumined and compassionate. But Sophie's expression was serious; I watched her face contort into a grimace, yet expected her to say something like, "You got it, Gene. You understand!" Instead she said, "Oh! That poor young man! He must have been so embarrassed."

I was shocked. It had never occurred to me that Lamont might have been embarrassed. Since 1968 I had remembered him simply as an oversensitive and angry young black man. And now I was upset that Sophie didn't praise me for being enlightened.

Up to that moment I had thought my understanding about racism was substantial. I had been trained to be a race unity workshop facilitator and recognized some of the effects of racism, but Sophie's response to my story suggested I was missing something, and I felt that an enormous deficit had been exposed. I was so humiliated I wanted to quit working for racial unity. But when I thought about Sophie's reaction to my story, I had to ask myself, *What kind of feedback did Lamont get from his friends? Did they say, "Told you not to trust a white guy!"? Was he embarrassed that he'd judged me wrong? Had he looked foolish in their eyes?*

I've had many disconcerting moments since that conversation with Sophie, and in every instance I've wanted to quit race unity work and cut my losses. But what are the losses? Time? The expense of books and training? The real loss if we quit is that we remain ignorant and pass up the chance to develop competence in our relationships. In matters of race, competence requires humility, the willingness to learn. It's different than humiliation. Humility is a character quality, a feature of our design as humans that we possess inherently but that often remains undeveloped, like a muscle that's never been used.

July 2005
Phone call from California to Tennessee

A careless word or comment—even in the context of a solid friendship—can cause problems. I'm thinking about a phone conversation with Deborah, an African-American woman Phyllis and I met in California. We became close friends before she moved back to her hometown in the South, and I call her occasionally to chat. A problem for me when I'm talking on the phone is that I can't see the facial expressions and body language I normally depend on to judge the impact of my words and to be sure I've been understood.

A few minutes into our conversation, Deborah said, "You should meet my friend James. You and he have a lot in common."

His name sounded familiar; she had mentioned James to me before, and I accessed the information about him I had filed away in memory. In an effort not to slow down the conversation, I sorted quickly through details about James: African-American; about Deborah's age; musician; educator; ah, yes, she'd once said something about him being an intellectual with strong opinions on education. I finished my summary, and in an attempt to express everything in one word—my verbal shorthand—I said, "Oh, you mean the guy who's uppity?"

I held the phone to my ear waiting for Deborah's "Yeah, that's him." But there was only silence, a silence that was as deafening as if my head were the clapper in a huge church tower bell, tolling the message for everyone in the community to hear: "Unterschuetz said the word!" "Unterschuetz said the word!"

Oh, Damn. Damn! I did say the "word," and I knew exactly what form that shape-shifter demon had taken on this time—"uppity."

Speaking is the physical act of exhaling air from the lungs past the vocal cords, which impart the air with a vibration. The lips sculpt the air into a particular sound that is then carried by waves to another person's ears and received as something meaningful—language. The miracle of modern technology is that this process can take place over incredible distances, such as past the earth's atmosphere into outer space—and even across a continent. I sensed that something was not right as the "word" left my mouth and escaped, as if part of a well-planned prison break, to resume its thuggish activities on the outside. I regretted my hasty choice of verbal symbol the moment my breath, charged with a precise vibration, expanded in my mouth and made its way past the final fortifications of my lips. Then those three fugitive syllables were whisked away by cell towers and finally delivered into the ear of my friend, two thousand miles across the country, only moments later.

The "word" vibrated Deborah's auditory nerves and was then de-coded by some apparatus of her brain; its content was interpreted then evaluated and passed on to her heart. In the meantime I was left to imagine the response she was having. Was she hurt, angry, disappointed that she had trusted me as a friend? I wanted to be trustworthy, and I felt that the only way I could be certain of success was to see trust reflected in her eyes. But, now, separated by distance, I was unable to see the visual cues upon which I so heavily depended.

Some ten to fifteen seconds of silence had elapsed.

"Uh, I think I said something that might have hurt you," I finally managed to mumble. "And I think it was the word *uppity.*"

"Yeah, that's an interesting word," she said.

"I know better than to use that word; I know that historically it's been used maliciously, and I know that its effect cuts deep. I'm really sorry."

"It's all right, Gene. I know your heart. I know you weren't trying to hurt me."

I apologized again and then asked, "Are we still OK?"

"Yes, we're OK," she said.

"You're sure?"

"Yes."

"Sure?"

"Yes."

We talked about the "word" for another hour and a half. When I hung up, I was still unsettled, but I had to trust that Deborah had told me the truth when she said she forgave me and loved me. To doubt her sincerity would inhibit the growth of our friendship.

Phyllis and I recently visited Deborah. Our time together was precious but too brief. We ate delicious Southern-cooked meals, talked about the challenges and joys of life, attended a devotional gathering, and watched a movie. All three of us are committed to our friendship, and we've come to a joint conclusion: Love is stronger than the "word."

COMMENTARY

In discussions about the word *uppity*, I've heard white folks say, "My grandma used that word all the time to refer to people in town who thought they were better than others. Why, she even called me 'uppity' sometimes when she thought I was getting too big for my britches. I know she didn't hate me. It's just a word people use."

So why would African-Americans have a strong reaction to the word *uppity*? What I've read is that if a slave learned to read and write or add and subtract—in short, if he or she displayed intelligence beyond what was required to do the work at hand—white owners might have said that slave was being "uppity." This was not a harmless observation about someone displaying arrogance or self-importance. It was a warning and might even have foreshadowed dire consequences. The message to the slave was, "Stay in your place, or else." For some that message is still attached to the word *uppity*.

Words can humiliate, terrorize, enrage, or crush the human spirit. I did not consciously choose to hurt my friend with the word *uppity*; in a sense, racial conditioning and ignorance had made that choice for me. Nevertheless, I have to be accountable for the impact of what I say. Although I could not see my friend's face, I knew she was struggling. Fortunately, I had learned something over the years, and I was able to quickly review the words I chose and determine what was causing my friend distress. And I apologized. To be able to address my upsetting behavior relatively quickly was an important milestone for me.

The work of eliminating racial prejudice requires tact, sensitivity, discretion. The Bahá'í writings offer the following guidance for black and white Americans: "Let neither think that anything short of genuine love, extreme patience, true humility, consummate tact, sound initiative, mature wisdom, and deliberate, persistent, and prayerful effort, can succeed in blotting out the stain which this patent evil has left on the fair name of their common country."[1]

The American right to freedom of speech is our priceless heritage. But that doesn't mean I can be insensitive and irresponsible and say anything I want, without regard for the impact of my words on others.

After four decades, I remember Lamont—his initiative, his indignation, and his embarrassment. And what has remained—besides the details of that event and the many other situations in which I uttered the "word" in one of its insidious mutations—is a tremendous sense of loss.

26

SAFE HAVEN

Phyllis, June 2007
Chicago, Illinois

"Just get your gas and leave," my son told me on the phone. "Don't stay there any longer than necessary." Then, as I was imagining how I would do this, he continued in a reassuring tone, "I'm not trying to scare you; I just want you to be aware."

How does that work, exactly? I wondered as I started driving. *How does a person acknowledge a statistical reality yet not use it to reinforce a stereotype? How do I accept that there's a legitimate need to protect myself without letting that make me feel afraid?*

Gene and I had just left our son's apartment. It was very late— around 2:00 in the morning if I remember correctly—and I'd forgotten to get gas earlier. The moment I started the car I remembered that we had to drive from the black neighborhood where he lived in a high-crime part of the city to the relative safety of suburbia only twenty minutes away, which we would never accomplish with an empty gas tank. So, still parked in front of his building, I'd called

him on my cell phone and asked where the nearest open gas station was. For we were past empty; the little amber light had been
glowing steadily for the last several miles of our drive into the city,
and I didn't think I'd make it even as far as the big, brightly-lit gas
station at the interstate entrance a few miles away. Our son had given
me directions to a gas station located just around the corner at an
intersection that was, statistically speaking, not the safest place in the
neighborhood this late at night.

I felt great relief as I pulled up next to the gas pump, glad that
we hadn't sputtered to a stop in the middle of the street somewhere.
Gene got out the passenger side door and walked around the car to
the pump. I could see in his movements an even balance. He was
aware, as our son had advised, but not nervous; he was alert to his
surroundings, yet casual.

A little too casual, actually. He swiped his credit card and pushed
the button for 87 octane.

"Wait!" I called out the window, envisioning my car chugging
along pathetically on inferior-grade gasoline. "You need to put in the
higher octane gas."

So much for keeping a low profile. He stopped the pump, then
pushed the button for the manufacturer's recommended grade of
fuel. The pump would not start. So he took his receipt for $0.16,
and I drove around the island to the pumps at the far side of the
lot, where he again ran his credit card through the reader. This one
refused his card altogether, thanks to our bank's fraud protection
policy. After several unsuccessful attempts to restart the pump,
Gene gave up and went into the station to prepay our purchase
with cash.

It was a warm summer night, and I leaned my elbow out the car window as I watched him walk across the cement and in the door, then take his place at the end of a long line of people. He was so *noticeable*, so obviously not from here. I could see him greeting his fellow line-standers and knew he was feeling a level of comfort gained in black communities in the Deep South. Neither of us felt afraid. At this point, however, any attempt to avoid drawing attention to ourselves was futile. We'd drawn it the moment we drove up to the first gas pump, denied from the beginning any hope of blending in.

I was acutely aware of the eyes on us and imagined I could hear people asking each other what we were doing here in their neighborhood. I wondered briefly if I should try to appear more alert, however that looks; or should I be monitoring my facial expressions, making a conscious effort to give the impression of nonchalance? A little comedy monologue played in my head—my own private stand-up routine: *Yes, we are here. We are white. We're just getting gas. We are not afraid, but we are aware. We'll get in and get out. We are not prejudiced. We love black people. We fully reject the notion that you are all criminals, so please don't shoot us.*

Perhaps at some point during the night, this spot would become the scene of a crime; it was even statistically likely. But right now it was as peaceful as any lazy Sunday morning I remember from my childhood. There were men and women, elders and youth, pumping gas, buying lottery tickets or cigarettes, speaking to each other in passing.

As I watched them coming and going, a man who appeared to be about my age stepped out of the gas station door and fixed his gaze on me through the open window of my car. And when I looked back

I felt that click—the barely audible but unmistakable sound that indicates a locking-in of frequencies. No jumble of thoughts, no chaos of feelings, no questions in my mind about what he was thinking. Just a looking, one into the other. A *seeing*. Then he nodded. I nodded back.

"Good morning, Mother," he said.

"Good morning, Sir," I responded.

That's all. Not even a smile, just a casual statement of truth: we are related. And there is a recognition of my place in this family.

How was it that I heard his voice so clearly? We were separated by a distance of maybe fifty feet, an island of gas pumps and a spread of concrete between us, yet his voice carried through the darkness and fell on my ear with the clarity of a whistle, with the intimacy of a whisper. At that moment, if a drug-crazed gangster had come squealing around the corner—guns blazing like Al Capone's—this man would have stepped into a bullet's path to save my life, as I would have done to save his. I felt as safe as if cradled in my mother's arms, safe because with one word of greeting I had been taken in and was now woven into the fabric of this neighborhood. In fact, I felt safer here than I did in a statistically nonviolent place where there was no sense of community, no awareness of people watching out for one another.

Gene returned and filled the gas tank, then got into the car. I looked back on the peaceful scene as I pulled out into traffic; everything appeared the same as it had when we'd pulled in. But I was changed.

So I will continue to reassure white folks that they don't have to stroll the 'hood at night in order to unlearn racial prejudice. I will continue to duck accusations that I am naive and foolish. Let them think what they will. I know where I'm safe and where I'm not. I know security when I feel it.

COMMENTARY

I originally began this commentary with the statement that not everyone agrees with my choices. Then I realized that if I made a disclaimer about every point people might disagree with, this book would become a 12-volume set. Suffice it to say that there are all kinds of folks, not just whites, who think we were insane to be at that spot so late at night. I'm sure there are even other residents of the neighborhood who would never go there after dark.

On another visit to our son's home, I was standing outside his front door, getting ready to retrieve something from my car, when I heard "BANG! BANG! BANG!"

"Was that gunfire?" I asked him. I've never heard gunfire in real life except during hunting season.

"Could be a car backfiring or someone shooting off firecrackers," he answered. I could tell he was irritated. He's tired of listening to people's stories of being on the South Side and hearing gunshots. He tries to teach me something about street smarts, of which I have none: Look around, keep your eyes open. He's not fearful living there, but he certainly stays alert, ready to avoid a dangerous situation if one comes up. Just like the other residents of the neighborhood.

I, on the other hand, am not only lacking street smarts, I'm often accused of being over-trusting to the point of self-endangerment—a Pollyanna. I looked up the reference online and found a definition from Wikipedia. Apparently the term *Pollyanna* comes from the novel of the same name and is used to describe someone who is "cheerfully optimistic and who always maintains a generous attitude toward the motives of other people. It also became, by extension—and contrary to the spirit of the book—a derogatory term for a naive optimist who always expects people to act decently, despite strong evidence to the contrary."[1]

That would explain the problem, then; I don't see enough strong evidence of people acting indecently. Maybe if I did, I would have different expectations.

Women particularly take exception to my habit of looking men in the eye. The argument goes like this: "I'm a woman, and I'm not going to make eye contact with *any* man when I'm alone, I don't care *what* color he is."

"Of course not," I placate. "I'm not suggesting any such thing." But this is not the truth, and at some later point in our conversation, it usually becomes obvious that I think it's a really good idea.

Once when I was talking about making eye contact, a woman said to me, "Well, you can do that; you're unusual." What did she mean by "unusual"? That I have some unique ability to sniff out and ward off evil intentions? That I'm just plain stupid? Or simply unappealing?

Another variation of the same argument I hear frequently from women is, "I'm not going to look any man in the eye, I don't care if he's black, white, or . . ." and here, in an effort to convince me that her fear is not in any way about skin color, she inserts some unlikely combination of hues and design elements. My favorite is always green with purple polka dots, which is vaguely reminiscent of the lilac bushes that grew in the backyard of my childhood home, and which lends a pastoral, dreamlike quality to the rest of the conversation.

I guess I do have a disclaimer after all, and also an apology if I've offended anyone. It's not my intention to demean or disrespect the experience of any woman who's been hurt by a man and as a result feels cautious or even fearful. It's just that I've never been attacked or even threatened, which certainly has a lot to do with my Pollyanna approach to life. I offer my experiences and theories in the hope of stimulating awareness and discussion, not with the idea that everyone should see things the way I do.

The other point I want to address is a tendency I've noticed in white people (and no, I haven't forgotten that I'm one of them) to think that any place with a majority of black residents is dangerous— a theory that has been disproved to me over and over in all parts of the country. Frequently the fear is focused on the "inner city," as if that were the only place African-Americans live. Whether in a workshop or an informal context, someone will protest vigorously that we seem to be suggesting they go wandering alone at night in search of new friends in the 'hood / inner city / ghetto that is infested with gangs / drive-by shooters / drug addicts, exposing themselves foolishly to all manner of violent crime. And although we respond each time with a gentle suggestion that they begin instead by initiating conversations in the grocery store, leaving the outing to the 'hood for another time, the look of panic stays with them and continues to color our discussion.

I know there is a reality that cannot be ignored, but if I try to talk myself into being wary, the conversation turns absurd. *Just pay attention. This is like a war zone here. Anyone would be vigilant in a war zone. It's about gangs and drugs, not about race. I'm sure even the black residents of this neighborhood are cautious when they come here at night. I'm sure many of the gang members and bad guys are white. OK, maybe not the ones right here, but somewhere there are plenty of bad white guys.*

Then I come to the conclusion—not for the first time—that racism has robbed us all, whatever our color, of the freedom to behave in a reasonable and spontaneous manner. In fact, sometimes I think it has turned me into a blathering idiot.

It's not my purpose here to address the issue of inner-city violence. There are plenty of books if you want to research its origins. White authors have been expounding their hypotheses for decades, but they can see the problems only from a white perspective; even black authors disagree among themselves about the underlying causes and solutions.

My purpose is rather to present for your consideration my small experience of truth: that even in what might appear to be the most unlikely of places, you will find others who not only recognize our relatedness but are not afraid to name it and extend it to you on a silver platter of trust; that while the conditions in these neighborhoods have been responsible for the deaths of a horrifying number of African-Americans, they have not succeeded in killing the pull of kinship in everyone who lives there; that the simple recognition of another soul—I am here; yes, I see you—has the power to overcome any fear that the society or the media can throw at us. We are family. When we acknowledge this, we become the very superheroes we've been looking for, capable of audacious acts of sacrifice and love. And is this not exactly what we need to pull ourselves out of the collective mess we've fallen into?

27

LIGHTNING ROD

Gene
Part 1: October 2000
Tennessee

When we walked into John's office, he was on the phone. He smiled when he saw us and gestured that his conversation was almost over. As soon as he finished, he got up from his desk, walked over and hugged us. "Man, it's good to see you two!" he said. "How y'all doin'?"

"Just great!" Phyllis said.

The three of us stood in the middle of John's large work area engaged in an animated exchange, laughing and blurting out quick reports of recent adventures. We had been going on like that for several minutes when John looked over my shoulder to the doorway of the office and called out, "Hey, man, come over here. I want you to meet some friends." I turned around to be introduced, and my eyes were drawn up to take in a man's face. He was solidly built and tall—a full head taller than I am. When I talk to tall people, I generally look up into the person's face with my eyes only—without tilting my head. In this instance, however, that tactic only enabled me to greet the top button of the man's shirt.

"Phyllis and Gene," John said, "this is my colleague, Robert. Robert this is Phyllis and Gene, the folks I was telling you about. They travel around the country doing race unity workshops."

"How ya doin'? Nice to meet you," I said. My hand felt tiny in the grip of Robert's handshake.

"Nice meeting you, too," Robert said. "John's told me about some of the work y'all do."

Robert took a couple of steps toward his desk to put down some papers. I followed him, and Phyllis walked with John to his workspace to hear about his current project. Robert sat on his desk so that we were almost at the same eye level. I was still looking up at his face, but at least I didn't have to tilt my head.

"That sounds like interesting work you and your wife do," Robert said. "So what kinds of things do you tell people in your workshops?"

I gave Robert an overview of the content of our presentations and stressed that one of our goals was to impress upon other white folks that we have to step up to our responsibility to eliminate racism. Robert's eyes opened wider as he listened, and I could see he had some things he wanted to express.

He crossed his arms and drew in a long breath, and as he began sharing his observations of white America's racist attitudes, he made statements that started with "What I see white people doing is . . ." and "White people say . . ." Robert's voice got louder as he continued to express the multitude of thoughts that seemed to be flooding his mind. Then he stood up to make a point, and there was a sense of urgency in the way he spoke. Now his statements started with, "When I see white people doing..." and "When I hear whites say..." and were followed by descriptions of how he felt as a result of their actions and words. Gradually Robert's intense but analytical demeanor gave way to a rising passion. Already towering over me, he now leaned forward, his face contorted into a clear expression of anger, and wagging his finger in my face he shouted, "And you shouldn't be doing...! And you should never say...!" I felt my face flush and my teeth clench. As I pulled my hands free from my pockets, my arms tensed up—ready to push him away from me—and I stepped back to get better footing. But although my body was bracing itself for a strike, I wasn't afraid.

I wondered how this scene might appear to an outside observer. A white onlooker might conclude that I was about to be hit. White men can get very nervous around black men, especially tall, assertive black men like Robert. His anger was justifiable; however, I knew I was safe. While I'm not a therapist, I was fairly certain that what I heard was not an accusation directed at me, but pain. And I knew what was required. I listened. As Robert kept talking, the sense of urgency gradually subsided, and he finally grew silent. He put his hand on my shoulder and said, "You know I don't mean you personally, don't you?"

"Yeah," I said. "No problem."

John and Phyllis walked over to Robert's work area. "We should probably let you guys get back to what you were doing," I said.

"Well," said John, "we do have a lot to keep us busy. But it was sure good to see y'all again."

"Right," said Robert. "I really enjoyed the conversation. Y'all take care." He bent over and hugged me, then Phyllis. "How long y'all staying in town?" he asked.

"Another week," Phyllis said.

"Well, be sure to come back and visit before you go," he said.

As we drove away, I reflected on the exchange with Robert. I was exhausted. The muscles in my neck and shoulders were still tight, and I was reminded of the aftereffects of accidentally touching the hot wire of an electrical outlet. I was aware that I had responded to someone's anger differently than I had in the past; that was a milestone for me. I realized that I had withstood a heavy dose of rage and not come unraveled. It seemed I had rendered a service—as if I had been used as a lightening rod, and thereby safeguarded a relationship—no damage sustained. I felt grounded. I wasn't completely sure what had happened during our brief visit, but I knew that in time I'd get my brain around it.

COMMENTARY

Even before we started traveling, I had observed that black acquaintances might suddenly shift from a cordial mood to a state of distress. Whites would then ask each other, "What's wrong with her?" or "What's his problem?" In my own experience, if a white person displayed intense emotion, I could usually identify the cause, and the behavior made sense to me. But with black people, it just seemed as if they were angry, and I didn't know why.

I remember once being with a group of friends and having a discussion about race that started out relaxed and rather academic. But at one point, a black woman in the group became very distraught. In a loud voice she spoke candidly about the indifference of whites to the plight of their black friends. Finally she paused and asked a white man, a long-time acquaintance, what he thought about her comments.

"Well, first of all," he said, "I didn't know you felt that way. You never said anything. But why do you have to be so angry?" I was familiar with this response. I had frequently wanted to ask the same question myself.

I've realized that I don't necessarily need to understand all the reasons a person feels angry. Often it's enough to just listen. Something I learned from a lecture on emotional healing is that there is a belief in our society that we will be destroyed by listening to the pain of other people, when in fact we will be recreated. We might be disturbed, we might even be in pain ourselves, but we will be changed. When we listen to someone's pain, we acknowledge that person's truth and create an opportunity to establish a powerful connection.

Part 2: May 2007
California

"Man, things have really changed," Brad said. "I used to hang out with all kinds of people when I was younger. A lot of my friends were black; we had great times together. But you couldn't pay me to socialize with blacks today. It's too dangerous now. I don't trust them."

Brad became agitated and spewed out a stream of "information" about the black community and black men in particular—proof, in his mind, that any association with them was life-threatening. Like many other whites, he had come to certain conclusions based on statistics he'd read in his local newspaper or heard on the evening news.

"Most of them are in prison. They're all addicted to crack. They commit crimes to support their addictions. They're irresponsible."

My stomach knotted up. I wanted to say something to contradict his erroneous generalizations, but I had long ago learned that confronting someone with facts when he is filled with emotion is fruitless. Again, I'm an artist, not a therapist, but as I listened to Brad, I thought I heard him express a feeling of loss. I prayed silently, "God, help me offer something—anything." And while I prayed, I saw in my mind the faces of black men I knew. I felt their presence and their support.

Finally Brad was spent. He was silent for a moment, then looked at me and asked, "So, do you have any black friends?"

I smiled; my prayer had been answered. I said, "You know we travel all over the country." Brad nodded. "Well, if I think about the people I consider my friends in all the places we've been"—I paused to be sure he was listening—"I'd have to say that most of them are black."

Brad's jaw dropped. "Really?" he asked. "Why?"

I told him that after meeting many African-American men, my experience did not support the belief that they are patently violent and dangerous. On the contrary, I found black men to be loving and generous. They had invited me to church and into their homes, where we had become acquainted during long conversations at the dinner table. And they perceived something of value in me and made me aware of it.

Brad stood quietly and listened. When I was finished, he adjusted his cap, walked over, and clapped me on shoulder. "You're alright, man," he said.

That little affirmation marked another important milestone for me. As I've previously mentioned, talking with other white folks about race has often led to verbal sparring in which I attempted to "impress" my understanding on others. It seemed that after Brad had been heard, he was able to listen to something that directly contradicted his perspective on the topic.

What I think Brad meant with his final words was that he had found something of value in my description of black men. Hopefully he would rethink his conclusions about them.

COMMENTARY

Brad relied on statistics he'd heard or read to help him make sense of things. Statistics inform us about the truth, but facts, figures, graphs, and percentages can give rise to a multitude of interpretations. In the commentary to Robert's story, I suggested that emotions also reveal truth. When Robert talked about the racist things white people say and do, he was angry. For men, blowing off steam is often how we express emotional pain. Where do we find that pain neatly graphed on x-y coordinates, or quantified and represented on a pie chart as a percentage of the findings in some study? It appeared that Brad was not able to factor that kind of truth into his assessment of black men.

Brad also sounded angry, but I sensed a mixture of fear and loss as well, perhaps related to separation from his friends of color. I knew that my role with Brad was to listen. However he was making erroneous statements that he applied to the entire black community. I needed to respond in a way that pointed to a more complete picture of the truth. These situations have always been a bit tricky for me.

When I feel that someone is trashing something I cherish, I feel hurt, and my first impulse is to respond with stinging repartee. As much as I want to justify that tendency as righteous indignation, it never creates harmony. Someone always walks away a loser—usually me.

There's an interesting distraction, which I've heard referred to as "find the racist," that stifles peoples' participation when the subject of race is being discussed. If some white person inadvertently lets loose with something ignorant—or honest—other white members of the group might be seen looking down in embarrassment for that person, but also in relief that the "racist" has been identified and it's someone else—not them. Everyone can relax now because the "racist" will receive a lecture that serves to illustrate some important lesson. This method is similar to training a puppy not to pee indoors. Whereas the puppy gets swatted with a rolled up newspaper, the racist gets bopped with the superior racial insights of some knowledgeable person in the group. The puppy eventually pees only outside, and the "racist" shuts down. The real lesson learned is: don't let people know what you're really thinking and feeling.

If our goal is to create harmony and unity, can we listen to a white brother's or sister's pain, then acknowledge and validate it? Even when it sounds ignorant? It might be the only way the truth will come out.

28

OF HORSE RIDERS AND KINGS

Phyllis, July 2007
Chicago, Illinois

I grew up in a town where status—at least among us children—was determined by the number of lessons we took. Scouts didn't count, nor did team sports. It was all about lessons. Surely this idea did not originate with us but was something we absorbed from our parents as we overheard them comparing our various accomplishments. Our park district offered every kind of lesson imaginable. There were classes for ballet, tap, and ballroom dancing; several types of acrobatics; arts and crafts; and others too numerous to mention. At the tender age of six, I acted in television commercials for the studio where my dad worked as a director. So when my parents said I could keep $100 of my earnings to spend on myself, I used it for lessons, thereby upping my status considerably.

I think I stretched the money out over a number of years; one hundred dollars went a long way back then. Sadly, I've since forgotten how to tap dance, and doing a three-point headstand now would surely result in serious injury; however, if you put a baton in my hand, I can still twirl it like a drum majorette—I actually know three twirling patterns, although while practicing in the trailer I tend to leave out the part where you throw the baton in the air and catch it behind your back.

My horseback riding lessons, though, turned into one of the greatest loves of my life. I learned how to trot, canter, and gallop; I could ride English or western. When I was a teenager, my family visited my grandparents in Arkansas every summer, and there I could rent a horse for $2 an hour. My friends and I trotted our steeds through the woods, jumped tiny streams, and galloped across the dam that separated sparkling, man-made lakes. During the school year, I would babysit Friday and Saturday nights and make enough money to go riding on Sunday at my favorite stable. My most passionate dream—the thing I wished for as I blew out my birthday candles every year until I turned twenty, the item on every single Christmas list—was my own horse.

It was apparently not meant to be. Where I lived, the only people who owned horses were wealthy, and my family dangled precariously from the bottom rung of the middle class. The dream lives on regardless, and I occasionally find myself thinking that someday—maybe when I'm seventy—I'll be able to afford my own horse.

Once when we were driving through the Navajo Reservation, we stopped to fill up at a little gas station off the interstate. On one wall of the small store were taped about a dozen stories, printed carefully in pencil on lined paper and illustrated with crayon drawings. The old man who owned the station saw me reading and told me the students from the local elementary school had presented him with their essays so he could think about them while he was working. Most of the children had written stories of riding their horses to school; in their pictures, drawn with surprising detail for such young kids, they rode bareback and carried their backpacks or lunch boxes in one hand, holding the reins in the other. I asked the owner, "Do these kids really ride horses to school?"

"Well sure they do," he answered. "How else would they get there?"

"And those are their own horses?"

"Well sure they are. Who else would they belong to?"

I felt the old dream rise up in me, and at that moment would have gladly changed places with one of those children, just so I could ride my own horse to school each day.

In the summer of 2007, Gene and I went into Chicago for Ghana-fest—an annual event that draws Ghanaians from all over the United States for a celebration of their culture—held at an expansive park on the city's South Side. We pulled up to look for parking just as the Ghanaian chiefs and queens were getting out of one limousine after another and processing toward the venue. They wore robes and headpieces of bright primary colors, and some of them carried golden scepters. They seemed to feel right at home in this park crowded with African-American families having picnics and playing baseball.

We enjoyed wandering around the festival, tasting specialty dishes from different regions of Ghana, listening to the music, and strolling among the vendor's booths. The high point of the afternoon came when chiefs and queens from different tribes filed with spectacular pageantry into the middle of the circle of onlookers. Accompanied by musical fanfare, these members of African royalty were honored and the names of newly elected representatives were announced over loudspeaker. It appeared to me as if the entire ceremony had been lifted out of Africa and dropped into the city of Chicago.

After several hours, we decided to go to a restaurant for dinner and started walking along the sidewalk back to our car, parked a half mile away. Ahead in the distance, I saw horses and riders. My vision is keenly attuned to the sight of people on horseback, and I adjusted my heading so I could pass near them. There were many more than I'd realized at first, and I could see others coming toward us from farther down the street. The riders' complexions were indiscernible through my dark sunglasses; I just assumed they were white.

When I got closer, I saw to my astonishment that they were black. All of them. The sentence that rose into my conscious mind was *I didn't know black people rode horses.* I was even more shocked to hear myself think that than I was to see the black equestrians.

My surprise was not great enough, however, to eclipse my envy. I approached one couple astride tall thoroughbreds; they wore jaunty riding outfits and helmets and exuded an air of graceful leisure.

"Oh, you're so lucky!" I said in my best eight-year-old voice, looking way up at them from my place on the ground. "I always dreamed of having a horse."

The man explained that they boarded their horses on a farm in Indiana and belonged to an equestrian club that came to the park occasionally to ride.

"These are your *own* horses?" I asked. I'm sure he heard the skepticism mixed in with the envy.

"Of course."

I wonder if he also heard what I didn't say out loud: *How come you have achieved my dream and I haven't?*

There were dozens of black equestrians in the park that day, and every time I passed another one, I was amazed all over again. The monologue running through my mind never let up, and I listened to it oddly detached, as though I were eavesdropping on someone else's private thoughts: *Not only are they riding horses, they're riding their own horses. And they're riding well. How did they learn to ride so well?* We came to a spot where an entire family of riders had gathered, some still mounted, others standing in the grass holding their horses' reins. A young boy of maybe eight years sat astride a feisty, full-sized stallion that was either agitated or just anxious to run. It was spinning and bucking slightly, and the boy nonchalantly controlled that big, restless horse as though he'd been riding since he was a toddler. *How the heck did that little boy learn how to ride like that?* Apparently I'd forgotten that I was riding at the same age, although not nearly as adeptly as he was.

Once we had passed all the riders and climbed into our car, I stopped being surprised and started in on the self-recriminations. *What the hell is wrong with me? I think I'm such an ally, supposedly so aware, impatient with whites' ignorance, and now it seems I just can't believe my eyes. I know there are plenty of rich black folks, so why am I surprised? Do I think they just wouldn't like horseback riding? But I've never seen black riders before!*

When satisfied that I'd beaten myself up sufficiently, I soothed my ego by recalling the words of an African-American friend in college who told me that black people aren't good swimmers—something about the structure or direction of their muscles, or the ratio of fat to muscle, something like that. "We just can't swim," he'd said. I thought it sounded unlikely, but because he was telling me, I believed it. I tucked this piece of information away so neatly that when I saw a black diver on TV, I thought it was a trick. Then there was the African-American woman who told me confidently, "Black folks don't have cats. We don't put up with animals in the house, walking all over our kitchen counters. No cats. Black folks just don't have them."

By this point, I was seriously in the mood to dispel some stereotypes, and I looked around intently as I drove away from the park, hoping to see a family walking back to their car in their swimming suits with dripping wet cats under their arms.

COMMENTARY

As I was writing this story, I thought of the two black students who went to my high school. I never talked to either of those students, but I do remember that one of them played the drums for a talent show. I had always loved the drums. At a parade, I would locate the best drum line and accompany it down the street, feeling the pounding of the percussion throughout my body. I was told in junior high that I would never play drums because only the boys could do that. I could choose flute or clarinet if I wanted to play an instrument. So when the curtain opened to reveal this student at his drum set, I was surprised but envious. He played wonderfully and was rewarded with a standing ovation. The same kind of question came into my mind then as when I saw the little boy on his horse: *how did he learn to play the drums like that?*

Over the past ten years, I have met African-Americans from every social stratum, some with levels of education I could not achieve in two lifetimes, working in every conceivable occupation. I thought I was free of stereotypes. And yet my now broad image of African-Americans was still not broad enough to comfortably encompass a whole bunch of black folks on horseback.

How often have I heard condescending remarks about women? "I didn't know women could fix their own cars." "Look at that woman driving that great big RV!" Not so long ago it was, "I'd never go to a woman doctor." People of my generation—men and women alike—are still surprised to see a female truck driver. We would argue that this is not about sexism; we're just surprised because it's new and unusual. We agree that women have been kept from certain occupations by institutionalized gender discrimination and that they are now finally able to compete with men for most jobs. We celebrate their advances, but there is a lingering fear—way deep down—that they can't do it quite as well. Even I, seeing the uniformed crew emerge from the cockpit of a large commercial jetliner, cannot imagine that the woman walking with her three male colleagues could possibly be the captain, the one who actually *flew* the plane. We cling with ferocity to stereotypes not only about others but about our own selves as well.

I don't want to be too hard on myself here; it serves no purpose, and besides, I'm sure there were plenty of black folks in the park that day who were just as surprised as I was, if that makes it any better. Or maybe the families from the neighborhood had seen the equestrians before and were more surprised to see African royalty with golden scepters.

I also don't want to leave you feeling despondent over the tenacity of stereotypes. It is an undeniable fact that the way we're conditioned to see people is a very difficult thing to unlearn. But it's not impossible, and we are apparently all struggling with the same kinds of issues.

And we were all there together in the park on that hot summer day. Ghanaian chiefs and queens, who had chosen to come here within the past few decades, were celebrating in their colorful robes. Descendants of Ghanaians who'd been brought here in chains centuries ago were barbecuing with their families and riding their expensive horses. There were also a few of us with paler skin, whose connection to Africa had been interrupted by the great migrations that took our ancestors into northern Europe, where the climate eventually repressed the visual evidence of our ancestry. The spacious park served as a kind of matrix, and I could see the threads that connected all these dark-skinned people to one another and to the grown-up, envious white girl from the suburbs.

I wasn't sure at first how these two images were connected—the equestrians and the African royalty—knowing only that there was some significance because I saw them in the same place at the same time. What I finally came up with, besides admitting to you that in spite of all my efforts I'm still struggling with stereotypes, is that this story is about me trying to understand who black folks really are, which means understanding who I really am. And that brings me back to the Vanguard of the Dawning Conference and to the awareness I had on that day: until I reconnect with the brothers and sisters from whom I was separated at birth, I can never really know my own self. So whether these lost siblings are Ghanaian chiefs and queens, affluent riders, or residents of poverty-stricken neighbor-hoods, we do not yet—any of us—know our full potential. Because our potential will be achieved only when we figure out how to behave like members of one family.

When I think of Bahá'u'lláh's words—"True loss is for him whose days have been spent in utter ignorance of his self"[1]— I realize that the longing I've been talking about in all these stories is a complex thing. It's the force of attraction that draws us to one another and calls us to overcome separation. But it's also a yearning to heal the separation between who we are and who we might become. It explains that feeling of loss when we can't seem to find our most noble selves. The longing urges us to emerge from a self-image that is obsolete and restrictive. It makes us believe we can become something new.

29

ASSIMILATION

Gene, August 2005
California

During a visit with friends, a white couple about our age, we were
engaged in a stimulating conversation over breakfast. They were particularly curious about our race unity work and asked well thought-
out questions; it appeared they had discussed the topic of race before
and were seeking answers. We shared some of the things we had
learned about the dynamics of racism, and mentioned how grateful
we were to the African-Americans we had met who helped us understand this complex issue. I was glad that our friends were comfortable
discussing a topic that white folks normally avoid.

But when our host started a sentence with "if," I tensed up, anticipating that what followed that small, two-lettered word would
require a response I was not up to. The rest of the sentence seemed
to come out of his mouth in slow motion: "If . . . they—would—
only—want—to—assimilate." It was clear from our discussion that
"they" referred to African-Americans. The last word, "assimilate,"

felt like an ambush, the preceding words having somehow sneaked up on me disguised as civility. I'd been left defenseless. My mind went momentarily blank, but even in that dazed condition I heard the words "dress" and "language" and "attitude" come out of the man's mouth. I could feel my face getting hot as I realized that he was reciting the standard laundry list of "requirements" that often make it impossible for black people to get jobs for which they are fully qualified.

I recalled a workshop Phyllis and I conducted in South Carolina that was attended by both blacks and whites. As a final exercise one evening, we asked all of the African-Americans to sit facing the white participants. Then we asked them to take turns addressing the whites using statements that began with, "I want you to always . . ." and then completing the sentence. Each person was told to make as many requests as he or she desired. I was aware that every speaker's list of requests included this one: "I want you to always correct misinformation about black people!" It was a powerful exercise—much more than a purging of feelings. I felt I had been given a mandate that clearly stated how to work toward eliminating racial prejudice.

Then I thought of friends who had done all the right things to qualify for career opportunities, only to meet with rejection when prospective employers found out they were black. I wanted to stand up, lean over the table, and scream at our host.

The challenge for me was this: If I didn't scream, how should I respond? If I said nothing, my silence might be understood as agreement. I couldn't do that, because as I've stated, I feel I've received a mandate from black friends to correct misinformation or at least offer a different perspective.

If only I could show this couple a video journal of what I've experienced. They could meet my friends and acquaintances, hear their intelligence, feel their compassion, become acquainted with their endeavors and values, and perhaps come to appreciate the unique gifts they have to offer.

In the video, they would see a black friend and his family move into a predominately white suburb. They would hear him describe how, on moving day, he noticed a neighbor, an elderly white lady, peeking out her window. "She watched us move in from behind the curtains. After the weekend, when we were finished with the work, I went over to introduce myself. She opened the door, and I could see she was frightened. I did everything I could to assure her she was safe, that she needn't be afraid of us. A couple days later, there was a *For Sale* sign in front of her house. I went back a few times hoping she would get to know me and wouldn't have to go through all the trouble of moving. I always went over when I knew she was home, but she never came to the door. Within a month, she was gone."

They would see me conversing with a talented young black man who was offered a high-paying teaching job—if he agreed to cut off his dreadlocks.

They would meet the Mayan medicine woman with one master's degree in biology and another in education, who can't get a job commensurate with her qualifications because she's Native American.

And a Lakota woman who broke down in tears while she recounted her childhood and youth as a resident of a boarding school that attempted to "beat the Indian out of her" and other Native youngsters.

The African-American man who, in addition to his civic contributions in local government and church, was a Scoutmaster. And when he tried to bring black boys and white boys together for Scouting activities, he was met with resistance from white parents who refused to allow their sons to participate.

The young Asian Ph.D. student who stayed on campus, because when she made trips into town, she was called names and terrorized.

The Hispanic man who beamed with pride as he told me how successful his boys were in school. Then a cloud of sadness passed over his face, and he pointed to his arm, touching his brown skin with his index finger, and said, "But they'll have to deal with this, like I have."

The white man who remembered turning five, entering school, and being told he may no longer invite his best friend for sleepovers because that friend is black.

The biracial woman whose father is white and thinks she is too sensitive when she tries to tell him about the racism she experiences.

The black businessman who visits a white college buddy in an unfamiliar suburb, gets lost and pulls into a driveway, and before he can walk from his car to the house to ask for directions, the white homeowner steps out the front door and points a shotgun at him.

And the black professor who reveals—to the astonishment of white colleagues who have worked with him for years—how much frustration he'd experienced at having been consistently passed over for advancement.

They would meet these friends and hundreds more, and hopefully they would be moved to reexamine the notion of assimilation—as I have. Perhaps, in a moment of reflection, they might ask themselves, "Is this thing we want—assimilation—realistic or even desirable? Are we missing something essential when we demand of others that they acquire our ways of doing things?" Maybe the video would encourage our hosts to replace the stereotypical images of people of color they'd seen in films and media with images of real people who love their families and help them recognize that all of us have the same kinds of aspirations. Hopefully the couple could then acknowledge the burdens placed on people of color that frustrate their efforts to contribute to a vital, healthy, creative community life.

So, in the end, I didn't scream at our host, but I was able to use the energy generated by my anger to illustrate the truth as I understand it, through storytelling and conversation. A dear friend once referred to it as witnessing—testifying to what I've observed. We should all be witnesses. And at this particular time in history, we should be comparing what we see and experience so that we can get an accurate idea of what's really happening in our community and in our country.

COMMENTARY

There's a difference between feeling belligerent because someone disrespects a principle or belief you cherish, and feeling indignant because someone is judging your friends with a contrived standard he believes is all-embracing. While writing this story, I remembered vividly the encounters with the people portrayed in my "video" as they related their experiences to me. Because I had connected with them, the pain they expressed moved me deeply—even if I didn't completely understand it.

At the breakfast table, I was moved not just to defend a principle, but to expose a distortion of the truth that prevented our hosts from seeing injustice. I tried to help them understand that African-Americans and other people of color want to play a constructive role in their communities. But nobody should have to sacrifice his identity and pretend to be someone else in exchange for access to opportunities. We should all be allowed to express our uniqueness.

30

REFLECTIONS FROM THE ROAD

Phyllis, June 2008
Oregon

Gene and I have come to the end of this phase of our journey and are taking a break from traveling to get our book ready for publication. As I write my final chapter, I'm looking back over the past ten years and trying to decide what thoughts I want to leave with you before we part ways.

I've shared some of my most embarrassing moments—my doubts, mistakes, and self-recriminations—the painful experiences that I could have avoided altogether if I'd chosen a different path. I've let you in on some of my toughest struggles. Perhaps you're wondering why I would put myself in situations that caused me so much anguish. I recall the words of an African-American friend who had listened to us describe the work of eliminating racial prejudice and asked why anyone—actually, I believe she specified anyone who is white—would choose to make this effort and experience this discomfort.

"I just don't think people are going to do it," she admitted, avoiding my eyes. "I think you need to forget about all that healing and just tell people to do no harm, tell them to just make the right choice and at least—or at first—to simply do good and be fair. The ideal of intimate friendships will come later."

It's something I've heard many times—this wistful thought that everything would be OK if people would just do good and treat each other fairly. But I think even that basic wish is not going to be fulfilled until we've uncovered the conditioning written in our cells that can prevent us from making the "good" choices. This conditioning can be exorcised only when we know it's there, and we can only know it's there if we first suspect that it *might* be there and then consciously put ourselves in situations where it will become apparent.

And why should I hope that you would make such a choice, particularly given my belief that unity is inevitable? If this is all God's plan, as Bahá'ís claim, then it will happen whether we do anything or not. So why should we engage?

We should do it because we are present on this earth, in this country, at this particular time, and at this specific stage in the social evolution of humanity. Our loving Creator has deposited into the creation everything necessary to achieve the next level of maturity. To opt out creates an internal dissonance, while opting in—even at the most primary level—creates internal harmony and well-being. The more often we practice and strengthen the divine qualities that are latent in us and patiently waiting to grow, the better we feel.

So in the end, I'm suggesting that we do this for ourselves—individually as well as collectively. Because after all the struggle, when I look at who I am now compared to who I was a mere decade ago, when I think of the love and joy I might have missed, I realize there is nothing anyone could say to convince me to do things differently.

Is this healing from separation a realistic goal? Can we actually do this? It's not easy because these habits of thought, feeling, and behavior have been reinforced over a long period of time; they are present even at a cellular level. If all we had at our disposal was our physical selves, we would be doomed to function according to the dictates of those promptings. But our true essence is spiritual; we are souls having a brief material experience, and therefore we can draw on a power that is far more potent than that of our programming. If that were not the case, you would never see people giving up their lives for a loved one or a cause they believed in. The human ability to choose something other than what the body dictates is proof of our transcendence over our material nature.

And do we all need to be doing this work of creating racial unity? Or is it enough that only some people are doing it? I'm thinking of a conversation I had with a young white woman in New England. We had just met and had only a half hour together, during which time she asked about our travels, and I told her several stories of people we'd met along the way. After listening intently for some time, she said in a rather confrontational voice, "Here's what I want to know. How and where are you finding all these loving black men?"

It was the same tone she might have used if she'd asked, "How and where are you finding all these five-legged cats?" It actually made me laugh because it seemed at first such an absurd question, and I wanted to shout, "They're all around you!"

She was studying at a local college and I assumed she must have known at least a few friendly students of African descent, but the wording of her question apparently revealed something about her experience. And she was not at all curious about how I had found loving black women. At first, I thought maybe the stories I'd told her had all been about men, but that wasn't the case.

The longer I thought about her question, the more I realized it was the *idea* of many loving black men that threw her. She doubted the possibility of it and figured I must be making it all up. It was nearly time to part, so I gave her a quick explanation of how we always find ready-made friends in our Bahá'í communities.

Looking back, I deeply regret that answer because, while it was true, it also skirted the real issue. Whether out of carelessness or cowardice, I missed an opportunity. I could instead have talked about how stereotypes and fear merge to create an insidious type of brainwashing. I might have told her how that conditioning keeps us in our own comfortable reality where black men are all unloving and so no one in her right mind would seek them out. But I did nothing to help her see more clearly. Worse still, I imagine her thinking, "Ah, she's got her religious community. So this has nothing to do with my life. I have no responsibility here."

But as far as I can see, we are all accountable by virtue of the fact that we are human beings living at this time and place.

We are, each and every one of us, designed to strive for perfection, and when we ignore our inherent impulse to become more authentic, to mirror more clearly the image of our Creator, we are miserable. This urge to become ever more spiritually refined drives all of us at some level all the time, even when we are unaware of its presence, even when we try to thwart it.

I'm not proposing that you do everything we've done. These are our stories—our own journey to leave behind the unnatural state of separation and move toward connection. This journey has been different for me than for Gene, even though we've shared most of the experiences, because we are dissimilar in many ways. But both of us have been thoroughly changed. Responding to the longing is automatic now. We are sustained by our friendships with people of many colors, and we are unwilling to abide separation caused by the mythical concept of race. And our hope is that we've inspired you to undertake your own journeys and given you confidence in the outcome. Each of you will create your own stories in your own way, within the limitations of your own unique situations. The point is that it's time to connect. This is the urgent need and the responsibility of our present generation.

Building interracial fellowship is a kind of high-wire act; you slowly inch your way forward along an impossibly thin line, keeping your eyes always fixed on the goal. You are constantly searching for balance—trying to stay aware, tactful, and discerning without becoming so fearful of mistakes that you're afraid to reach out. That long heavy pole that helps you maintain your balance once you find it is spiritual guidance, whether it comes from your religious teachings or is whispered by your own soul. The safety net that will catch you when you fall is the intertwined arms of all those who are grateful for your efforts.

We have within us everything we need for this mighty undertaking. We have a tremendous power—the power of choice. We can choose to pursue new understanding and choose friends who will assist us in that pursuit. We can choose what kinds of images we allow into our brains, what we let our kids watch on TV, what kind of language we use in our homes. We can choose who we hang out with, where we live, how we respond to injustice, how we react to "harmless" jokes.

We also have courage, which can be ignited by even the smallest spark of faith and become a raging flame that quickly burns away any doubt or fear.

And we have the power of love—God's gift to us, and our gift to one another. It is sufficient to the task.

31

KEEP UP THE WORK

Gene, August 2008
Oregon

In a recent phone conversation with a white friend who has been a relentless advocate of racial unity for decades, I asked if there were any questions I might pose when we meet people in our travels. She said, "Ask the whites what motivates them to engage in this work of eliminating racial prejudice." I jotted down her suggestion and when our chat ended, I asked myself that question. What motivates me to engage?

As I have noted earlier, Toni Morrison's "Beloved" moved me and made me conscious about race; when I finished the book I had questions. The race unity workshop that followed provided certain answers, but something was missing.

When Phyllis and I started traveling and we met African-Americans and other people of color, I started understanding my own racial conditioning and some of the pieces began falling into place. As we moved from one community to the next we developed the habit of describing our recent encounters with African-Americans and explaining what we'd learned from them. At some point I realized that I had stumbled into an area of service that felt like a good fit, and I was confident that I was aligning myself with a cause that had widespread benefits.

I was engaged, but there were times when I wanted to disengage—like when I said something racist in the middle of a workshop we were conducting, or when I got into arguments with other white people about racial issues and lost. In either situation I was embarrassed and asked myself, "Why am I doing this race unity stuff? I'm such an idiot." At those times I had to draw on a source of strength that could revive my flagging commitment.

From the very beginning of our travels, black friends have been so supportive that I have a virtual suitcase filled with empowering memories: welcoming hugs, eyes full of compassion, marathon conversations and shared moments of insight, late-night laughter at diners, sweet tea, ribs, greens and sweet potato pie, painful images of friends sharing stories about the stress racism causes them and their loved ones, family celebrations, wisdom and encouragement. I carry all of these precious items with me for easy access. But there is one in particular that I draw upon frequently because of its special power to give me clarity of purpose.

Phyllis and I were in Arizona talking with an acquaintance about marketing our workshop; he suggested we should meet Joshua, a young African-American man in the area who was successfully conducting race unity workshops as a business venture. So I called and introduced myself, and Joshua invited Phyllis and me to stop by his house a couple days later. He said he was looking forward to getting together and having us meet his wife and children. When we arrived at his house on the day we'd arranged, Joshua welcomed us warmly, then apologized that our visit would have to be brief, as he had another commitment he couldn't get out of.

We had been traveling only about two years at that point, and my mind was still full of a lot of junk. It's not that I was anxious about being in his home; we had already been in South Carolina, where almost everyone we socialized with was black. But I was obsessing about saying something that would expose my unconscious racial prejudice.

Joshua told us briefly about himself, his personal struggles, and what had led him to the field of diversity training. His young face and warm smile revealed no evidence of the hardship that had already touched his life. But he seemed more interested in learning about us. I was conscious of how intently he studied me as I spoke, and it made me nervous. I knew that my understanding of racism was paltry and that I risked coming off as naive and inept, but I was also aware that this was an opportunity for growth. I shared what we had learned about the patterns of racism in the South from African-Americans we'd met and how we'd recognized the same patterns everywhere we traveled. I told him about our growing commitment to get white people to examine the dynamics of racism and make a personal plan of action. I admitted that we had been traveling only two years and we knew there was so much more to learn. He just nodded.

After a half hour, Joshua apologized again and said he had to leave. He and his wife walked with us out of the house to our car, and while Phyllis was saying goodbye to his wife, Joshua walked over, hugged me, and said quietly next to my ear, "Keep up the work. You might save some brothers' lives."

"OK," I said weakly, even as I felt a strange energy surge through me. I had no idea what his words meant, but I knew they were important and have never doubted their veracity. I have always relied on the energy of that utterance, whispered in my ear, to move my heart.

It's been over a decade since that brief half hour with Joshua; in that time we have talked with folks across the country about the elimination of racial prejudice. Some of these conversations occurred during workshops or after presentations at colleges and community organizations. A few were chance encounters at scenic roadside over-looks or truck stops, on mountain trails and beaches, in parking lots, grocery stores, and movie theaters. And many of these discussions have taken place around a table as we shared a meal with friends or new acquaintances. No matter where they happen, we always try to pass on something useful we've learned along the way. Most people seem to appreciate any information that provides added clarity about this unrelenting dilemma, and they will frequently tell us, "I'm glad you're out there doing the work you do." Every time we hear someone say that, we wonder *what do folks imagine actually happens "out there"?* The real work of eliminating racial prejudice is difficult to visualize because it happens inside us.

The idea of "work" calls forth specific images, such as the farmer plowing a field from sunrise to sunset or the corporate board of directors putting together a business plan. In every instance of work, the goal is a finished product or a desired result, and in the end one expects measurable benchmarks for success or failure that justify the expenditure of time, energy, and resources.

So what is the work required to eliminate racial prejudice? What are the short-term and long-term goals? What are the benchmarks of success?

Talking together is a vital element of the work. The notion that there are multiple races is fiction; there is only one humanity. However greed and exploitation, ignorance and deception have combined to enable racism—the belief that one group of the human family is superior to another—to take root in the psyches and hearts of Americans. Addressing this distortion requires that we find a method of distinguishing truth from fiction. Dialogue is one method; it involves a face to face encounter in which we have opportunities to talk about our pain, confusion, hopelessness, or fear around the issue of racism and to share insights and disprove the myths that keep us separated.

Sometimes when workshop participants become distressed about the pervasiveness of racism, they exclaim, "Racism is so huge! What can one person do?" It is our belief that if each of us makes a private commitment to 1) talk with others about the dynamics of racism, 2) become aware of how it touches everyone's life, 3) learn about past and current efforts in the field of race relations and 4) test new understanding in our day-to-day encounters by making insightful choices —particularly in relationships with people from whom we've been historically separated—then we are all engaged in the work of eliminating racial prejudice. This is a service that each of us can render.

Our capacity to choose is crucial to the work. No other individual or group can make the choices of conscience that are specifically ours to make. These choices include deciding how to deal with our awkwardness or ignorance and deliberately seeking opportunities to meet others who are different from us—even if it means leaving the comfort of our familiar circumstances. Each of us can initiate connections. We can make a strong effort while interacting with others to forego suspicion and to search for the integrity that lies at the core of every fellow human.

Individual transformation is the primary short-term goal. In the West, we count on expediency—quick results and fast turnarounds—to ensure a speedy delivery of profit. Transformation, however, is a process that requires patience. This is a goal that points us in the right direction, but we can never predict the duration of the process or the exact nature of the results with 100% accuracy.

Establishing racial unity is the long-term goal, and racial prejudice is an obstruction to its attainment. If we focus on the goal of racial unity we will be able to identify the benchmarks of progress along the way: trust in another's eyes, the absence of suspicion or fear in relationships, comfort in unfamiliar situations, unity of thought, and the ability to respond with compassion, patience, forgiveness, and justice in situations that were previously overwhelming. As we do the work, we should expect that we will develop enlightened ways of thinking and behaving. And if one day we observe in ourselves these benchmarks of success, then we can assume that we have become transformed, that is, we have changed into advanced versions of ourselves.

Collective transformation is the eventual result of our efforts. When transformed individuals serve in the community, it too becomes transformed. Eventually we will experience a shift in collective consciousness, which will have an effect on the entire world.

The Bahá'í writings assure us that the establishment of unity between blacks and whites in the United States will make a significant contribution to world peace. "Strive earnestly and put forth your greatest endeavor toward the accomplishment of this fellowship and the cementing of this bond of brotherhood between you. . . . Each one should endeavor to develop and assist the other toward mutual advancement. . . . Love and unity will be fostered between you, thereby bringing about the oneness of mankind. For the accomplishment of unity between the colored and white will be an assurance of the world's peace."[1]

The Revealers of all of the world's major religions have promised world peace, but the dismal condition facing the earth's inhabitants today challenges one's ability to imagine life without the constant horror of conflict. According to Bahá'í teachings, humanity has been developing in stages. Over millennia, it has passed through infancy and childhood, and it is now nearing the end of adolescence and entering maturity. Like a rebellious teenager, humanity has tried to do things its own way. But God has His own plan for the well-being of His creation.

In spite of its history of slavery, protracted racism, and stubborn attachment to the status quo, the United States has become home to people from virtually every country in the world. It appears that an awe-inspiring process is unfolding. It is a process that works invisibly, gradually raising our collective awareness of the benefits of working together to advance civilization. All of us—regardless of our racial, ethnic or cultural background—have a role in that process. Our first task is to investigate that role and then step up to the responsibility of making our unique contribution. Our real failure, individually and collectively, would be refusing to attune ourselves to an unfolding divine process that has unimaginable benefits for all of us.

An appreciation of the invisible forces operating in the universe can give us confidence as we strive to reach our goals. The writings of the Bahá'í Faith describe one of these forces that is crucial to the establishment of unity: "Love is the most great law that ruleth this mighty and heavenly cycle, the unique power that bindeth together the divers elements of this material world, the supreme magnetic force that directeth the movements of the spheres in the celestial realms. Love revealeth with unfailing and limitless power the mysteries latent in the universe. Love is the spirit of life unto the adorned body of mankind, the establisher of true civilization in this mortal world, and the shedder of imperishable glory upon every high-aiming race and nation."[2]

Is it possible that our understanding of the true nature of love is immature and might be related to the stage of adolescence in which humanity finds itself? Maybe we have confused the universal power of attraction with romance, passion, or superficial goodwill. As humanity enters the stage of maturity, we will surely come to understand love as the most practical force in the universe—a force that will empower us to embrace our differences, forge lasting relationships, and build communities committed to freeing the innate potential of every resident of the earth.

We are all participants in this current stage of social evolution. Today we have a window of opportunity in which to render a service that is essential to the development of our collective well-being. Will we search beyond the confines of the familiar and explore the possibilities of new relationships, thereby strengthening the fabric of our society? When we feel the force of attraction pulling us together as one family, will we respond or resist? This is the choice confronting each of us.

Sometimes responding to the force of attraction can pull you into challenging situations. I remember the workshop series Phyllis and I facilitated in South Carolina. It was the very first time we had presented a workshop since setting out on our journey. The participants were all African-Americans, with the exception of a handful of white Bahá'ís who traveled from neighboring towns to support the effort. For three weekly sessions in a row, we had emphasized the principle of unity in diversity and stated confidently that racism was an issue of the heart.

On this third evening, as I looked around the circle of attendees—all of whom we later found out were struggling to make ends meet in this rural area—I noted with satisfaction that everyone was nodding in agreement with what we had just said. I felt good that we were rendering this valuable service and invited everyone to share any thoughts and feelings that might have surfaced during the presentation.

A man named Harold, who was about my age, sat on the opposite side of the circle and smiled at me empathetically, yet resolutely. He raised his hand.

"Yeah, Harold. What do you have to share?" I asked.

"Well what y'all have been saying is all well and good. I've been to a lot of these diversity meetings and it's usually talk about the heart and such. But where racism is getting me is right here," he said, tapping the wallet in his back pocket.

I didn't know how to respond. All I had to offer at that time was workshop material and idealism. That was one of those times when I felt like disengaging. Harold had not intended to make me look ignorant—I *was* ignorant, and it seemed like my shallow awareness of racism had been exposed for everyone sitting around the circle to observe.

My bruised ego survived. Phyllis and I continued meeting with the group until the end of the workshop series. We decided that we would try to be less theoretical in our presentations and give participants plenty of opportunity to talk about how racism was impacting their day-to-day lives.

During the remainder of our time in South Carolina, our friendship with Harold deepened. We attended church services with him and his wife, and they invited us to their home to meet the rest of the family. When we went to visit, as we stood on the front porch, Harold's mother blocked our entrance into the house. "Hold on," she said. "Let's give the neighbors lots of time to see this." She told us that it was unusual for white people to even be in the neighborhood, much less to visit someone socially. When we were all inside and everyone got busy with the food preparation, Harold pulled their best cuts of beef out of the freezer. This was a special occasion for all of us.

At dinner I sat across the table from Harold. I waited until I was sure I had his attention, then said, "Hey, Harold. Tell me more about the stuff you brought up in the workshop. I think I can hear it now." I listened as he recounted one personal story after another that illustrated how racism had affected his life.

By the time the workshop series was finished, Harold's family had also become our friends. We drove to their house to say good-bye before our departure from the area. After we had all hugged and wished one another well, Harold and I stood face to face, reminiscing about our time together during the past couple of months. I realized that I had no idea when I would see him again.

"We'll be back." I said.

"Yeah. OK," Harold said. "Y'all take care of yourselves."

As Phyllis and I backed out of the driveway, I looked at our friends waving at us, and wondered, *What is the significance in my life of these two months we've spent here?*

A year later we returned, and after we got settled in, we drove to see Harold and his family. As we pulled into his driveway, I saw them all sitting in the back yard drinking lemonade and relaxing. We got out of the car. Harold looked up to see who was visiting, then recognized us and stood up. He walked toward us, smiling and shaking his head. I thought I heard him repeating something over and over, but I couldn't tell for sure until he was closer. When he was about twenty feet away, I could hear him saying, "I knew I'd see you again! I knew I'd see you again!" Maybe his belief in our friendship was the force of attraction that pulled me back.

CONCLUSION

Over the years, we've read many books that have helped us understand the dynamics of racism; most of them emphasized the intractable nature of a dilemma that has plagued the United States for centuries. Their purpose was to edify readers and to expose the grim realities of racism using facts, statistics, and descriptions of deplorable conditions that impact the lives of people of color. While these books have been important elements of our education, they often left us feeling overwhelmed by the enormity of the problem and frustrated in our efforts to find practical ways of addressing racial prejudice in our personal interactions. What was missing for us was the answer to the question we had heard so many times—what can one person do?

We wanted the book you have just read to be different. Although research and statistics are essential to understanding the scope of the disease of racism, information alone does little to help us address the cause—spiritual ill health. Over the past century, spirituality has somehow come to be regarded as a product of human frailty, impotent in the face of relentless social problems plaguing our communities. Rarely do our leaders of thought call on spiritual power to solve our current crises, which so severely impact our collective well-being and social stability.

In our book, we have described racism as a spiritual disease and stated unequivocally our belief that only by strengthening spiritual capacities, which lie at the core of our design as humans, can we unravel the complexities of racism and work together across ethnic and racial boundaries to find and implement lasting solutions.

We have recounted our attempts to use spiritual principles as tools for rooting out our own conditioning and creating integrity in our interactions with African-Americans. We've depicted, as candidly as possible, our awkwardness, ignorance, and fears that made those interactions challenging for us. It is our ardent hope that our stories have convinced you there is something we can actually do—that it is possible for all of us to develop new skills and behaviors that can result in purging racial prejudice from our hearts.

Racism has many layers and many solutions, most of which target a specific symptom of the disease. If we've told our stories well, hopefully it has become evident that the success of all these efforts rests on the foundation of healthy interpersonal relationships. Each one of us can do something to eliminate racism; we all have the power to initiate connections, struggle with our inexperience and discomfort, and make enlightened choices.

But our stories are also about something bigger—an unfolding process from which we can draw courage and strength, a divine plan for the coming together of humanity, an assurance that we have entered the stage of maturity in our collective evolution. It helps to know we are not alone; we are all participants in this process, and as we align ourselves with its energy, we gain access to a power that can inspire us and help us create new possibilities in our relationships.

CONCLUSION

We want to thank you for coming on this journey with us. May you find friends in unlikely places. May you respond to the longing and experience its confirmations. We wish you many wonderful adventures and great success in your efforts to transform yourselves and your communities.

NOTES

2 / Confrontations

1. Diagram "Cycle of Racial Conditioning" developed by Rita Starr, copyrighted 1986.

2. Personal notes from a talk by Nathan Rutstein given Feb 21, 1998 in New London, CT.

4 / A Window of Opportunity

1. 'Abdu'l-Bahá, *Paris Talks*, no. 42.5–9.

5 / Separated at Birth

1. "Abdu'l-Bahá, quoted in Shoghi Effendi, *The Advent of Divine Justice*, p. 37.

6 / A Leap of Faith

1. The Regional Bahá'í Council of the Southern States is a group of people elected to coordinate the work of teaching the Bahá'í Faith in the South.

7 / Looking For Simon

1. 'Abdu'l-Bahá, quoted in Shoghi Effendi, *The Advent of Divine Justice*, p. 37.

8 / Be Careful What You Wish For

1. Shoghi Effendi, *The Advent of Divine Justice*, p. 40.

14 / Eve's Little Serpent

1. Shoghi Effendi, *The Advent of Divine Justice*, p. 40.
2. 'Abdu'l-Bahá, *The Promulgation of Universal Peace*, p. 453.
3. 'Abdu'l-Bahá, in *Star of the West*, vol. 6, no. 6, p. 45.
4. 'Abdu'l-Bahá, *Foundations of World Unity*, p. 88.

15 / Electric Fly

1. The dance "Electric Slide" was created by choreographer Ric Silver.

19 / Body Language

1. Ralph Ellison, *The Invisible Man*, Prologue, p. 3.
2. Ralph Ellison was born March 1, 1913 and died April 16, 1994. When we started traveling in 1997, Ralph Ellison had already passed away. My hope of meeting him years later at the bookstore was in vain.
3. 'Abdu'l-Bahá, *Paris Talks*, no. 15.7.

20 / Snowbird

1. William James, quoted in "Michael Moncur's (Cynical) Quotations." *The Quotations Page*. Feb. 27, 2008. http://www.quotationspage.com/search.php3?homesearch=William+James.

22 / Moose Tracks

1. From a letter written March 25, 1949 on behalf of Shoghi Effendi to individual Bahá'ís, quoted in Bonnie Taylor, *The Pupil of the Eye*, p. 87.

25 / The Word

1. Shoghi Effendi, *The Advent of Divine Justice*, p. 40.

26 / Safe Haven

1. "Pollyanna." *Wikipedia.* Feb. 20, 2008. http://en.wikipedia.org/wiki/Pollyanna.

28 / Of Horseriders and Kings

1. Bahá'u'lláh, *Tablets of Bahá'u'lláh*, p. 156.

31 / Keep Up the Work

1. 'Abdu'l-Bahá, *Foundations of World Unity*, p. 35.
2. 'Abdu'l-Bahá, *Selections from the Writings of 'Abdu'l-Bahá*, pp. 30–31.

BIBLIOGRAPHY

Works of Bahá'u'lláh

The Hidden Words. Wilmette, IL: Bahá'í Publishing, 2002.

Prayers and Meditations. Translated by Shoghi Effendi. Wilmette, IL: Bahá'í Publishing Trust, 1987.

Tablets of Bahá'u'lláh Revealed after the Kitab-i-Aqdas. Compiled by the Research Department of the Universal House of Justice. Translated by Habib Taherzadeh et al. Wilmette, IL: Bahá'í Publishing Trust, 1988.

Works of 'Abdu'l-Bahá

Foundations of World Unity. Wilmette, IL: Bahá'í Publishing Trust, Fourth Printing, 1968.

Paris Talks: Addresses Given By 'Abdu'l-Baha in 1911. Wilmette, IL: Bahá'í Publishing, 2006.

The Promulgation of Universal Peace: Talks Delivered by 'Abdu'l-Bahá during His Visit to the United States and Canada in 1912. Compiled by Howard MacNutt. 2nd ed. Wilmette, IL: Bahá'í Publishing Trust, 2007.

Selections from the Writings of 'Abdu'l-Bahá. Wilmette, IL: Bahá'í Publishing, 2010.

Star of the West, Vol. 6, No. 6.

Works of Shoghi Effendi

The Advent of Divine Justice. Wilmette, IL: Bahá'í Publishing Trust, 1990.

The World Order of Bahá'u'lláh: Selected Letters. Wilmette, IL: Bahá'í Publishing Trust, 1991.

Other Works

Ellison, Ralph. *Invisible Man.* New York: Vintage Books / Random House, Inc., 1990.

Taylor, Bonnie. comp. *The Pupil of the Eye, African Americans in the World Order of Bahá'u'lláh.* Riviera Beach, FL: Palabra Publications, 1995.

Baha'i
PUBLISHING

AND THE BAHÁ'Í FAITH

Bahá'í Publishing produces books based on the teachings of the Bahá'í Faith. Founded over 160 years ago, the Bahá'í Faith has spread to some 235 nations and territories and is now accepted by more than five million people. The word "Bahá'í" means "follower of Bahá'u'lláh." Bahá'u'lláh, the founder of the Bahá'í Faith, asserted that He is the Messenger of God for all of humanity in this day. The cornerstone of His teachings is the establishment of the spiritual unity of humankind, which will be achieved by personal transformation and the application of clearly identified spiritual principles. Bahá'ís also believe that there is but one religion and that all the Messengers of God—among them Abraham, Zoroaster, Moses, Krishna, Buddha, Jesus, and Muḥammad—have progressively revealed its nature. Together, the world's great religions are expressions of a single, unfolding divine plan. Human beings, not God's Messengers, are the source of religious divisions, prejudices, and hatreds.

The Bahá'í Faith is not a sect or denomination of another religion, nor is it a cult or a social movement. Rather, it is a globally recognized independent world religion founded on new books of scripture revealed by Bahá'u'lláh.

Bahá'í Publishing is an imprint of the National Spiritual Assembly of the Bahá'ís of the United States.

For more information about the Bahá'í Faith,
or to contact Bahá'ís near you,
visit http://www.bahai.us/
or call
1-800-22-unite

OTHER BOOKS AVAILABLE FROM
BAHÁ'Í PUBLISHING

CHILDREN OF THE KINGDOM
A Bahá'í Approach to Spiritual Parenting
Daun E. Miller
$16.00 U.S. / $18.00 CAN
Trade Paper
ISBN 978-1-931847-75-9

Children of the Kingdom conveys a practical approach to educating children in a loving and supportive manner, with spiritual principles, virtues, and character development serving as the foundation for their learning and growth. Using the Bahá'í writings, as well as personal experience, author Daun E. Miller demonstrates that there is an alternative to the chaos and confusion that many parents see engulfing the world and that children can be raised to be guided by moral and spiritual principles. Parents and families often run into difficult questions regarding the best way to raise children, and this book provides spiritually based answers. Written in chronological order so that busy parents can find what they need quickly and easily. It designates each age group as an important stage in a child's life and one that demands specific action on the part of parents. The guidance shared in this book focuses on the nature of the soul and the vital reasons why we should educate our children spiritually.

THE FACE OF GOD AMONG US
How the Creator Educates Humanity
John S. Hatcher
$17.00 U.S. / $19.00 CAN
Trade Paper
ISBN 978-1-931847-70-4

The Face of God among Us is an examination of religious history that aims to find out exactly who the founders of the great religions of the past were, and what their role has been in the development of human society. Author John Hatcher looks at the lives and stations of the Prophets of the past—Buddha, Krishna, Zoroaster, Moses, Jesus Christ, Muḥammad, the Báb, and Bahá'u'lláh—and asks: Who exactly were these exalted beings? Were they ordinary humans, temporarily inspired by God? Are they God incarnate, as some believe? Or are they a different category of being all together? In the course of his investigation, Hatcher uncovers a pattern in religious history that seems to hold the answers to all these questions. In doing so, he offers a new insight into the method by which the Creator educates humankind, and provides us with a fascinating perspective about our existence on this planet.

ILLUMINE MY BEING

Bahá'í Prayers and Meditations for Health

Bahá'u'lláh and 'Abdu'l-Bahá

$14.00 U.S. / $16.00 CAN

Trade Paper

ISBN 978-1-931847-69-8

Illumine My Being is a collection of prayers and meditations from Bahá'í scripture that are intended to provide spiritual healing for the individual during times of crises. Many of these prayers ask God for the healing of the individual as well as the community, the nation, and the world. These extracts from the sacred writings explain how individual healing can be achieved through one's relationship with God, and they also elaborate on the nature of spiritual healing and how the healing of the entire human race can be achieved. Healing has always been an essential component of religion, and these prayers and meditations are meant to provide comfort, hope, and reassurance to anyone during these troubled times.

SELECTIONS FROM THE WRITINGS OF 'ABDU'L-BAHÁ

'Abdu'l-Bahá
$14.00 U.S. / $16.00 CAN
Trade Paper
ISBN 978-1-931847-74-2

Selections from the Writings of 'Abdu'l-Bahá is a compilation of correspondence and written works of one of the central figures of the Bahá'í Faith. 'Abdu'l-Bahá, meaning "Servant of the Glory," is the title assumed by 'Abbás Effendi (1844–1921)—the eldest son and appointed successor of Bahá'u'lláh, the Prophet and Founder of the Bahá'í Faith. After his father's passing in 1892, 'Abdu'l-Bahá assumed leadership of the worldwide Bahá'í community until the time of his own passing in 1921. During that time he corresponded with Bahá'ís all over the world, providing them with an abundance of practical and spiritual guidance. The works collected here cover a wide range of topics including physical and spiritual health, death and the afterlife, the spiritual reality of humankind, the oneness of humanity, and the elimination of prejudice. The wisdom imparted in this volume remains as timeless and relevant today as when it was first committed to paper.